D1360976

A GIFT FROM
ADVENTIST DEVELOPMENT
AND RELIEF AGENCY

NOT TO BE SOLD

FUTURE WAR

Armed conflict in the next decade

Copyright © Multimedia Publications (UK) Ltd. 1983, 1984

First published in the United States of America in 1984 by
Facts On File, Inc.
460 Park Avenue South
New York, NY 10016

All rights reserved. No part of this book may be reproduced
or utilized in any form or by any means, electronic or
mechanical, including photocopying, recording or by any
information storage and retrieval systems, without
permission in writing from the Publisher.

This book was devised and produced by Multimedia
Publications (UK) Ltd

PRODUCTION DIRECTOR: Arnon Orbach

DESIGN AND ART DIRECTION: John Strange

ORIGINAL ARTWORK:
Rich Blakeley
Phil Holmes
Rob Shone

PICTURE RESEARCHER: Sarah Waters

Library of Congress Cataloging in Publication Data
Main entry under title:

Future war.

   Includes index.
   1. War.   I. Barnaby, Frank.
U21.2.F88 1984 355'.02 84-1593
ISBN 0 87196 892 4

Typesetting by John Hills Typesetting, Sawbridgeworth, Herts.
Printed and bound by Sagdos SPA, Milan, Italy

FUTURE WAR

Armed conflict in the next decade
Edited by
FRANK BARNABY

Devised by **PETER NICHOLLS**

Facts On File Publications
New York, New York ● Bicester, England

CONTENTS

Chapter 1

Why Wars Might Go on Happening

What are armed forces for? To protect our national security, most would say. But against what? Military invasion and occupation by some foreign power is the stock answer. History shows that such fears are not unjustified. But they may be getting rapidly out-dated. There are increasingly obvious non-military threats to our national security. Perhaps the non-military threats will prove to be much more dangerous than any military threat. Particularly in the longer term.

The economic crisis, for example, with its high unemployment, its inflation, its wildly fluctuating interest and exchange rates, its falling living standards and its deteriorating international monetary system is an obvious threat to our 'way of life', our social and political values. It will probably lead to increasing political and social turmoil in the rich countries and worsening poverty in the poor countries. Tension between North and South may well become a greater threat to security than tension between East and West. These are the very kinds of circumstance under which countries resort to military action. Such action may actually be demanded by populations to ease their economic problems, by acquiring scarce raw materials for example. In fact, the competition for raw materials may become a frequent cause of future wars (but see Chapter Two). Military action may also be used by politicians to divert attention from worsening domestic problems. Some believe that the Falklands war is an example of this trend.

Ecological stress is another threat to security. For example, changes in world climate may come from the rapidly increasing levels of carbon dioxide in the atmosphere as we burn more and more fossil fuels. Such climatic changes may

well have bad consequences for food production in some regions.

The rapidly increasing number of people in the world has far-reaching implications for security. The USSR, for example, has about a thousand million (one billion) Chinese on one border and nearly a billion Indians on another. These statistics must worry the Soviet strategists as much as, or more than, the threats they perceive as coming from NATO.

Measures taken to deal with perceived military threats to security often worsen the non-military threats. Take North-South tension for example. To stop this tension increasing Third World development must be accelerated, so that health and prosperity are increased. But the financial resources and the manpower needed for this development are tied up more and more by the military, in the advanced countries as well as in the developing ones. The amount of government aid given to developing countries by rich countries amounts to about 25 billion (thousand million) dollars a year. The military in the industrialized countries spend this sum every two weeks. Third World countries themselves spend more on the military than they receive in aid. Unless some of these military resources are freed and used for improving industry and agriculture, it is hard to see how we can stop the poverty gap from widening indefinitely. There is a clear relationship between economic development and security.

Wars Over Oil

Of all raw materials, oil is the most obviously related to security, and will be at least for the next decade or two. Oil from the Persian Gulf supplies a significant fraction of the energy used by most

A Harrier jet is launched from the deck of HMS Hermes during the 1982 conflict between the United Kingdom and Argentina over the sovereignty of the Falkland Islands, or Malvinas..

Western European countries and other American allies like South Korea, Taiwan and Japan. The bulk of Gulf oil comes from Iran, Iraq, Kuwait, Saudi Arabia and the United Arab Emirates. These five countries hold us in the palms of their hands. Recent events in Afghanistan, Mecca and Iran, and the continuing Iran-Iraq war, show how very unstable the region is.

The USSR may become an oil importer towards the end of the 1980s. Its present oil exports to its East European allies and the West will dry up and the USSR will also compete for Gulf oil. Superpower rivalry in the Gulf area will become more intense.

A future conflict in a Third World region like the Persian Gulf may easily escalate out of control. It may begin as a conventional war and escalate to a local nuclear war in which nuclear weapons produced by the local powers are used. The war may then spread to Europe, begin there as a conventional war, escalate to a tactical nuclear war, and finally to an all-out strategic nuclear war between the Superpowers.

The involvement of the Superpowers is likely to come about because of the arms trade. The two Superpowers supply the bulk of the weapons used in the wars in the Third World. A characteristic of modern wars is that munitions, especially missiles, are very rapidly used up. Third World countries at war soon need to replenish their arsenals, or face defeat. This was dramatically demonstrated during the 1973 war in the Middle East. Within a few days of the onset of war both Superpowers had to fly in munitions to their respective clients to prevent their defeat.

The Superpowers thus become the guarantors of the survival of their clients at war. They cannot risk the loss of credibility, the loss of 'face', which would certainly follow a failure to prevent a client from being defeated. The arms trade is a major factor in international relations and a dangerous link between conflicts in

the Third World and a possible nuclear war between the Superpowers.

Another link is the spread of nuclear weapons. We seem to be on the brink of a new round of nuclear-weapon proliferation. It is becoming more easy to

get access to nuclear-weapon technology around the world, and this is related to the spread of nuclear energy for peaceful purposes, which is itself an off-shoot from military programmes. The more countries that have significant nuclear-power programmes, the more that will acquire the skills and the capability to produce the fissile material needed for the construction of nuclear weapons. Pakistan may be the next nuclear-weapon power. Few believe that it will be the last. As the number of countries with nuclear weapons grows, the probability of a nuclear incident increases.

New Developments in the Arms Race
Both the global arms trade and the spread of the capability to produce nuclear weapons are out of political control. So is the nuclear arms race between the USA and the USSR. The nuclear arms race is

The OPEC ministers meet, and their actions may determine the fate of the world. As oil becomes more scarce, the Western powers in particular feel the need to retain political influence in the Middle East – using the military as reinforcement if necessary.

fuelled by military research and development. Military scientists are developing nuclear weapons which are so accurate and reliable that they may be seen as more suitable for fighting a nuclear war than deterring one. Most important in this respect is the development of ballistic missiles with warheads that can be aimed with great accuracy at very small military targets. The day is coming when one Superpower might hope to destroy its enemy's nuclear warheads by striking first, thus ensuring the survival of its own cities. Some experts believe that the policy of nuclear *deterrence* by mutual assured destruction is fast giving way to policies based on actually fighting and winning a nuclear war. The more the two Superpowers adapt their military plans to nuclear-war *fighting* policies and integrate many types of nuclear weapons into their military tactics and doctrines, the greater will be the probability of a nuclear world war because the idea that nuclear war is both fightable and winnable will gain ground.

Military scientists are also developing technologies to support nuclear-war fighting weapons. The most important are anti-submarine warfare systems, anti-ballistic missile systems, and anti-satellite warfare systems. The new weapons and technologies are increasing the probability of a nuclear war caused by accident or miscalculation.

The most lethal threat to humankind is unlikely to be any of the factors discussed above taken in isolation. Many of them are mutually reinforcing, and the most likely cause of future war will be several of these factors in combination. Competition for raw materials is likely to be very intense when nations perceive that their first-strike technologies may be effective. An international crisis, irresponsible or incautious leadership in one of the Superpowers, and a conflict in a region where Superpower rivalry is at a high level, is a feasible recipe for world disaster.

The danger of conflict in the Third World expanding uncontrollably into nuclear war is heightened by the frequency of wars in the Third World. On average, a new war begins in the Third World every three months. Any one of them could escalate out of control. Human violence also includes civil war and genocide. Either one could escalate to a war across borders and they are, therefore, threats to world security in addition to being dreadful in themselves.

Bigger and Better Weapons

A nuclear world war is obviously the greatest single threat to humankind. But we should not forget other superweapons. Chemical and biological weapons are seen by some as the poor country's weapons of mass destruction, easier and cheaper to produce in strategic quantities. The spread of these weapons would have great dangers for regional security.

Looking further ahead, we can plausibly speculate that new weapons of mass destruction may be developed. Some people talk about the possibility of producing man-made tidal waves, or stimulating earthquakes, or diverting hurricanes from their paths for hostile purposes. No one knows which, if any, of these potential weapons will be developed. But what we can say is that conventional offensive weapons of the kind that already exist will become even more destructive. Already, such conventional weapons as fuel-air explosives, vacuum bombs and fragmentation bombs which can cause as much destruction locally as nuclear weapons are available. In a fuel-air explosive an aerosol cloud of an explosive chemical is produced and ignited when at its optimum size. By creating several adjoining clouds very large explosions can be produced, equivalent in explosive power to several tons of TNT. Some nuclear weapons now deployed have explosive powers equivalent to that of only about ten tons of TNT. The gap in destructive power between conventional and nuclear weapons is, therefore, almost

gone.

Many military technological advances in nuclear and conventional offensive weaponry may be lessening the world's precarious stability. Developments in microelectronics and computers are a main component of the current advances. We are all aware of how microelectronics has revolutionized peaceful activities. We know that the 'information society' of the Year 2000 will be as different from today's society as our society is from the agricultural society of the eighteenth century. We are less aware that microelectronics has revolutionized military activites. The characteristics of weapons have changed beyond recognition over the past few years. The wars in the Falkland Islands and the Lebanon gave some inkling in 1982 of the nature of high-technology missile warfare. But technology has outstripped tactics. Future warfare will be much more automated. So much more in fact as to raise fundamental questions about how victory on the automated battlefield will be defined. Will men still be involved in battles in the next century, or will warfare be left to robots?

The Bright Side
More immediately, there is a bright side to advances in military technology. Recent developments greatly favour defence rather than attack. Advances in microelectronics have revolutionized both missile-guidance systems and command, control, communications and intelligence systems. Using these new technologies it is now possible for nations or, say, the NATO powers to evolve a militarily credible defence posture against any threatened invasion. This could be both non-nuclear and unambiguously defensive with little, or no, offensive capability.

The adoption of a non-nuclear defensive deterrent could lead to the removal of nuclear weapons from the land-mass of Europe and, therefore, prevent their replacement by more modern, lethal nuclear weapons as is now planned. Since this imminent modernization will mean the deployment of nuclear-war *fighting* weapons in Europe

May Day parade in Moscow, and the usual display of Soviet military might. Most of the weapons paraded are out of date – otherwise they would not be on show.

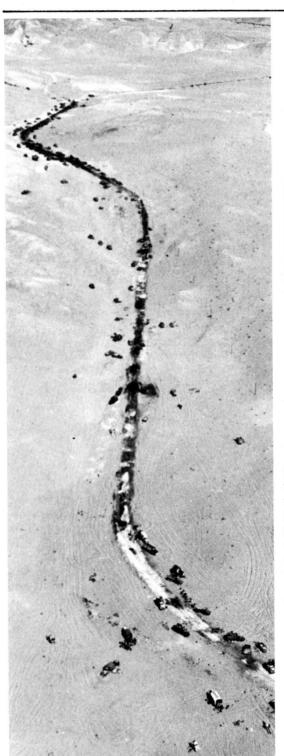

(as opposed to deterrents), and since those tactical nuclear-war fighting weapons will embody the most precise possible threat and will also entail a greater danger of nuclear war by accident or miscalculation, the prevention of their deployment would, many think, reduce the probability of a nuclear world war.

Why is the probability of a nuclear world war increasing, even though we know that it would be such an utter catastrophe? There are two possible explanations. One is that some political leaders actually want a first-strike capability, to give their countries world domination or strategic superiority. The other is that the nuclear arms race is out of control.

If the arms race is out of political control it is in part because of the enormous

During the Six-Day War of 1967, between Israel and Egypt, the destruction was enormous. Here, in the Sinai desert, lay literally hundreds of tanks and other military vehicles destroyed by the opposing forces.

British forces in the Falklands, during the final assault on Port Stanley, prepare to use the sophisticated Rapier system. Microelectronics promise more accurate, and therefore more cost-effective, guided weapons.

political lobbying power of those groups, especially within the USA and the USSR, which continuously press for higher military budgets and the use of all conceivable technological advances for military purposes. There are four main groups involved around the world: the military (any group which disposes of at least 600 billion dollars a year is bound to have immense political power); the defence industries (which gross about 160 billion dollars a year, which makes them the second biggest world industry after oil and, therefore, very powerful politically); the academics (about 25 per cent of the world's research scientists and engineers are funded out of military budgets); and the bureaucrats (about 27 million civilians work for the military and defence establishments, about the same number as that of the people in uniform).

Political leaders know that if they resist the demands of the military–industrial–academic–bureaucratic complex they will be thrown out of office or not re-elected, as the case may be. So the political leaders give in and agree to the deployment of the weapons the scientists develop. They then adjust their nuclear policies to rationalize these deployments. Of course tensions between East and West also fuel arms build-up; as the one side increases its arsenal, so does the other.

Why Not Disarmament?
Some political leaders are, of course, aware of the dangers of an uncontrolled nuclear arms race and look for ways of reducing domestic pressures encouraging the production of more armaments. Many pin their hopes on international negotiations for arms control and disarmament. The aim is first to stop and reverse the nuclear arms race (the building of more weapons), and then to reduce all existing nuclear arsenals. In the end, general nuclear disarmament can only come about as the result of a multilateral process involving all interested parties, although many feel that some steps could, and should, be taken

unilaterally by individual nations. Disarmament should take place in a way which reflects each country's legitimate demands for security. What we need – obviously – is a comprehensive programme of arms control and disarmament leading specifically to far-reaching nuclear disarmament. The programme should include a comprehensive ban on nuclear tests and a ban on chemical weapons as urgent first steps, followed by measures to prevent the further spread of nuclear weapons, measures to control the global arms trade, and then the disarmament of conventional weapons.

Over the past two decades or so, a number of arms-control treaties have been negotiated but they have had virtually no effect on the nuclear arms race or the military strength of states. The choice of measures adopted has been haphazard, and some of the activities that are banned have never even been seriously considered as methods of warfare. The negotiation of such small, unrelated steps cannot, it is now clear, produce significant disarmament. It has not even slowed down the arms race between East and West, which has continued virtually unabated for the past 35 years.

The main reason why there has been no progress in disarmament is a lack of political will, particularly on the part of the great powers. It seems unlikely that political leaders will move towards disarmament unless sufficient pressure is exerted on them by public opinion to persuade them to do so. Henry Kissinger said, in 1974: 'Throughout history men have sought peace but suffered war; all too often decisions or miscalculations have brought violence and destruction to a world yearning for tranquillity. Tragic as the consequences of violence may have been in the past, the issue of peace and war takes on unprecedented urgency when, for the first time in history, two nations have the capacity to destroy mankind. In the nuclear age, as President Eisenhower pointed out two decades ago, "there is no longer any alternative to peace".'

In the ten years since Kissinger made this statement the world has spent (in today's values) nearly six thousand billion dollars on the military. Nuclear arsenals have been built up to contain 50,000 warheads with a total explosive power equivalent to that of well over one million Hiroshima bombs. We have drifted closer to nuclear war. But still there is reason for hope. More and more people are realizing the dangers of an uncontrolled arms race and are working to stop it. If enough people join in, the politicians, even the reluctant ones, will respond.

Frank Barnaby

Members of the Greenpeace movement protesting against the further testing of nuclear weapons in the Nevada desert during April 1983. After five days, the protesters were arrested for having infiltrated a top-secret area.

Chapter 2

Where Wars Happen

Man is a rational animal and most wars happen for rational reasons (or at least rationalized reasons), and in logical places. Societies fight because they see advantage coming through battle, or to fend off the threat of some fate worse than battle. The locations of wars and battles have a historical rationale of their own that has held good since the days of classical empires, through the medieval times of warring baronies, through the embattled centuries of the nation state and to the campaigns of the new empires of the nineteenth and twentieth centuries.

Geography is one constraint, and logistics are another, and those constraints vary in importance as the mobility of armies increases, and the technology behind the soldiers develops. But the pattern remains much the same over the centuries, and it is worth looking at the kind of wars and battles that ensue.

The World's Most War-Torn Area
The cockpit of Northwestern Europe's lowlands is a relatively small area which over the past thousand years or so has seen more wars fought and more blood spilt than any other part of the planet. Some generals, like Marlborough, made their reputations there, and others like Haig and Ludendorff lost theirs in the same muddy fields of Flanders. The Dutch fought for their liberty among the tangled waterways against the Spaniards, against the Austrians, against the French, against the Germans and against each other. In 1914 and in 1940, it was the route the German armies took in their great attacks to conquer mainland Europe. In the 1980s, it is the area where any future land battle between NATO and Warsaw Pact will be decided.

Why should one spot of land be so important? Some of the reasons are logical enough. The first is geography. From the mountains of the Urals, all the way to the Atlantic Ocean, rolls a great plain, perhaps

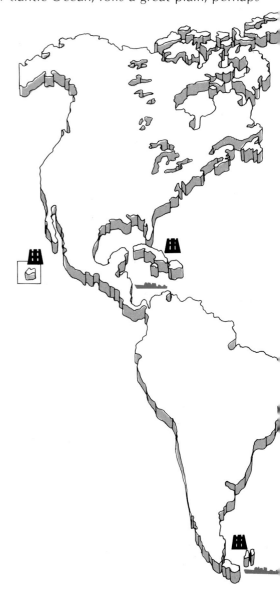

Many wars (though not all) occur at 'choke points' — comparatively narrow areas on trade routes. The classic choke point on land is the 'cockpit' of Europe's low countries. Some wars are fought at 'fortress points' — areas of great symbolic value like Israel and

the finest cavalry and tank country that armies have ever known. No mountain range and no unfordable river stands in the way of an army that comes from the heart of Asia all the way to the western edge of Europe. This North German Plain starts off in Russia over 1,500 km wide. In Germany, it is still hundreds of kilometers wide, but steadily narrowing. The Harz mountains and finally the River Rhine itself present natural defensive positions against attacks from either direction. The exhausted German armies of 1944 were able to hold the US and British allies for a long winter on the Rhine, just as the British, French and Belgians had held the Kaisers armies 30 years earlier.

The Rhine itself, and the other rivers of Europes cockpit, the Moselle, the Meuse, the Somme, the Sambre, the Scheldt and the Saar present a tangle of waterways

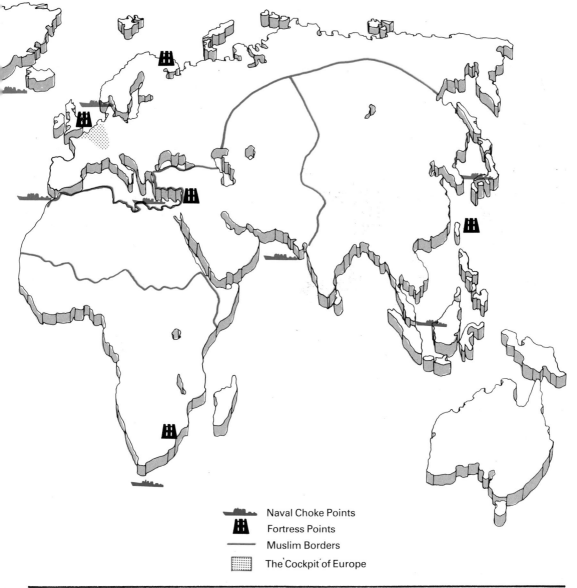

Naval Choke Points
Fortress Points
Muslim Borders
The Cockpit of Europe

the Falklands. There has been much fighting along the borders (marked above) between the Muslim and the non-Muslim world. War has geographical as well as economic causes.

that slowed armies long before the Dutch built their canals and dykes and learned to protect their land by flooding it. And the rivers also brought wealth, with the Rhine itself as the railroad of medieval Europe.

Long before trade made the Low Countries into attractive possessions in themselves, the Romans built their great fortress and base against the barbarians over the Rhine at Trier. And after the collapse of the Roman Empire, Charlemagne the Great made Aachen the centre of his new Empire. A thousand years later, the empire of Napoleon was finally defeated at Waterloo, a battle which saw the British and the Prussians defeat the French. The presence of the British, a maritime people, points to the further significance of the cockpit of Europe. Not only is it the area where the North German Plain runs to the sea, it also represents the classic point of entry for the maritime powers into European affairs. Henry V at Agincourt, Queen Elizabeth I at Zutphen, Cromwell at Dunkirk, Marlborough at the battles of Ramillies, Oudenarde and Malplaquet, Wellington at Waterloo, Haig at the Somme and Montgomery at Arnhem – this has been the route of the British invasion, the interface between the oceanic and continental powers of Europe. And from 1942 to 1944 it became the scene of the first strategic air battle as the RAF and American bombers fought their way across to the Central European heartland.

As a historic battleground, it is unique. It is in one sense a logical place to have a war, because historically, whichever power has dominated the Low Countries and the Rhineland has dominated the whole of Europe. But it is an area without significant raw materials. There is little in the land itself worth fighting for. This seems odd. When strategists and statesmen in the 1980s talk of likely trouble spots, they talk for example of the Persian Gulf, the source of more than half of the world's oil. But traditionally, men have chosen not to fight for raw materials, or at least, not to fight for them in the places where they are

found. The only major war which was fought directly to win territory which contained raw materials was the Japanese campaigns of World War Two. But for the most part, there are other ways of controlling raw materials, whether buying them, or taxing them, or best of all, dominating the great trade routes between the raw materials and their markets.

It is a logical process. For a conqueror to take over the mines where the raw

materials are produced means taking on himself the cost of extraction, the problems of the labour force and so on. For him to take over the markets for the product, the cities where people live or the adjacent factories where they work, is an expensive and complicated business. But to control the route between the two and to tax everything that passes produces the biggest income for the smallest outlay. Just before the great expansion of the British Empire in the nineteenth century, the highly patriotic Foreign Secretary Lord Palmerston warned his countrymen against the temptations of Empire. 'Trade without rule where possible, trade with rule where necessary', was his advice.

16

The Battle of Waterloo (1815) – here painted by Sir William Allan – was only one of a long series of battles fought by the European nations in the world's cockpit. This part of the Low Countries is traditionally an area in which the British fight their continental foes.

Between the German robber baron of the fourteenth century, taxing every barge that passed by his castle on the Rhine, and the British Empire's dominance of Gibraltar, the Suez Canal, Singapore, the Cape of Good Hope and the Falkland Islands, there is very little difference. They are each institutions which exercise control over a choke point. Most wars are fought over choke points, and a remarkably high proportion of battles is fought in them.

When the Persians invaded Ancient Greece they had to come twice through choke points. The first was their crossing of the Dardanelles near the site of the future fortress city of Constantinople. The second was their progress through the pass of Thermopylae, where three hundred Spartans could hold off an army. The cockpit of Europe is a classic choke point, and so are the Panama Canal, the Malacca Straits, and the Straits of Hormuz at the entrance to the Persian Gulf. Perhaps the most important military campaign that Britain has fought since 1945, far more vital than the battle for the Falklands, was the long guerrilla war between 1968 and 1977 in Oman, a war

to keep a pro-Western ruler in charge of the country which dominated the Straits of Hormuz.

Choke Points at Sea
Naval warfare is also based upon finding the choke point and applying pressure through blockade. The first task in naval war is to take command of the sea, so that the only ships which pass are the ones your side permits. The enemy's ports are then under blockade. He cannot trade by sea, and if the blockade be effective enough, he starts to starve. Victory or defeat in a naval battle is of less importance than this capacity to impose a choke point. In 1916, the two most

Manhandling an eighteen-pounder out of the mud near Langemarck during the Battle of Poelcappelle, Ypres, in late 1917.

powerful fleets in the world met in the North Sea. The battle was indecisive, but the British fleet suffered much heavier losses than the German. Nonetheless, the Germans were sufficiently chastened by the encounter that they never challenged the British fleet again. The British blockade was allowed to tighten. By the end of 1916, there had been 61 food riots in German cities. So even at sea, where there are no rivers or mountains to impose geographic constraints, the strategic objective remains.

Nor was this strategy limited to the age of battleships and aircraft carriers. It remains valid today, when naval warfare has become increasingly a matter of submarines. The standard NATO scenario for a conventional war in Europe illustrates the process precisely. NATO doctrine says that the German, British and US armies in central Europe must hold a Warsaw Pact attack long enough for reinforcements of men and supplies to get across the

Atlantic from the United States. Whatever the losses on the way, the United States will have to ferry troops across by an air bridge, and to carry heavy equipment and strategic supplies by sea.

So it will be the Soviet objective to impose a choke point in mid-Atlantic, using submarines and air attack to sink the transport ships and the NATO escorting warships. Equally, it will be NATO's objective to impose a choke point on the

WHERE MAJOR WARS HAVE HAPPENE

Guatemala
El Salvador
Nicaragua
Colombia
Chile

The Battle of Trafalgar (1805), during the Napoleonic Wars, took place at an obvious 'choke point', near Gibraltar: the French fleet in the Mediterranean was effectively barred from invading Britain. Nelson's 27 ships sank 20 out of 33 French vessels, suffering no loss – although Nelson himself died.

access routes of the Soviet submarines before they can reach the Atlantic. That means in the Channel, in the Iceland-Faroes gap and up to Greenland. If there is a NATO war, it is here that the great naval battles will take place. For all the expanse of the ocean, the location of that battle can be predicted with some precision.

Such naval battles are predictable in any war. In the days of Nelson and Napoleon, the key choke points were Gibraltar, the mouth of the Channel at Ushant, and the Dutch coastal waters. If the French were to invade England, they would need to combine their three fleets. They had one in the Mediterranean, which could be blockaded from Gibraltar. They had another in the port of Brest, by Ushant, and they had the use of the Dutch fleet. The major naval battles of the war took place in the inevitable places, at

1945

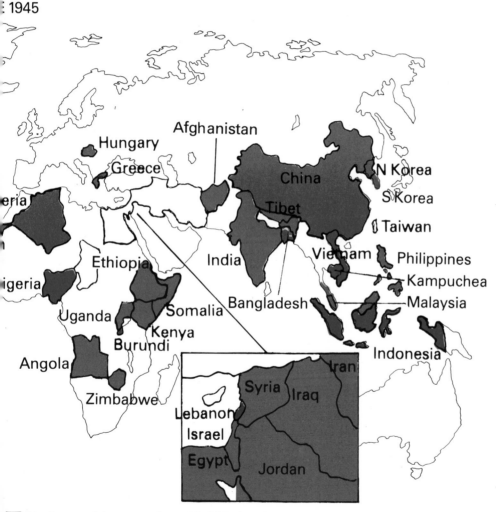

■ Nations with more than 10,000 dead since 1945
■ Nations with more than 100,000 dead since 1945

The end of World War Two did not bring peace on Earth. The map shows those nations involved in major wars, including civil wars, since 1945. The only nations included are those estimated to have lost more than 10,000 people in warfare since 1945. There have often been as many as twelve wars a year in this period, and smaller conflicts, such as the Falklands war and the various civil wars in Chad do not appear. If all wars had been included, the whole of Latin America, Africa, Asia and the Middle East, with only twelve exceptions out of more than 100 nations would have been marked on the map. Nobody knows exactly how many died in these wars – probably more than six million.

Trafalgar, near Gibraltar, at Camperdown, in Dutch waters – and the Brest blockade continued. Earlier, in the sixteenth century, when Philip of Spain sent his Great Armada against the England of Elizabeth in 1588, the rules were the same. His army was in the Low Countries, and his fleet in Spain. To reach the troops, the Armada had to pass through the Channel. The English had to make sure that fleet and army did not meet, and they had the long killing ground of the Channel in which to do it.

The choke points of future naval battles can be defined today. The Straits of Malacca, and the nearby base of Singapore, will see the battle that decides whether Japan and the fast-growing states of the Pacific rim can continue to be supplied with oil from the Middle East. If the tankers cannot be fought through, then the route will have to shift to Australia, and then north via Hawaii and across to Japan, some 24,000 km of sea lanes in which to defend the tankers against submarine attack. Meanwhile, between the islands of Japan and the Siberian mainland, one of three naval battles of constriction will be taking place to see whether the Soviet Navy can be blockaded in port. In this area around Vladivostock, and also in the long gap between Scotland and Greenland in the North Sea, and up in the Mediterranean,

the Soviet Navy will have to try to break out of the blockade which throttled the land empires of Napoleon, the Kaiser and Hitler. Its chances of success must be rated as slim, because for the Soviet Union sea power is a luxury. For the much-extended West, which is as much a global confederation of trading partners (and occasional rivals) as an alliance, sea power is a vital necessity which it cannot afford to forgo.

War Across Vast Distances
There are wars where a long land frontier on a vast plain imperils normal strategic logic. The very size of Russia meant that in the wars against Napoleon and against Hitler, the loss of territory did not prove decisive. Tsar and Stalin alike could retreat endlessly, trading space for time until the Russian winter came to savage the enemy. Napoleon did better than Hitler; his armies at least occupied Moscow, whereas Hitler's were halted on the outskirts. But even had Moscow fallen, Stalin was ready to continue the war from behind the Urals.

This pattern of war, ranging across vast distances, has recurred whenever two great empires have become neighbours. The Romans and the Persians fought spasmodically across the Middle East for centuries, with their frontier now in Judea, and then at the mountains of Kurdistan.

The steppes of Russia, by their very vastness, have defeated would-be conquerors such as Napoleon and Hitler. Slowly retreating, and constantly harrying, Russian forces have always been able to rely on the eventual intervention of 'General Mud' and 'General Winter'.

The long conflict between the Chinese and Russians, stretching from the Mongol invasions of the middle ages to the border skirmishes and long tensions of the last twenty years, falls into a similar pattern.

For the Moors and Saracens and Christians who lived and fought through them, the Crusades and the wars in Spain and the Balkans must have seemed like separate campaigns, separate wars, divided by centuries. But with hindsight, it makes more sense to see them as a single thousand-year war between two religious empires, from the first explosion of Islam in the seventh century to the siege of Vienna in the seventeenth. Wherever the two cultures met, they fought. The Moors held a bridgehead in Spain for six centuries before the Christians finally threw them back to North Africa. Constantinople and the Byzantine remnants of the old Roman Empire held the Moors back from crossing into mainland Europe for seven centuries before the fortress fell, and the Ottomans surged into the Balkans.

The only illogical place for the two cultures to fight was in the Holy Land. The Crusaders first reached the area by land, but then they had to sustain and reinforce it by sea. Their initial success in doing so led the Moslems to develop a naval power of their own, and the clash of cultures which had fought at the Spanish and Balkan peripheries for centuries finally had to meet in grand naval battle off the coast of Greece at Lepanto in 1571.

The Crusades were not simply about religion. They represented the clash of different cultures and different races. It is striking that in the Arab world in the late twentieth century, the view is commonplace that the Crusades are not over, and that modern Israel is the physical heir of the Crusaders' twelfth-century kingdom of Outremer – which occupied the same territory. Outremer and Israel – outposts of a Western and alien culture, sustained by an advanced military technology and by support and reinforcement from the European heartland. The concept is the more plausible in that it ignores the symbolic and religious basis of the Middle Eastern troubles – the ownership of a territory that is a Holy Land for Christian, Jew and Moslem alike.

The parallel between Outremer and Israel throws into relief the way that humankind is shaped and governed – in whatever century – by certain historical continuities. In the late twentieth century, the civil wars in the Sudan, in Chad, in Niger and Mali between the Arabs and the blacks echo a racial and cultural clash that has been under way for centuries. Until the European came to exert his own brief dominance, the Arabs were everywhere

The Statue of Unity at Juba, in the Sudan, gives an idealized picture of the spirit of cooperation between Arab and black African. But still Sudan is riven by civil uprising, as the black population (30 per cent) of the south resists domination by the Moslem peoples (70 per cent) of the north and west.

The Battle of Lepanto – strictly speaking, an unnecessary and useless battle – was fought on 7th October, 1571, between the Christian fleet, under the Spanish military commander John (Juan) of Austria, and the Turks. The defeat demolished Turkish dreams of becoming a maritime power.

the masters, and the blacks were more or less slaves. When the white man left, power was usually inherited by the tribal group whose land enclosed the white man's capital or administrative centre. So a hundred years ago, the black men of

Niger and Mali and Chad were slaves. Today they persecute the Arabs. And along Africa's Sahel, the long shore between the desert of the nomad Arabs and the semi-fertile savanna of the black tribes, a sputtering kind of war is likely to continue, until the desert itself expands enough (through overgrazing) to make the squabbles over wells and land into a dispute of purely academic and historical significance.

This kind of tribal dispute over land has its ugliest echo far to the South, in what is likely to be one of the most war-prone regions of the Year 2000 – the enclave of the white tribes of South Africa. Echoing Israel, a technically advanced minority imposing their will on a hostile regional majority, the South Africans are preparing themselves for two kinds of war.

The first is the classic war of Europe, the final confrontation of wills between organized armies – what Clausewitz called the *Hauptschlacht* – the ultimate slaughter. (Ironically, Southern Africa has a spot that could have been named after it – Bulawayo, the place of skulls.) In the rest

of the twentieth century this is unlikely, simply because there is little prospect of black Africa developing the kind of social and technical sophistication that could withstand a South African army, unless the Russians and their Cuban clients were to intervene on a vast scale. The more likely alternative is that standard response of the weak to the military overlord – popular resistance and guerrilla war.

The Limitations of the Guerrilla

The two great victories of the Vietnamese after World War Two, against the French and against the American and South Vietnamese allies, were not guerrilla successes. The war of the guerrilla simply bought time for the organization of classic standing armies. At Dien Bien Phu, the French were beaten by artillery and infantry attacks; in 1975, Saigon fell to an armoured division.

There is no reason to think that this pattern will ever change. Guerrillas have the limited role of keeping alive the flame of resistance, of buying time, of sapping enemy morale and of preparing the way for the enemy's armies to be more easily beaten. But the limits of guerrilla war were simply explained by the future Field Marshal William Slim, in charge of the 14th Army in Burma in World War Two. Brigadier Wingate, leader of the Chindits, a British guerrilla force which harassed the Japanese in the jungles, argued that the whole of the British forces in South East Asia should become guerrillas. Idiocy, replied Slim. The Japanese would simply march into India, irrespective of losses, and occupy the airfields and bases from which the guerrillas were supplied.

There can be little doubt that some kind of guerrilla war will develop against the white tribes of Africa, and that it will have a degree of success. But the war of the guerrilla is an explicit denial of the *Hauptschlacht*; it is an admission that one is not yet ready for the decisive campaign. If the black Africans can combine guerrilla tactics with a progressive move towards formal warfare, backed up by diplomatic

Women guerrilla fighters of the Vietnamese National Liberation Front. Guerrilla forces are ill-equipped to win decisive victories, but their spectacular, if localized, actions help keep their cause in the public eye. The high level of commitment by individual fighters, too, is a prime propaganda weapon, lending the guerrilla cause a human, heroic dimension.

and propaganda campaigns, then it can expect – eventually – to meet the kind of success that Robert Mugabe's guerrilla war enjoyed in Zimbabwe. But it is likely to take very much longer, to be more bitter, and to see widespread devastation of neighbouring black African states as white South Africa mounts incursions against 'terrorist bases', as in the South African air raid on a suburb near the capital of Mozambique in May, 1983. And terrorism itself is always a two-faced weapon, inflicting as many ugly changes on the terrorist as on his target.

It is a striking feature of warfare that where there is no logical or decisive place for a battle to take place, men tend to invent one. In one sense, the Crusaders' battles for the Holy Land were just such an invention. More precisely, the battle for Verdun in 1916, and for Madrid in the Spanish Civil War, were battlegrounds imposed by propaganda rather than military logic. The German Field Marshal von Falkenhayn chose to make cynical use of the patriotic symbol of Verdun to make it a killing ground. The French strove to hold a ruined landscape that the German artillery could devastate at will. Ironically, the French commander Marshal Joffre had not wanted to defend Verdun, just as he had not wanted to risk his total defeat in the defence of Paris in 1914. 'Paris is a town like any other', he told his political masters.

Joffre's military logic cannot be gainsaid. It is a difficult business for an army to defend a great city. Either you devote half your troops to organizing and carrying out the evacuation of the civilians, or you massively complicate the logistics problem, somehow keeping enough food and water for the civilians coming into the city along with your ammunition and reinforcements. But the politicians overruled Joffre in 1914 over Paris, and overruled him again in 1916 over Verdun, just as the political leaders of Republican Spain insisted in 1936 that Madrid be held against Franco. In 1941, it was Stalin himself who insisted that the

cities of Leningrad and Moscow be held against the Germans, no matter what the cost. For the citizens of Leningrad, the cost was 600,000 lives lost from starvation, bombardment and exposure. It was a desperate price to pay, and in

return, Stalin could only claim the moral victory of having denied the German invader the capture of a city.

Was it worth it? At Leningrad probably not, because the Germans did not expose their own troops to similar casualties by attacking fortified Leningrad. But at Stalingrad, in the winter of 1942, von Paulus's German VIth Army bled itself to death in its long, vain assaults upon the city. The rubble defences of the city chewed up the tanks and *Panzergrenadiere.* who had been trained for a war of movement. The Germans had accepted Stalin's moral valuation of the city that bore his name. They fought for it, and sustained a strategic defeat when there was no need to do so. Stalingrad could have been by-passed, surrounded, and left to surrender.

Similar symbols are likely to feature in the wars of the future. Indeed, some of them already do. Both Afghanistan and Vietnam became major symbolic battlegrounds for the two great powers, although it was plain that neither Superpower had a vital strategic interest at

23

Between February and December, 1916, well over 700,000 people died in the Battle of Verdun. The French, under Joseph-Jacques-Césaire Joffre, were the heavy losers; ironically, it was a battle which Joffre, who resigned in the wake of the defeat, had advised should not be fought. No real advantage was gained by either side.

risk there. The island of Taiwan, grudgingly supported by successive United States governments in the teeth of Peking's hostility, is a classic example of the symbolic focus of potential war. The Falkland Islands became the focus in 1982 of a sharp little war which was basically over national pride and political 'face', notwithstanding the grand talk of Antarctic oil reserves and potential riches. The wiliest of German statesmen, Count Bismarck, once dismissed a major diplomatic issue as 'not worth the bones of a single Pomeranian grenadier'. In and of themselves, many issues are just as worthless. But men choose to invest them with mystical significance, to make of a place name on a map a test of national virility – just as Britain and France almost

as West Germany is now the second economic (and non-nuclear military) power of NATO, so East Germany is the second economic and military power of the Warsaw Pact. The presence of British, French, American and Soviet troops in Berlin ensures that the division of Germany will continue. Perhaps the most alarming result of an American disengagement from Europe would be the resulting dominance of Western Europe and the EEC by West Germany. Traditionally, such a dominance by any one power has been seen as a *casus belli* (occasion of war) by Britain and by Russia. The inevitable pressure towards German re-unification would, with memories of 1941-45 so strong in the Kremlin, provoke a dramatic Soviet response. The symbol of

went to war in 1898 over a godforsaken oasis in the Sudan called Fashoda, never heard of before nor since, simply because two flag-bearing expeditions had happened to arrive there at about the same time.

There is one such symbol of East-West virility which retains its potential capacity to plunge the world into war. The enclave of West Berlin symbolizes the continuing division of Germany into two halves. Just

West Berlin – which is not worth the bones of anyone's grenadier – could become the trigger of a desperate confrontation.

The Floating Fortresses

Where geography has not made a choke point for men to fight in and over, generals hasten to supply one in the shape of a fortress. Whether as in Wellington's bloody assault on Badajoz

The Battle of Stalingrad, fought from August 1942 to February 1943, was a battle over a symbol – the city named for Stalin himself – rather than a conflict for tactical gain. The slaughter was enhanced by Goering's assurances to Hitler that the Luftwaffe could airlift supplies to the German troops. As was obvious, and as it proved, the Luftwaffe could not.

and Cuidad Rodrigo in Spain in 1811, or Haig's crashing through the Hindenburg Line in 1918, they have to be taken – usually at a time and place of the enemy's choosing. The future of warfare is likely to revolve around just such fortresses.

In naval war, the aircraft-carrier groups – which will command the sea lanes in the widest parts of the oceans where submarines may expect to find their sanctuary – will become mobile fortresses which the enemy must besiege and take (see Chapter Seven). If the carrier groups survive, as the British carriers did in the Falklands sea battles, their side is likely to win. The defence of the sea lanes to the Persian Gulf where the oil is will be fought by carrier groups in the Indian Ocean – supported by island bases like Diego

besieging them. Whether the satellites carry surveillance cameras or laser beams, the same principles will apply. They will have to be assaulted, and protected. Julius Caesar used to mount sieges while deploying a flank army to guard against Gallic relief columns; the generals of space battles will have to do the same thing.

In warfare, only the weapons change. The locations, the principles and, above all, the raw material of men remain the same. As long as there are men – unless our slow cultural evolution sickens us of war at last – Gibraltar and Suez and Panama and Singapore and the Low Countries will have their garrisons and their predators – even if surveillance platforms in space allow them a swifter response against attackers.

Garcia and Singapore.

In space, the same kind of mobile-fortress principle will apply (see Chapter Eight), with satellite stations occupying the commanding heights, and the enemy

Martin Walker

Aircraft carriers, such as the Russian vessel above, together with their support ships, comprise veritable 'floating fortresses'. Their survival or destruction is likely to determine the outcome of future non-nuclear wars.

Chapter 3

Will There be a Nuclear War?

Most of us believe that a nuclear world war is the greatest single threat to our society, if not to humankind, and many believe that the probability of a nuclear world war is steadily increasing. They believe that the major reason for this growing danger is that the nuclear arms race between the USA and the USSR is out of political control. Only if, and when, this arms race is brought under control, these people say, will the danger of a nuclear holocaust begin to recede. It is, therefore, crucially important to understand the nature of the nuclear arms race between the Superpowers and to try to fathom its causes.

There are a frighteningly large number of ways in which a global nuclear war might break out. Nuclear war could start with the deliberate decision of one Superpower to attack the other; or by the escalation of a conventional war; or through mechanical error or malfunction in a nuclear-weapon system; or because of irrational behaviour by the people controlling nuclear weapons; or through an error by humans or computers controlling the nuclear alert and firing systems; or by the acquisition and use of nuclear weapons by irresponsible governments; or last, but by no means least, by the use of nuclear explosives by terrorists.

The danger of a nuclear war starting by 'accident, miscalculation or madness' is ever-present. But the escalation of a regional conflict fought with conventional weapons to an all-out nuclear war between the Superpowers is generally thought to be the most likely scenario – more likely than a direct attack by one Superpower on the other. This is the situation as it looks today and for the rest of this decade. But will it remain true into

The characteristic mushroom cloud of a nuclear explosion. Some of the warheads currently possessed by the Superpowers have, individually, an explosive capacity equivalent to, or greater than, the sum total of all the explosives used in warfare throughout human history, to date.

the 1990s? Or will a nuclear attack out of the blue, a 'first strike' in the jargon of the experts, become the greatest danger? And if one side does develop the capability to make an effective first strike, or even develops the perception that it can do so, would it be likely to resist the temptation to attack? To answer these and similar questions we must understand the nature of nuclear weapons and the changes and improvements made to these weapons over the years.

The nuclear weapons now in the arsenals of the nuclear-weapon powers vary considerably in their explosive power – the smallest have a power equal to that of ten tons of TNT, and the largest are equivalent to at least twenty million tons (twenty megatons) of TNT. It is difficult to appreciate what destructive power a twenty-megaton nuclear warhead has. It might help to know that the total weight of all the explosives used in war by man throughout history is roughly twenty megatons. The Superpowers really do have nuclear warheads each of which contains as much explosive power as *all the explosives used so far in war put together.*

The Nuclear Arsenals
Nuclear warheads are of two types – strategic and tactical. The range of the missiles that carry them is their main distinguishing factor, strategic weapons having very long (intercontinental) ranges, greater than say 6,000 kilometers. But the existence of such intermediate-range missiles as SS-20s and cruise missiles confuses the distinction between different types of weapons. The strategic–tactical distinction is, in any case, artificial.

Strategic nuclear weapons[1] are deployed on intercontinental ballistic missiles (ICBMs), submarine-launched ballistic missiles (SLBMs), and strategic bombers. Soviet and American ICBMs have ranges of about 11,000 kilometers; modern SLBMs have ranges of about 7,000 kilometers, and strategic bombers have ranges of about 12,000 kilometers.

Some ballistic missiles carry many warheads – up to fourteen. Modern multiple warheads of a single missile can be directed at targets hundreds of kilometers apart. These are called multiple independently-targetable re-entry vehicles, or MIRVs in military jargon.

A Minuteman-III intercontinental ballistic missile in its cocoon. The guidance systems for this missile are so precise that, even over intercontinental distances, each missile has a 50 per cent chance of landing within 200 meters of its target.

Strategic bombers carry not only free-falling nuclear bombs but also air-to-ground missiles armed with nuclear warheads. The most modern of these missiles is the American air-launched cruise missile (ALCM) carried by the B-52 strategic bomber. The ALCM has a range of about 2,500 kilometers.

The USA at the end of 1982 had 1,596 strategic ballistic missiles – 1,052 ICBMs and 544 SLBMs. Of these, 1,094 (544 SLBMs and 550 ICBMs) are fitted with MIRVs. There are 316 B-52s operational as strategic bombers; they carry 1,264 nuclear free-fall bombs, 1,114 short-range attack missiles with nuclear warheads and 192 ALCMs.

These American strategic nuclear forces carry between them about 9,400 nuclear warheads – 2,100 on ICBMs, 4,700 on SLBMs and 2,600 on bombers. These warheads can deliver a total explosive power of 3,500 megatons; 1,500 by ICBMs, 300 by SLBMs and 1,700 by bombers.

The USSR at the end of 1982 had 2,335 strategic ballistic missiles – 1,398 ICBMs and 937 SLBMs. Of these, 930 (260 SLBMs and 670 ICBMs) are thought to be fitted with MIRVs. Some 150 Soviet long-range bombers may be assigned an intercontinental strategic role.

These Soviet strategic nuclear forces carry in all about 8,500 warheads on ballistic missiles – about 5,700 on ICBMs and 2,800 on SLBMs. These warheads can deliver about 6,400 megatons, about 5,500 by ICBM and 900 by SLBM. The bombers may carry an additional 300 nuclear weapons – about one half as free-fall bombs and the rest as short-range attack missiles. The explosive power of these aircraft-delivered warheads totals about 300 megatons.

A MIRV (multiple independently-targetable re-entry vehicle) warhead. Thanks to MIRVs, which allow a single missile to carry warheads destined for a plurality of targets, arms-reduction talks have shifted emphasis from numbers of missiles to numbers of warheads.

A B-66 thermonuclear bomb is loaded onto an FB-111. Approximately half of the megatonnage deliverable by the American strategic nuclear arsenal is carried aboard aircraft.

Tactical (as opposed to strategic) nuclear weapons are deployed in a wide variety of systems – including howitzer and artillery shells, ground-to-ground ballistic missiles, free-fall bombs, air-to-ground missiles, anti-aircraft missiles, atomic demolition munitions (landmines), ground-, air-, and submarine-launched cruise missiles, torpedoes, naval mines, depth charges, and anti-submarine rockets. Land-based tactical systems have ranges varying from about twelve kilometers or less (artillery shells) to a few thousand kilometers (intermediate-range ballistic missiles). The explosive power equivalent of tactical nuclear warheads varies from about ten tons to about one megaton of TNT.

The USA deploys tactical nuclear weapons in Western Europe, Asia and on its own territory, and with the Atlantic and Pacific fleets.

We know a great deal about the American nuclear arsenal from official and semi-official sources. We know very little about the Soviet nuclear arsenal from official sources. It is, in fact, quite extraordinary how much information is publicly available in the USA about American military affairs. The Soviets, on the other hand, are obsessively secretive about military matters. This is not only a communist habit; it has been true of the Russians for hundreds of years. Sadly, the defence establishments of the other established nuclear-weapon powers (the United Kingdom, France and China) like secrecy almost as much as the Soviets do. The world would be a safer place if the major powers followed America's example and were more open about their military arsenals and manpower.

Data on nuclear-weapon stockpiles are crucial for an informed debate on nuclear-weapon issues. Much information about the nuclear arsenals of other nuclear-weapon powers has been made publicly available by American intelligence agencies. Available public information about American nuclear stockpiles has been recently collated by the American scientists W.M. Arkin, T.B. Cochran and M.M. Hoenig in the *Nuclear Weapons Data Book* (1983).[2]

American Plans

The US nuclear arsenal hasn't changed much in quantity and quality for a decade or so. But very considerable changes are planned for the next ten years. According to some experts the deployment of their new weapons is changing United States policies from nuclear deterrence based on mutual assured destruction to nuclear-war fighting. A similar argument applies of course to Soviet nuclear policies.

Currently, according to Arkin and his colleagues, the US nuclear arsenal contains about 26,000 nuclear weapons – down from the peak of some 32,000 reached in 1967. Today's weapons are spread over 25 types – ranging from portable landmines, weighing a mere 70 kilograms, to strategic bombs, weighing about 3.6 tons. As we have seen, the explosive power of the weapons varies considerably – from the equivalent of about ten tons of TNT for the W54 atomic landmine to the equivalent of nine million tons of TNT for the B-52 strategic bomb. Twelve types of US nuclear weapons are currently deployed at bases throughout NATO countries.

The number of nuclear weapons of different types in the US stockpile varies considerably. The numbers range from 3,500 for the W48 155-mm nuclear artillery shell to 65 for the W53 Titan-II ICBM warhead. The number of nuclear free-fall aircraft bombs deployed is about 7,500 spread over five types.

The number of tactical nuclear weapons (about 16,000) is only 60 per cent more than the number of strategic nuclear weapons (roughly 10,000). About 6,000 tactical nuclear warheads are deployed in NATO

Six of the 25 types of nuclear weapons in the American arsenal are still in production – the warhead for the air-launched cruise missile, the warhead for the Minuteman ICBM, the warhead for

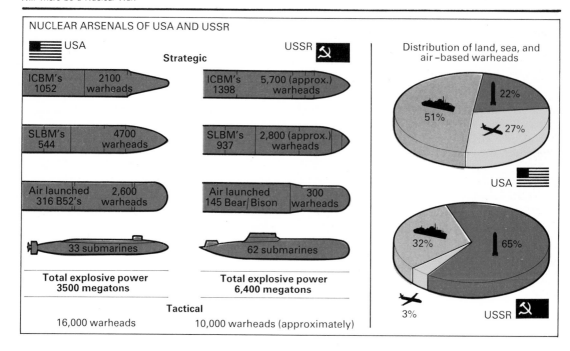

NUCLEAR ARSENALS OF USA AND USSR

USA | USSR

Strategic

	USA	USSR
ICBM's	1052 — 2100 warheads	1398 — 5,700 (approx.) warheads
SLBM's	544 — 4700 warheads	937 — 2,800 (approx.) warheads
Air launched	316 B52's — 2,600 warheads	145 Bear/Bison — 300 warheads
	33 submarines	62 submarines

Total explosive power 3500 megatons | **Total explosive power 6,400 megatons**

Distribution of land, sea, and air–based warheads

USA: 51% / 22% / 27%

USSR: 32% / 65% / 3%

Tactical

16,000 warheads | 10,000 warheads (approximately)

the Trident SLBM, the enhanced radiation warhead (neutron bomb), the 8-inch enhanced-radiation artillery shell for the Lance ground-to-ground missile and a free-fall bomb.

Four types of nuclear weapons are being, or soon will be, withdrawn from the American arsenal – the Nike-Hercules ground-to-air (anti-aircraft) missile, an atomic landmine, a strategic bomb, and the Titan-II ICBM. Ten other types will be replaced, and three others partially replaced.

Seven more types of nuclear warheads will be produced over the next five years. These are warheads for the submarine-launched cruise missile, a nuclear ship-to-air missile to defend warships against air attack, a 155-mm artillery shell, warheads for the ground-launched cruise missile,

An air-launched cruise missile (ALCM). Although the air-launched cruise missile weighs less than 1,360 kilograms, it has a range of some 2,500 kilometers and can deliver a 200-kiloton 'package'.

The Soviet and US nuclear arsenals. Between them, the two Superpowers have deployed more than twenty times more nuclear weapons than the other nuclear weapon nations put together. The combined explosive power of these weapons is equivalent to no less than one million Hiroshima bombs.

warheads for the Pershing-II ground-to-ground missile, warheads for the MX ICBM and a new strategic bomb.

According to current plans, about 9,000 new warheads of the six types now in production will be built. The plans call for the production of a total of about 10,000 warheads for the seven new types to be produced over the next five years. Looking further ahead, to the late 1980s and 1990s, Arkin and his colleagues list another seven types of nuclear weapons for production – for anti-submarine warfare weapons, the low-altitude air-defence system (an anti-ballistic-missile system), the lethal-neutralization system, the corps-support weapon system, advanced tactical air-delivered weapons, tactical air-to-surface munitions and advanced cruise missiles. They estimate that about 10,000 nuclear warheads will be produced for these future weapon systems.

It can be seen that the planned changes in the American arsenal are spectacular in their scale and their variety. These new weapons would amply suffice for the near destruction of humankind, as would their Soviet equivalents.

All in all, projected nuclear-warhead production in the USA from now until about the mid-1990s may involve the production of some 30,000 new warheads, of which about 14,000 are for weapons in current research and development programmes. The likelihood is that the US will deploy 23,000 new nuclear warheads by the end of the 1980s. Making an allowance for the fact that about 17,000 warheads will be withdrawn from the stockpile, or replaced, during this time the number of US nuclear warheads will grow from the current 26,000 to 32,000 by 1990. The Soviet nuclear arsenal will also expand dramatically within the same time horizon.

Three Tons of TNT for Everyone
Currently, the Soviet and American nuclear arsenals are roughly the same size. This means that together the Superpowers have deployed about 45,000 nuclear weapons. In contrast, the nuclear arsenals of the other three established nuclear-weapon powers (the United Kingdom, France and China) contain a total of about 2,000 nuclear warheads. The total explosive power of the American and Soviet nuclear arsenals is roughly 15,000 megatons. Some authorities say 20,000. This is equivalent to over one million Hiroshima bombs, or putting it another way, to over three tons of TNT for every man, woman and child on earth. This is 750 times all the high explosives used in all the wars in history. Many critics believe that the nuclear arsenals are, and have for many years been, much larger than needed for military, political or strategic purposes.

Because of the amount of 'overkill' in the nuclear arsenals, any further increase in the number of nuclear weapons deployed is very much less important than today's improvements in the quality of the weapons themselves. It is these qualitative developments which are causing the current changes in nuclear policies.

The blast-off of a Trident missile. Each submarine-launched Trident has, on average, eight independently targetable warheads, with each warhead having an explosive capacity equivalent to that of one hundred thousand tons of TNT.

For many years now the balance of nuclear power has worked as a deterrent to war, because of the fear (to use the jargon phrase) of 'mutual assured destruction'. In other words, if one of the two Superpowers launched a series of nuclear missiles at the major cities of the other Superpower, then the other Superpower would immediately retaliate by sending missiles to destroy the attacker's cities. Nobody has been ready to start a nuclear war, because it would promptly result in the destruction of the attacker's own cities.

The only strategy would be to knock out the retaliatory nuclear missiles of the enemy, preferably before they left the ground, as a very *first* step to an attack. If this could be done, then the side that first pressed the button would have an excellent chance of winning the war with little or no retaliation. Fortunately, up to now, this has been impossible. The missiles of both Superpowers are well concealed, protected in massive concrete bunkers, and extremely difficult to knock out. Only an extremely accurate attack could knock them out.

It is for this reason that the new developments in nuclear weapons are so very worrying. The most important advances, which are taking place right now, are radical improvements to their accuracy, reliability and targeting flexibility. Many of these new types of nuclear weapons are likely to be perceived as accurate enough – with their warheads delivered very precisely, even over vast, intercontinental distances – to knock out very small military targets, as opposed to big cities. If this becomes possible, then it is possible for one side to destroy the retaliatory power of the other at the very beginning of a war, especially if it is a surprise attack. According to some experts he who makes the first strike, for the first time in the history of nuclear weapons, stands a real chance of winning. For this reason there are uncomfortable signs of new policies being developed. The near-future emphasis will quite possibly change from the idea of using nuclear weapons to deter war to the idea of using them to win a war. This was quite impossible with the previous generation of weapons.

It is not necessary for one side to possess the ability completely to destroy the other side's retaliatory capability for such a first strike to be contemplated. It is sufficient for the attacker to believe (even if wrongly) that a surprise attack will reduce the enemy's capacity to fight back to the point where the attacker's casualties, caused by any retaliatory attack, will be 'acceptable' for a given political goal. Some writers have been ready (in theory) to sacrifice a great many of their fellow citizens in exchange for such a victory. We shall have more to say on this vital topic later on.

In this context one must remember that, in times of crisis, political leaders are more apt to listen to the advice of their military chiefs than to their civilian scientific advisers. The calculations of casualties which affect military decisions are quite likely to be based on wrong assumptions about the military performance of both sides. The performance of the enemy's weapons is likely to be overestimated and the performance of those on 'our' side underestimated: this is a 'worst-case' analysis for our performance and a 'best-case' analysis for theirs. On the other hand, military calculations about the effects of nuclear weapons are likely to emphasize estimates of immediate deaths and injuries and ignore the uncertain long-term effects, even though these long-term effects may well be ultimately more lethal. In addition, the serious sociological and psychological consequences of the total loss of social and technical services and the trauma of nuclear war are likely to be ignored as unquantifiable and therefore unimportant!

The New Generation of Ballistic Missiles
The accuracy of a nuclear missile is normally measured by its circular error probability (CEP). This is defined as the

radius of a circle centred on the target, within which half of a large number of warheads fired at the target will fall. In both the USA and the USSR, the CEPs of ballistic missiles (ICBMs and SLBMs) and of tactical nuclear weapons are being continually diminished as missiles become more accurate.

In the USA, for example, improvements have been made in the guidance system of the Minuteman-III ICBM which involve better mathematical descriptions of the performance of its inertial platform and accelerometers during flight, and better pre-launch calibration of its gyroscopes and accelerometers. With these improvements, the CEP of the Minuteman-III is about 200 meters, compared with 400 meters for the Minuteman-II. At the same time the design of the Minuteman warhead has been improved so that for the same weight, size, radar cross-section and aerodynamic characteristics, the explosive power of the warhead has been increased from 170,000 tons (170 kt) of TNT-equivalent to 330 kt.

These new Minuteman-III warheads delivered with their higher accuracy could destroy Soviet ICBMs in their silos (hardened to withstand over-pressures of 1,500 pounds per square inch) with a probability of success of about 57 per cent for one shot and about 95 per cent for two shots.

The improved land-based ICBM force significantly increases US nuclear-war fighting capabilities. These will be further increased by the MX missile system now under development. The American House of Representatives and the Senate voted in May, 1983, to allot further funds for this development. The guidance for the MX will be based on the advanced inertial-reference sphere (AIRS), an all-altitude system which can correct for movements of the missile along the ground before it is fired. A circular error probability of only 100 meters should be achieved with this system. If the MX warhead is provided with terminal guidance (using a laser or

radar system to scan the ground around the target, lock on to a distinctive feature in the area, and guide the warhead with great accuracy onto the target) CEPs of a few tens of meters are feasible.

The MX is a large missile, with a launch weight of about 86,000 kilograms, about 2.4 times heavier than the Minuteman-III, and a throw-weight (the weight the missile can carry as warheads) of about 3,500 kilograms – more than three tons. The three MX booster rockets will use advanced solid propellants, very light motor cases and advanced nozzles to propel the missile twice as efficiently as the Minuteman is propelled. The MX will carry up to twelve warheads, each with a yield of 330 kt.

American military planners have been very worried about the vulnerability of these massive weapons, even in concrete silos, and some spectacularly expensive schemes have been formulated to protect them. The MX missiles could, in fact, be fitted in the original Minuteman silos, but a mobile-basing system is more likely to be used. A typical design consists of a loop of roadway about twenty km long and ten km wide, with slip roads along it to each of 23 underground shelters. Each missile could be continuously moved from shelter to shelter, so that the enemy would have to knock out 22 empty shelters to be sure of getting the right one. The whole system in some versions would be underground, and the cost would be as much as 50 billion dollars! The most often quoted numbers are 200 MXs and the construction of 4,600 shelter points to house them. This system may well prove too dramatically expensive to be installed, but some system of ensuring the survival of many MX missiles in the case of a surprise Soviet attack is bound to be demanded by the military, and although the final decision about the basing of MX missiles is yet to be made, it is quite likely to be mobile.

The most formidable of Soviet ICBMs is the SS-18. This is thought to have a CEP of about 400 or 500 meters, with the accuracy soon being improved to about 250 meters. Each SS-18 warhead probably has an explosive power of about 500 kt. With the higher accuracy a typical SS-18 warhead would have about a 55 per cent chance of destroying a US Minuteman ICBM in its silo. Two warheads fired in succession would have about a 95 per cent chance of success.

The USSR also has the SS-19 ICBM, which is thought to be somewhat more accurate than the SS-18 and equipped with a similar warhead. Some of both the SS-18s and SS-19s are MIRVed, each missile carrying six, eight or ten warheads. In one of the single-warhead versions, the SS-18 is thought to carry a twenty-megaton warhead. This would have the dubious distinction of being probably the biggest bomb in the world, equal in power to *all* the explosives ever used previously in warfare.

The other Soviet MIRVed ICBM, the SS-17, carries four warheads, each with an explosive power of 750 kilotons. So far, about 670 of the Soviet ICBMs have been MIRVed, compared with 550 United

States MIRVed ICBMs. The Soviet MIRVed ICBM force carries a total of about 4,400 warheads. The US MIRVed ICBM force carries 1,650 warheads.

The Soviet strategic ICBM force is an increasing threat to the 1,000-strong US Minuteman ICBM force, as the accuracy and reliability of the Soviet warheads are improved. On both sides, these increasingly accurate ballistic-missile forces based on land may bring the prospect of a supposedly 'winnable' nuclear war much closer. Land-based missiles are increasingly being aimed at small, hardened military targets, in an attempt to create a situation where retaliation would be impossible. However, submarine-based ballistic missiles are still in many cases targeted on cities. This is, in a limited way, reassuring! It means that the risk remains – for the moment at least – that any first-strike attacker would suffer the loss of its own major cities in retaliation. It is very difficult indeed to be confident of knocking out all the enemy's submarines in a first strike.

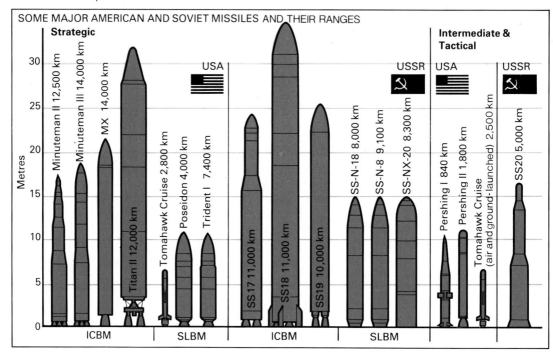

SOME MAJOR AMERICAN AND SOVIET MISSILES AND THEIR RANGES

Strategic — USA

Minuteman II 12,500 km
Minuteman III 14,000 km
MX 14,000 km
Titan II 12,000 km
Tomahawk Cruise 2,800 km
Poseidon 4,000 km
Trident I 7,400 km

SS17 11,000 km
SS18 11,000 km
SS19 10,000 km
SS-N-18 8,000 km
SS-N-8 9,100 km
SS-NX-20 8,300 km

Intermediate & Tactical — USSR / USA / USSR

Pershing I 840 km
Pershing II 1,800 km
Tomahawk Cruise (air and ground-launched) 2,500 km
SS20 5,000 km

ICBM | SLBM | ICBM | SLBM

(Opposite left) Circular Error Probability (CEP) is defined as the radius of a circle, centred on the target, within which half of a given number of warheads fired at the target will fall. In these three scenarios a missile is fired at an enemy missile protected in a hardened silo. Explosive yield is symbolized by the red circles

Strategic Nuclear Submarines

The Soviet and American navies operate between them a total of 95 modern strategic nuclear submarines, equipped with SLBMs. Their ballistic missiles are normally targeted on the enemy's cities and industry, and provide the assured destruction on which nuclear deterrence currently depends. A single US strategic nuclear submarine, for example, carries about 200 warheads, enough to destroy every Soviet city with a population of more than 150,000 people. American cities are hostages to Soviet strategic nuclear submarines to the same extent as Soviet cities are to American strategic submarines. Just four strategic submarines on appropriate stations in the oceans could destroy most of the major cities in the Northern Hemisphere.

The most advanced and newest class of Soviet ballistic-missile submarine in active operation is the Delta-class. Each one carries twelve or sixteen SLBMs, the missiles having ranges of about 8,000 kilometers. The SS-N-18, the missile carried by Delta-class submarines, is the first Soviet SLBM to be MIRVed. These missiles could hit most targets in the USA from Soviet home waters.

At the end of 1982 the Soviets had 240 SS-N-18s deployed, each equipped with seven MIRVs, each MIRV having a yield of about 200 kt. The SS-N-18s are carried on fifteen Delta-class submarines. The other main operational Soviet SLBM is the SS-N-8, with a range of about 8,000 kilometers and a single one-megaton warhead. There are 289 SS-N-8s deployed, mainly on 22 Delta-class submarines. The USSR also operates 24 Yankee Class strategic nuclear submarines, each carrying sixteen SS-N-6 SLBMs, a 3,000-kilometer range missile carrying either a 700-kt warhead or two 350-kt warheads. The two warheads cannot, however, be independently targeted and thus can only hit targets not very far apart.

In 1980, the USSR launched an extremely large strategic nuclear submarine, the Typhoon. This 170-meter long boat displaces, when submerged, 25,000 tons and carries 20 SLBMs. It will become operational in about the mid-

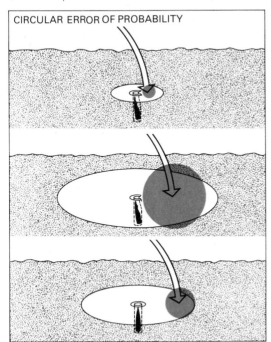

CIRCULAR ERROR OF PROBABILITY

and the CEP is the radius of the unshaded black circle. Top: a missile of small yield and small CEP destroys the target; this is what the Americans hope for. Middle: a less accurate (larger CEP) but very powerful missile also destroys the target; this is what the Russians, whose missiles are often much bigger, *hope for. Bottom: a medium-sized missile with a large CEP fails to destroy the target; neither side wants this. (Above) One of the first MX ICBMs in its gantry. The USA has decided to go ahead with building MXs, but the nature of their deployment is not yet settled.*

1980s and be equipped with a new, more accurate ballistic missile, the SS-NX-20. This SLBM will probably carry twelve warheads with a range of about 8,000 kilometers.

By the end of 1982, the USSR had deployed 937 SLBMs, 260 of them MIRVed, in its 62 strategic nuclear submarines. These SLBMs are capable of delivering about 2,800 nuclear warheads, about 33 per cent of the total number of

become operational at the rate of about one a year.

Trident-I SLBMs are being retro-fitted into Poseidon strategic nuclear submarines. So far, twelve Poseidons have been fitted with the new ballistic missiles. Nineteen other Poseidon boats are operational. Each carries sixteen Poseidon missiles, with ranges of about 4,500 kilometers.

The extra range of the Trident SLBMs

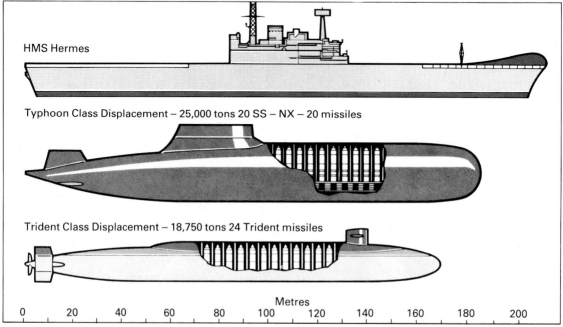

HMS Hermes

Typhoon Class Displacement – 25,000 tons 20 SS – NX – 20 missiles

Trident Class Displacement – 18,750 tons 24 Trident missiles

	Metres	
0 20 40 60 80 100	120 140 160	180 200

warheads in the Soviet nuclear arsenal.

The United States now operates two types of SLBM – the Poseidon and the Trident-I. Each Poseidon carries, on average, nine MIRVs, each with a yield of 40 kt. Each Trident-I carries, on average, eight MIRVs, each with a yield of 100 kt.

Trident-I SLBMs are deployed on Trident submarines and on Poseidon submarines. The Tridents are new boats. Two are now in operation. They are approximately twice as large as the Poseidon missile submarines which they are replacing. Each Trident carries 24 Trident SLBMs, with ranges of about 7,300 kilometers. Seven more Trident submarines are being built. They should

allows the submarines carrying them to operate in very much larger areas of the oceans and still be within range of targets in the USSR. The submarines do not then have to expose themselves to the same extent as their predecessors to Soviet anti-submarine warfare systems.

The US Navy can deliver 544 SLBMs, carrying a total of about 4,700 warheads, with a total explosive power of about 300 megatons. Nearly 50 per cent of American strategic nuclear warheads are carried on submarines.

The Americans plan to increase the accuracy of their SLBMs so that they will become as accurate as land-based ballistic missiles. The CEP of the Poseidon SLBM is

According to US intelligence the first of the new Soviet mystery submarines, the Typhoon class of SLBM launchers, will be fully operational with the Soviet Northern Fleet by the end of 1983. Published estimates of its length have varied from 170 meters to 200 meters; we have shown a compromise. It is almost as third as heavy again as the largest US SLBM launcher, the Trident class, but carries fewer missiles. A senior British submariner has commented 'What a gigantic target!' HMS Hermes, a light aircraft carrier, is shown for comparison.

about 550 meters; that of the Trident-I is probably about 500 meters at maximum range. The CEPs of SLBMs will be further reduced by the use of mid-course guidance techniques together with the more accurate navigation of the ballistic-missile submarines. The deployment of terminal guidance on the warheads will give CEPs of a few tens of meters. SLBMs will then be so accurate as to cease to be only deterrent weapons aimed at enemy

as accurate as American ones. The Soviets are said to have tested already a new SLBM, the SS-NX-17, with a CEP of about 500 meters.

Strategic Bombers
The USA is continually modernizing its strategic bomber fleet. Currently, B-52s are being provided with air-launched cruise missiles (ALCMs). The plan is to deploy some 3,000 cruise missiles, 25 per

cities. They will become nuclear-war-fighting weapons able to destroy enemy strategic nuclear forces.

Soviet SLBMs are significantly less accurate than their American counterparts. Operational Soviet SLBMs are thought to have CEPs exceeding 1,000 meters. But the accuracy of the missiles will steadily improve and they will eventually become

bomber.

The Reagan Administration also plans to build 100 B-1B bombers to replace some of the ageing B-52s. The first of this new generation of strategic bombers should be operational in 1986 and they too will carry ALCMs. The Administration is also encouraging intensive research into the Advanced Technology Bomber, or 'Stealth'

The B-1B bomber. The Reagan Administration plans to build 100 of these bombers over the next few years in order to replace the B-52s, many of which are to be phased out. The first B-1B bombers should be in operation sometime in 1986.

aircraft. This programme involves the development of radar-absorbing materials and aircraft shapes which give a very small radar cross-section. Terrain-following (low flying, following land contours) and other systems to avoid detection by Soviet air-defence systems are also being developed for 'Stealth' aircraft. The term 'low-observable' is used of any aircraft whose characteristics detectable by radar can be reduced ten times. This in turn reduces the time which a hostile air-defence system has available in which to engage a fast, low-flying aircraft to about half. As an example, the radar cross-section of the air-launched cruise missile is only one thousandth that of a B-52 bomber.

The air-launched cruise missile is a long-range, sub-sonic, nuclear-armed, winged vehicle, about six meters long, weighing less than 1,360 kilograms, with a range of about 2,500 kilometers, and a nuclear warhead of about 200 kt. The ALCMs could be launched from outside Soviet territory to attack Soviet air-defence systems, their radars and anti-aircraft missiles. Following waves of B-52 bombers would then be able to penetrate into Soviet territory to attack other targets with their nuclear bombs and ALCMs. The missiles are accurate enough to be used against small, hardened military targets and, because cruise missiles have relatively small radar cross-sections they are difficult to detect by radars on the ground.

Unlike the USA, the USSR maintains an extensive air-defence system based on a family of surface-to-air missiles and a large number of interceptor aircraft. The Soviets will probably extend their air-defence system to be able to cope with the cruise missiles now being deployed by the USA. This will probably involve the deployment of Airborne Warning and Control System aircraft to constantly patrol the Soviet borders to detect incoming air- or ground-launched cruise missiles, and alert and control fighter aircraft and surface-to-air missiles to shoot the enemy missiles down.

PERSHING II, CRUISE-MISSILE AND SS-20 — PROPOSED D

Netherlands

United Kingdom

Belgium

West Germany

Proposed Cruise missile deployment

Proposed Pershing II deployment

The believed current deployment of Soviet SS-20 missiles. These missiles, of which more than half are trained on Western Europe, have a range of about 5,000 kilometers and (usually) three independently targetable warheads, each with a yield of about 150 kilotons.

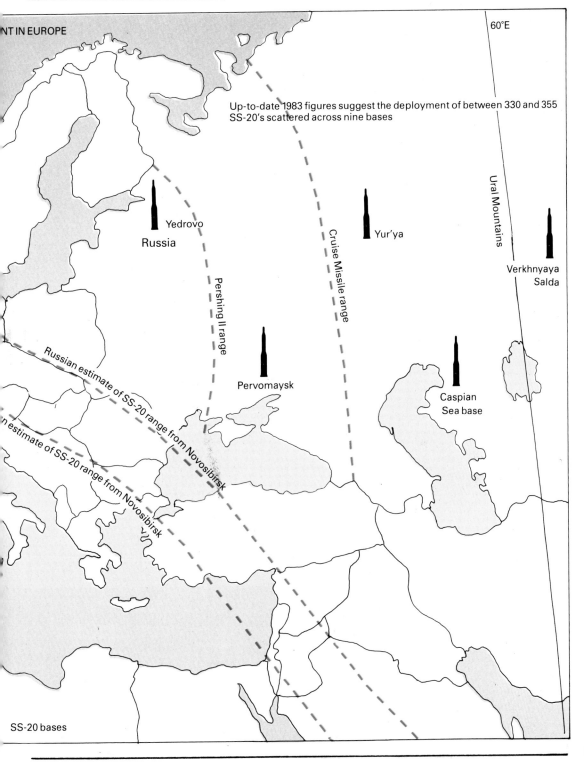

NT IN EUROPE

60°E

Up-to-date 1983 figures suggest the deployment of between 330 and 355 SS-20's scattered across nine bases

Yedrovo

Russia

Yur'ya

Ural Mountains

Verkhnyaya Salda

Pershing II range

Cruise Missile range

Russian estimate of SS-20 range from Novosibirsk

n estimate of SS-20 range from Novosibirsk

Pervomaysk

Caspian Sea base

SS-20 bases

There are those who believe that the main reason for the deployment by the USA of cruise missiles is to provoke the USSR into spending very large sums on these complex countermeasures.

Updating the Tactical Arsenal

Both the USA and the USSR are modernizing their tactical nuclear arsenals. Tactical nuclear weapons have a shelf-life of only twenty or so years, after which they must be withdrawn from the arsenal or replaced. This is because the fissile and fusion material in the weapons, particularly tritium, undergoes radioactive decay and other materials also deteriorate. Modernization is, therefore, inevitable if nuclear weapons are to be continually deployed.

Among the new types of nuclear weapons planned for NATO forces are Pershing-II missiles and ground-launched cruise missiles. These weapons are so accurate as to be perceived as nuclear-war-fighting weapons, like some of their larger strategic missile relatives. Both have a CEP of about 50 meters. Although less accurate than these American missiles, the Soviet SS-20, an intermediate range ballistic missile, is accurate enough, or soon will be made so, to be a nuclear-war-fighting weapon also, given the relatively large explosive power of its warhead.

The Soviet SS-20, first deployed in 1976, is a two-stage mobile missile, with a range of about 5,000 kilometers. About 330 of the missiles are deployed as of early 1983. Around 60 per cent are targeted on Western Europe (from sites west of the Urals) and the rest are targeted on China and possibly on other Asian targets (from sites east of the Urals). It is important to remember that it is not only America and its allies that are perceived as potential enemies by the Soviets. Each SS-20 normally carries three MIRVed warheads, each with a yield that is said to be about 150 kt. The CEP of the SS-20 is thought to be about 500 meters.

The Pershing-II, due to replace the Pershing-I missiles deployed by the USA in West Germany, will be provided with a sophisticated new guidance system called RADAG. When the warhead approaches its target a video radar scans the target areas and the image is compared with a reference image that was stored in the warhead's computer before the missile

An artist's impression of the deployment of Soviet SS-20 missiles, ready for use. Because the launchers of these weapons, like those of their NATO counterparts, are so highly mobile it is impossible for the opposing forces to 'knock them out' before launch.

was launched. This computer controls aerodynamic vanes which guide the warhead onto its target with an accuracy unprecedented in a missile with a range of 1,800 kilometers. The missile, due for deployment from the end of 1983, although described as tactical will be able to penetrate a significant distance into the USSR; it could, for example, reach Moscow from its sites in West Germany. The plan is to deploy 108 Pershing-IIs with warheads having yields in the low kilotonnage range.

NATO also plans to deploy 464 ground-launched cruise missiles between 1983 and 1988, in West Germany, Italy, the United Kingdom, Belgium and the Netherlands. The missiles will have ranges of about 2,500 kilometers and carry warheads with a yield in the kiloton range.

This concludes a brief survey of the nuclear arsenals presently deployed and about to be put into operation by the two Superpowers. Even in a severely condensed form, the variety and nomenclature of the various nuclear-weapon systems is enough to make the average person's head spin! The main danger of this is that people tend to turn

The launch of a Pershing-II missile. In spite of widespread protest in the countries concerned, 108 of these weapons will be deployed in Europe, starting from the end of 1983. The missile has a range of about 1,800 kilometers. Recent reports suggest, however, that its reliability may be questionable.

away from the nuclear debate because it seems so intricate and technical. We make no apology for presenting this catalogue of nuclear weaponry, however, for it is extremely important that everyone should try to understand at least the basic facts on which any judgment of the nuclear situation must be formed. This is especially true since the facts themselves are changing radically in these early years of the 1980s, with consequences that could bring the prospect of future war much closer. Yet these changes have not received a great deal of public attention, even in, for example, the 1983 United Kingdom election campaign.

The Drift from Deterrence to Dreams of Victory

Until the end of the 1970s the nuclear policy of the USA was nuclear deterrence by mutual assured destruction. Nuclear deterrence depends as we have explained on the belief that the enemy will not attack suddenly (pre-emptively) if he knows that most of his cities and industry will be destroyed in retaliation. Cities are the hostages to mutual assured destruction. If the enemy no longer fears that his cities are at risk nuclear deterrence by mutual assured destruction no longer works. This is precisely what happens when accurate and reliable nuclear weapons are deployed.

Deterrence is essentially a matter of psychology. What matters is what the enemy believes. It is impossible to maintain a policy of nuclear deterrence by mutual assured destruction once truly accurate weapons are introduced, simply because the enemy will assume, willy nilly, that the other side's nuclear warheads are targeted on his military forces and not on his cities. The cities then cease to be the hostages. Accuracy, in other words, kills deterrence. Nuclear-war fighting based on the destruction of hostile military forces, then becomes the only credible, and, therefore, the only feasible policy.

As we have seen, the current American nuclear policy is a complex mixture of nuclear deterrence by mutual assured destruction and plans for actual nuclear-war fighting. SLBMs provide the deterrence element, being still targeted on cities, while ICBMs are nuclear-war-fighting weapons, targeted on enemy strategic nuclear forces. But when the Trident-II missiles are deployed, about five years from now, SLBMs will also be accurate enough to be nuclear-war-fighting weapons and the US nuclear policy will become pure nuclear-war fighting.

A dangerous situation would be the deployment of significant numbers of tactical nuclear-war-fighting weapons in Europe, together with the deployment of strategic nuclear-war fighting weapons in the USA and the USSR. If tactical nuclear-war-fighting weapons are deployed in Europe they will be integrated into military tactics at low levels of command. Then, not only would a war in Europe almost inevitably escalate to a nuclear war but the military will more readily come to believe that a nuclear war is fightable and winnable, and that a protracted nuclear war limited in area (that is, to Europe) is possible.

Philip Williams[3] has pointed out that the four main requirements of United States strategic policy are as follows. Firstly, to have a capacity to 'render ineffective' the total Soviet (and allied) military and political power structure through attacks on the political and military leadership and their associated control facilities, on nuclear and conventional military forces and on industry critical to military power. Secondly, to possess nuclear forces 'that will maintain through a protracted conflict and afterward the capability to inflict very high levels of damage against the industrial and economic base of the Soviet Union and her allies so that they have a strong incentive to seek conflict termination short of an all-out attack on US cities and economic assets'. Thirdly, to 'maintain in reserve under all circumstances nuclear offensive capabilities so that the US would never

emerge from a war without nuclear weapons while still threatened by enemy nuclear forces'. Fourthly, to improve command and control facilities to a point where they are capable not only of 'supporting controlled nuclear attacks over a protracted period but of maintaining links with those SLBM forces which would be held in reserve throughout the conflict'.

War-fighting deterrence, as the present policy has been called, is giving way to war-winning strategies, in which it is argued that victory is possible in a nuclear war. Typical advocates of the possibility of nuclear victory are Colin Gray and Keith Payne.[4] In a nuclear war, they argue, 'the United States should plan to defeat the Soviet Union and to do so at a cost that would not prohibit US recovery'. They go on to say that 'a combination of counterforce offensive targeting, civil defense, and ballistic missile and air defense should hold US casualties down to a level compatible with national survival and recovery'.

Over the next five years the US Administration plans to spend about 250 billion dollars on strategic nuclear systems, including nuclear defence and command, control, and communications systems. A range of military technologies is being developed that will strengthen military and political perceptions about the possibility of fighting and winning a nuclear war. The most important of these technologies are those related to anti-submarine warfare, anti-ballistic missile systems and anti-satellite warfare systems.

If one side could severely limit the damage that the other side's strategic nuclear submarines could create in a retaliatory strike, and if it believed that it could destroy – by, for example, high-energy lasers in space – any enemy missile warheads which survived a surprise attack, then the temptation to make an all-out first strike may become well-nigh irresistible, particularly during a period of international crisis.

Are the Politicians in Control?

Many people believe that the progression from deterrence policies to nuclear-war winning policies is considerably increasing the danger of a nuclear world war. Not only is the danger of a deliberate attack by one side on the other increasing as both sides move towards a first-strike capability but, perhaps more seriously, there is an increasing danger of nuclear war caused by accident, miscalculation or madness. We have seen that this situation is coming about because the nuclear arms race is continually producing improvements in nuclear weapons. Even if political leaders wanted to maintain their old policy of nuclear deterrence by mutual assured destruction they would be prevented from doing so by the characteristics of the new nuclear weapons developed by military scientists. Military science, it could be argued, is no longer under political control. (It is interesting – and perhaps cheering – to recall in this context the remark of Lord Carver, ex-Chief of Staff of the British forces, that if he had received an order to use nuclear weapons he would not have obeyed it, since it would have proved that the Prime Minister was insane!)

Today, about 500,000 scientists around the world work on military research and development. This is about 25 per cent of all scientists employed on research. This large group of scientists is a powerful political lobby. Moreover, vast bureaucracies have grown up in the great powers to deal with military matters. Academics and bureaucrats join with the military and the weapons industry to form a giant academic–bureaucratic–military–industrial complex intent on maintaining and increasing military budgets, and agitating for the use of every conceivable technological advance for military purposes. This complex has so much power as to be politically almost irresistible. If this is so, the nuclear arms race is now totally out of the control of political leaders. And this is as true in the Soviet Union as it is in the USA.

In fact, because similar military technological developments are taking place in the USSR, Soviet and American nuclear policies can be expected to develop in roughly the same way. In most areas of military technology the USA is ahead of the USSR but only by a few years. The knowledge that the other side could catch up will increase the temptation to make a surprise nuclear attack once the perception of a first-strike capability fully develops.

Frank Barnaby

References

1   The data in this chapter come mainly from **World Armaments and Disarmament, SIPRI Yearbook 1983,** Taylor and Francis, London, 1983
2   Arkin, W.M., Cochran, T.B. and Hoenig, M.M., **Nuclear Weapons Data Book,** Ballinger, Washington, 1983
3   Williams, P., **Deterrence, Warfighting and American Nuclear Strategy,** ADIU Report, Jan. 1983
4   Gray, C.S., and Payne, K., 'Victory is Possible', **Foreign Policy,** Summer 1982

Chapter 4

New Members of the Nuclear Club

The expertise to design and construct nuclear explosives is quite easy to find. So much so, that the authorities are now worried that terrorists or even criminal groups will build nuclear devices. Few governments would have any difficulty in finding people to design and construct efficient nuclear weapons.

The central threat of the nuclear age is that plutonium can be used as a very powerful explosive. A nuclear weapon of the type and explosive power that destroyed Nagasaki, and killed about 80,000 people, could, for example, be made using just a few kilograms of plutonium. In an atomic bomb of modest efficiency, about twenty per cent of the plutonium is detonated. Such a device would typically use about five kilograms of plutonium to produce an explosion equivalent to twenty kilotons of high explosive. Such is the awesome efficiency of nuclear explosions that a grapefruit-sized chunk of plutonium can be made to explode with a power equivalent to the amount of high explosive that would fill a train eight kilometers long. And this would not be a very remarkable device. Today's nuclear-weapon designers would regard it as primitive indeed.

If a terrorist group exploded a nuclear device containing just five kilograms of plutonium with an efficiency as low as one tenth of one per cent, it would still explode with the power of one hundred tons of TNT – a big enough explosion to shatter the centre of a city, and to cause a great deal of radioactive contamination. One does not have to be very expert to do much damage with a relatively small amount of plutonium. You would have to be prepared to take some risk with your own life and be prepared to disregard other lives. But this is just what terrorists *are* prepared to do.

It seems very probable that the leaders of terrorist groups have at least thought about using nuclear and other mass destruction devices. Presumably, they have until now decided that killing, or threatening to kill, large numbers of people indiscriminately would not further their ends, but there is reason to believe that this attitude may change. The presence of large amounts of plutonium and its frequent transportation may tempt terrorists to steal it to build, or threaten to build, nuclear explosives. The main bugbear in guarding against this is the very small amount of plutonium needed to build a bomb.

Plutonium – the Dangerous Element
Plutonium does not exist in nature except in very minute amounts, but it is produced as an inevitable by-product in nuclear reactors. The fuel in a reactor is normally uranium, a widely distributed element. As the fuel is burned up in the reactor, nuclear fission occurs in the uranium. Fission produces heat. The heat is used to produce steam which drives a turbine and produces electricity. But as the uranium is used up plutonium is produced.

For the most efficient nuclear weapons, plutonium rich in the isotope plutonium–239 is required; preferably, the proportion of plutonium–239 should exceed 93 per cent of the total fissile material. Such plutonium (called weapons-grade) can be produced from a nuclear-power reactor normally used to produce electricity commercially by limiting the burn-up of the uranium fuel, that is, the amount of energy released by the uranium. The fuel elements would be removed after they had been in the reactor for a period of weeks.

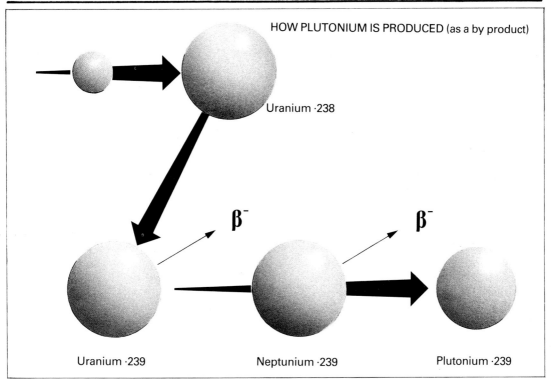

HOW PLUTONIUM IS PRODUCED (as a by product)

Uranium ·238

β^- β^-

Uranium ·239   Neptunium ·239   Plutonium ·239

When a power reactor is operated under normal conditions for the generation of electricity, the fuel elements are left in the reactor for three or four years. The plutonium in the fuel elements then contains much less of the isotope plutonium–239. This plutonium could still be used to produce effective nuclear weapons, although the explosive power of the bomb would be less for a given amount of plutonium, and also less predictable.

Any nation which has nuclear-power reactors is accumulating plutonium on its territory which could be used in nuclear weapons. It could, of course, choose to produce weapons-grade plutonium at any time. Such countries are also producing scientists and engineers with nuclear skills, some of whom could be recruited into a nuclear-weapons programme. The military use of nuclear power is intimately linked with its peaceful use. The Nobel prize winning physicist, Hannes Alfven, commented that 'the peaceful atom and the military atom are Siamese twins'.

Plutonium could also be obtained clandestinely from a reactor, acquired specially for the purpose. A typical nuclear-power reactor generates about 1,000 million watts of electricity (MWe), and produces each year about 250 kilograms of plutonium. A small reactor with a power of about 40MWe could produce enough plutonium each year for two 20-kt atomic bombs. The components for such a reactor can be easily, and secretly, obtained on the open market for a cost of 30 million dollars or so. The reactor and a small chemical reprocessing unit to remove the plutonium from the reactor fuel elements could be clandestinely constructed and run by, say, the military. The units could be effectively disguised or hidden in a building or underground. It was in this way that Israel acquired and operated the reactor at Dimona, from which it produced the plutonium for (it is usually assumed) a nuclear-weapon force.

Plutonium – the isotope Pu-239 which can be used for making nuclear weapons as in the Nagasaki bomb 'Fat Boy' – is a natural by-product in all nuclear reactors which use uranium-238 as fuel. The normally stable U-238, which usually constitutes about 97 per cent of a reactor's fuel, is partly converted into Pu-239. (A fast neutron enters a U-238 atom, which then emits two beta-particles – electrons – to become a Pu-239 atom.) This effect can be increased in so-called fast-breeder reactors by wrapping a blanket of U-238 around the reactor core. It is easy to separate out the fissile Pu-239 in a reprocessing plant for use in weapons.

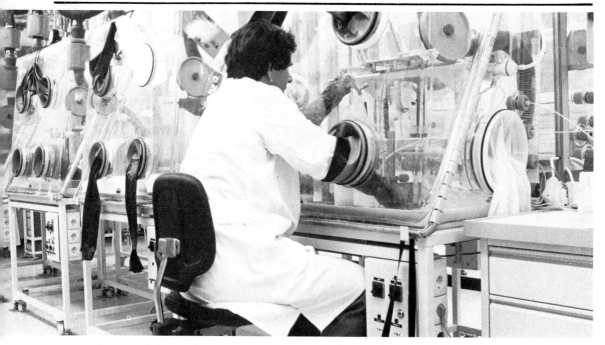

Uranium enriched with the rare isotope uranium–235 can also be used to construct nuclear weapons. A small plant to enrich uranium could also be constructed clandestinely for a nuclear-weapon programme. It is generally believed that Pakistan is now doing just this and that South Africa has already done so.

Because the facilities to produce plutonium and enriched uranium for nuclear weapons can be built and operated secretly and simply, we do not certainly know which countries have nuclear weapons and which do not. There is no system of nuclear safeguards which can bring such clandestine nuclear operations to light.

A system of international safeguards *is* operated by the International Atomic Energy Agency (IAEA) but it can only detect the diversion of plutonium or uranium from the plants it safeguards after the event. It cannot prevent such diversion, and the little it can do depends on the co-operation of the country being inspected.

The Nuclear Third World

In 1983 about 260 nuclear-power reactors are operating in some 27 countries. Another 250 or so power reactors are ordered or are under construction. So far, about 150,000 kilograms of plutonium have been accumulated world-wide from civilian electricity-producing nuclear-power reactors. (Incidentally, this is roughly the same as the amount of plutonium now in the world's nuclear-weapon arsenals.) The civilian reactors world-wide are now producing about 30,000 kilograms of plutonium a year, which is theoretically enough to manufacture an atomic bomb of the Nagasaki type every three hours. Most of this plutonium is being left in spent reactor fuel elements, stored under water near the power reactors from which they have been removed, until decisions are made about the construction of new commercial reprocessing plants. These decisions will have a great bearing on the future spread of nuclear weapons, both to governments and to terrorist groups.

At present, twelve nuclear-power reactors are operating in six developing

The International Atomic Energy Agency (IAEA) applies its safeguards to well over 800 nuclear installations outside the nuclear-weapon states. This figure represents 98 per cent of the installations the IAEA knows about: none the less, it is believed that some states are dodging the safeguards and manufacturing nuclear warheads using the products of their power stations.

countries – Argentina, Brazil, India, South Korea, Pakistan and Taiwan, with a total generating capacity of about 6,000 MWe. About twenty plants with a capacity of some 16,000 MWe are under construction in these six countries and also in Cuba, Mexico, the Philippines and South Africa. These nuclear plants contribute very little to energy production in the Third World countries: a mere one per cent of the total electricity in Third World countries is generated by nuclear power (compared with about ten per cent for the whole world). This raises the suspicion that at least some Third World countries want nuclear power to give them the option of constructing nuclear weapons if they take the political decision to do so.

The emergence of new nuclear-weapon powers in some regions would have very serious ramifications for the security of those regions. This is perhaps most true for the Middle East. Nuclear developments in this area are, therefore, of particular interest and concern.

Most observers believe that Israel already has a nuclear-weapon force, containing, some say, twenty or so nuclear weapons, presumably constructed with plutonium from Israel's small reactor at Dimona.

Egypt, Libya, and Iraq plan significant nuclear-energy programmes which will eventually give them the expertise to design, and the capability to produce the plutonium for, nuclear weapons. Nuclear developments in the Middle East are likely to depend to some extent on Pakistan's nuclear programme, which is known to include the building of a small uranium-enrichment plant near Karachi. Enriched uranium from this plant may be used, and many would say will be used, for a nuclear explosion.

A Pakistan nuclear bomb would have considerable consequences in the region. There are said, for example, to be close Libyan and Saudi Arabian links with Pakistan's nuclear programme.

Libya already operates a small research reactor at Tajura. It plans to construct a 440-MWe nuclear power reactor, to be imported from the USSR, on the Libyan coast. This reactor will produce about 100 kilograms of plutonium a year, theoretically enough for ten or more

Nuclear India: a peaceful power station or a plutonium factory? In the Third World, twelve nuclear reactors (soon to become 32) are in operation, yet they contribute only one per cent to national power usage. India exploded its first nuclear bomb in 1974; are more in manufacture?

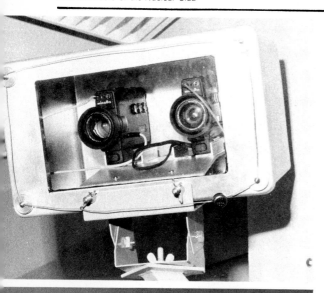

nuclear weapons a year. Officially, the reactor's purpose is to provide electricity for tourist resorts and also possibly to desalinate water.

nuclear weapons a year. Officially, the reactor's purpose is to provide electricity for tourist resorts and also possibly to desalinate water.

The fact that Libya has large oil resources and, therefore, no obvious need for nuclear power for electricity generation, is enough to raise the suspicion that Libya's nuclear interest is related mainly to nuclear weapons. Moreover, Libya has had a long-standing interest in nuclear weapons. Some years ago it made an unsuccessful attempt to buy one from China.

from Niger to Pakistan via Libya. In this way Pakistan gets more of Niger's uranium than it officially admits. Libya pays for the extra, secret amount. The IAEA then has no accurate idea about the amount of uranium entering Pakistan, for Libya does not allow IAEA inspectors to account for the uranium it transfers.

Tough Action from Israel

It is a fundamental goal of Israel's foreign policy to prevent any other country in the Middle East from acquiring nuclear weapons. The lengths to which Israel will go to achieve this goal are shown by its raid on Iraq's nuclear facility. On June 7, 1981, Israeli aircraft attacked and destroyed Iraq's Osirak research reactor – an act justified by Prime Minister Begin as necessary to assure Israel's survival. Israel believed that Iraq would use plutonium produced by the reactor, or enriched uranium fuel supplied (by France) for the reactor, to build nuclear weapons. Actually, the Israeli raid may have been even more dramatic than is generally believed. The aircraft may have been a cover operation. The reactor may have been destroyed by explosives placed by Israeli agents inside it and detonated by radio signal from Israel at the precise moment that the Phantom aircraft were dropping their bombs.

A double camera in use as part of the IAEA's surveillance system. Sadly, it is virtually impossible for the IAEA to detect the diversion of plutonium for military use until after the event. By that time, of course, it is too late.

An IAEA inspector – Keisuke Kaieda – at work in the Austrian nuclear-power station at Zwentendorf.

There is an element of speculation in this scenario. First suspicions that the blowing-up of the reactor was accomplished by sabotage were aroused when Jordan reported having detected an Israeli radio signal at that moment. Certainly, the bombing was suspiciously accurate for a single, high-speed bombing run. If there was such a deception (to protect Israeli intelligence agents) it was certainly a brilliant diversionary tactic to send in aircraft. These were flown to Iraq, incidentally, in a formation that simulated the radar image of a commercial airliner, and were so reported by radar operators in Jordan, over which they flew.

Iraq has rather ambitious nuclear plans, involving eventually the construction of a number of nuclear-power reactors. Egypt, which has been operating a research reactor at Inhas near Cairo since 1961, also plans to erect a nuclear-power reactor, to be imported from the USA.

Egypt, Iraq, and Libya have ratified the Nuclear Non-Proliferation Treaty (NPT). Many argue, though, that the treaty is not necessarily effective, because it allows each party to withdraw from it after giving three months' notice if a member nation decides that 'extraordinary events' have 'jeopardized the supreme interests of the country'. The treaty allows its parties to construct all the parts of a nuclear weapon. Only the assembly of the weapon is prohibited. Thus a member nation could legally produce all the components of a number of nuclear weapons, and then withdraw from the treaty and assemble them.

Because Egypt, Iraq, and Libya are in the NPT, all their nuclear facilities are inspected by the IAEA. But they can, and do, choose the nationality of the inspectors they will accept on their territory and the timing of any inspection. For these, and other reasons, the NPT is regarded as a weak barrier unlikely to prevent a country from acquiring nuclear weapons if it took the political decision to do so.

In 1974, India exploded a nuclear device. This nuclear explosion used exactly the same techniques as those used in nuclear weapons and, therefore, India demonstrated her capability to be a nuclear-weapon power. It was generally expected that Pakistan would be provoked by this event to do the same.

Currently, Pakistan has two reactors operating – one research reactor and one power reactor. The 125-MWe power reactor, which has been operating since 1972, produces plutonium very efficiently, and Pakistan is accumulating plutonium at a significant rate. Another power reactor (600 MWe) is being built at Chasma and should soon be operational. According to the chairman of the Pakistan Atomic Energy Commission, Pakistan will have 24 nuclear-power plants in operation by the Year 2000, an optimistic prediction.

Pakistan does not have a commercial reprocessing plant. A contract was signed with France in 1976 to buy one but was later abandoned because of American pressure. The Americans were afraid that Pakistan would use the plant to produce plutonium for nuclear weapons. Pakistan could, of course, build a small reprocessing plant of its own for military purposes but it might then be refused further foreign nuclear assistance because the plutonium they were processing was originally produced in imported reactors subject to IAEA safeguards. It is to avoid this problem that Pakistan, financed, it is reported, to the tune of a few hundred million dollars by Saudi Arabia, is constructing a plant to enrich uranium. Pakistan is building this plant itself and, therefore, need not put it under IAEA safeguards. The enriched uranium may then be used (instead of plutonium) for a nuclear explosion. Pakistan, like India, has not joined the NPT. If Pakistan does explode a nuclear device, it could possibly start a nuclear arms race on the sub-continent with unpredictable consequences.

Latin America and East Asia
A nuclear arms race may also be under

nuclear weapons into the South Atlantic during the Falklands war. Argentina has, over the years, built up a significant nuclear programme, including five research reactors (two of Argentine design) and two power reactors. A 300-MWe reactor has been in operation in Lima, Buenos Aires, since 1974. A 600-MWe reactor will soon be operating at Embalse Rio Tercero at Cordova. And a 700-MWe reactor is scheduled for operation in 1987 in Lima. The power reactors are of a type that produces plutonium efficiently and is convenient for the production of weapons-grade plutonium.

Argentina, which has considerable nuclear assistance from Canada, Switzerland, Spain, India, the USSR, and particularly West Germany, has nearly completed a new reprocessing plant at Ezeiza, which will not be under any international safeguards. The plant is relatively large; it will produce roughly 300 kilograms of plutonium a year, enough for 30 or so nuclear weapons a year. Suspicions that much of Argentina's interest in nuclear technology is to acquire the capability to produce nuclear weapons

way in Latin America between Argentina and Brazil. This is because they are vying for prestige in the region; there have been no actual hostilities between the two countries in recent history. Argentina felt an especially strong provocation to go nuclear when the United Kingdom carried

are strengthened by the fact that Argentina has not yet ratified (although it has signed) the Treaty of Tlatelolco for the Prohibition of Nuclear Weapons in Latin America. Nor has Argentina joined the NPT.

Argentinian enthusiasm for nuclear

HMS Invincible, with her supporting ships, heading for the Falkland Islands in preparation for the 1982 conflict between the UK and Argentina. It is virtually certain, although the UK government has failed to confirm it, that Invincible was carrying nuclear weapons.

In his notorious 'If . . .' cartoon in the London Guardian, Steve Bell has frequently criticized the British military campaign to recapture the Falkland Islands from the Argentinians. Here the jingoistically patriotic 'King Penguin' discovers one of the hidden and less savoury facts of the campaign.

weapons will have been increased by its experiences in the Falklands war. Some of the ships in the British naval task force sent to the Falklands were equipped to carry nuclear weapons, including the aircraft carrier *Invincible* and some destroyers and frigates. One must assume that these ships carried their nuclear weapons. The presence of hostile nuclear-capable warships in its vicinity may well hasten the day when Argentina produces nuclear weapons. Brazil will almost certainly follow suit.

Brazil's first nuclear-power reactor, generating about 600 MWe, will soon start operating at Itaorna, Rio de Janeiro. Two others are under construction at Itaorna. When all three are operating, a few years from now, Brazil will have over 3,000 MWe of nuclear power.

Two of the Brazilian power reactors are to be supplied by West Germany; the other is American. The West German reactors are part of a deal signed in 1975 by which West Germany will provide Brazil with a reprocessing plant and a uranium-enrichment plant. This multi-billion dollar deal has been severely criticized by a number of countries,

decide to do so. Included in the deal is an option for six more nuclear-power reactors to be completed by 1990, a hopelessly optimistic timetable.

The nuclear programme of Brazil, with its plans for reprocessing and uranium enrichment, will certainly give it the capability to produce nuclear weapons. The fact that Brazil, like Argentina, has not ratified the Tlatelolco Treaty or the NPT, indicates a desire for a nuclear-weapon option.

The other countries in Latin America with plans for significant nuclear-power programmes are Mexico and Cuba. Mexico is constructing two 650-MWe reactors at Cardel, Veracruz; the reactors are being imported from the USA. Cuba's 440-MWe reactor will come from the USSR.

At the opposite side of the world, South Korea and Taiwan also have ambitious nuclear plans. South Korea has had an American 560-MWe power reactor in operation near Pusan City since 1978. A Canadian 630-MWe reactor is virtually ready at Ulsan and an American 600-MWe reactor is under construction near Pusan City. When these reactors are operating,

especially the USA. It will be the first time that an enrichment plant or a reprocessing plant has been exported. Many fear that, even though the facilities will be under IAEA safeguards, the nuclear know-how acquired by Brazil will greatly help it to construct nuclear weapons if it should

South Korea will have about 1,800 MWe of nuclear power. The plan is to have four more reactors in operation by 1990, giving South Korea a total of over 5,000 MWe of nuclear power.

Taiwan has two nuclear-power reactors, imported from the USA, in operation at

Nuclear power stations in Brazil (left) and Argentina (right). Neither country has signed the Treaty of Tlatelolco for the Prohibition of Nuclear Weapons in Latin America, and it seems likely in both cases that their interest in nuclear power is purely a product of the desire to become nuclear-weapon states. Since neither has a need for nuclear weapons, this is probably an example of international 'face' fuelling the arms race.

Shihmin Hsain, each with an output of about 600 MWe. Another is almost ready and yet another is under construction at Wanli Hsain. When all four reactors are operating Taiwan will be producing over 3,000 MWe by nuclear power. Taiwan constructed a small reprocessing facility at the Lung Tan Nuclear Energy Research Centre but it was dismantled some time ago. It shows, however, that a small Third World country like Taiwan is well able to handle the technology of nuclear reprocessing.

A South African Bomb

On July 3, 1977, the Soviet spy satellite *Cosmos 922* passed over the Kalahari Desert in South Africa. The sky was cloudless and conditions were ideal for space photography. On July 20, a week after *Cosmos 922's* mission ended, *Cosmos 932*, a manoeuvrable satellite carrying close-look photographic equipment, was launched. Two days later it was directed over the Kalahari. *Cosmos 932* was recovered on August 2, 1977. Four days later Soviet officials informed the Americans that a South African nuclear test was imminent. Pressure was then applied by the Superpowers on South Africa to persuade them not to go through with a nuclear test – if it had intended to do so. There was, in fact, no nuclear explosion in the Kalahari. But two years later an explosive event occurred over the Indian Ocean that was registered on scientific equipment in a satellite. Many scientists still believe that this was a nuclear test – probably South African – even though a White House committee of scientists has judged the evidence to be inconclusive.

In fact, South Africa has had the technical capability to produce nuclear weapons for many years. A research reactor has been in operation at the National Research Centre at Pelindaba, near Pretoria, since as early as 1964. A second research reactor has been in operation at Pelindaba since 1967.

If South Africa has produced nuclear weapons, as many believe it has, they may well have been made from enriched uranium produced from a pilot plant which became operational at Valindaba in 1976. How much uranium is produced, like all nuclear matters in South Africa, is kept a closely guarded secret. The plant is subject to no international safeguards.

A South African nuclear-power station has been under construction at Koeberg, near Cape Town, since 1976. Two power reactors, each producing nearly 1,000 MWe, are being built there by a French consortium. One will soon be switched on, thanks to the recent release of uranium fuel from France by the Mitterand government. The other should be ready in 1984. The reactors will produce 400 kilograms of plutonium a year, theoretically enough to produce a Nagasaki-type bomb each week. Given South Africa's huge deposits of coal, the use of comparatively expensive nuclear energy for electricity generation makes no economic sense.

There is strong speculation, though no positive proof, that there has been secret international co-operation between Israel, Taiwan and South Africa in nuclear weapons. The Anti-Apartheid movement thinks this is certain; others think it is probable. Though there is no direct confirmation, the nature of scientific and military visits between the three nations is regarded by many as circumstantial evidence almost as strong as finding a trout in the milk would be of a lesser conspiracy. The supposed collaboration is between Israel and South Africa on the one hand, and South Africa and Taiwan on the other. There is no good evidence for a direct Israel Taiwan link.

Military links of a lesser kind have long been alleged between Israel and South Africa. It has been suggested that United States arms dealers have used Israel as a 'proxy' for getting undercover arms shipments to South Africa. The Israeli government has denied any recent arms deal of this kind.

In many ways, of course, Israel, Taiwan

and South Africa have little in common. However, all three are small powers living in close proximity to hostile nations, and all three are regarded to a degree as 'pariah' nations by the great powers. It may very well be that this has led to a degree of communal feeling between the three countries.

Why Should a Country Want the Bomb?

The Third World countries that most experts believe are immediately likely candidates to produce nuclear weapons are Argentina, Brazil, Egypt, Iraq, Libya, Pakistan, South Korea and Taiwan. India, which has already exploded a nuclear device, and Israel and South Africa, which are generally assumed to have nuclear weapons already, are excluded from the list.

The most important reasons why these countries may go nuclear are (i) prestige, and (ii) a need to solve real or imagined security threats. There is also likely to be a 'domino' effect in some regions. If one country acquires nuclear weapons, a neighbouring one may feel obliged to do the same. Thus, Pakistan, the next most likely country to explode a nuclear device in the near future, will do so in the first instance because of India's nuclear explosion.

Countries like Israel have, or perceive that they have, security problems which they think may be helped by the acquisition of nuclear weapons. Taiwan and South Korea may eventually acquire nuclear weapons for similar reasons.

Prestige is an important stimulant for nuclear-weapon proliferation. The fact that

THE NUCLEAR POWERS – Who Has The Bomb?

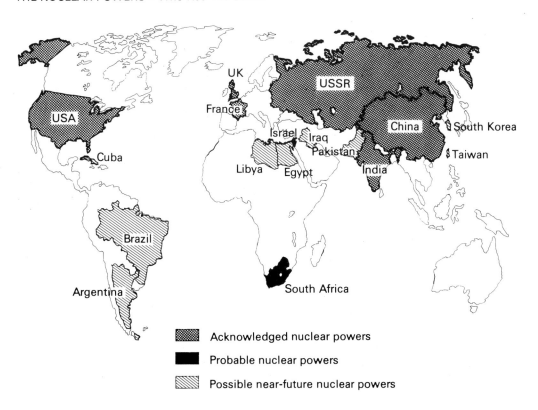

- Acknowledged nuclear powers
- Probable nuclear powers
- Possible near-future nuclear powers

The world's nuclear powers—as of 1984.

all the permanent members of the United Nations Security Council are nuclear-weapon states has a potent symbolism that is not lost on those countries without nuclear weapons. Prestige was the main reason why the United Kingdom acquired nuclear weapons, and it may (ironically) play a substantial role in the nuclear thinking of Argentina. If Argentina acquires nuclear weapons to enhance its prestige in Latin America, Brazil will probably feel impelled to do the same so as not to fall behind in the competition for regional status.

Political leaders may want to explode nuclear devices for internal political reasons – to boost their domestic political prestige or to distract the attention of the population from worsening internal social or economic problems. India very likely exploded its nuclear device partly for this reason, partly to impress Pakistan, and partly to try to enhance its security against China.

South Africa is a rather special case. The use of nuclear weapons in southern Africa would make no military, or other, sense, although some diehard white South African fanatics may argue fiercely for its potential in any last-ditch military effort. This argument is certainly likely to come up if internal pressures from black liberation movements become very strong. There is, however, little doubt that Soviet and American policies towards South Africa, whether they desire to influence events directly or by proxy, will be affected by the acquisition of nuclear weapons by the Pretoria regime. The South African government may imagine that the threat to use nuclear weapons may at some future time provoke the Americans to support it. This would be out of fear that the use of nuclear weapons in South Africa might escalate to a nuclear world war, as indeed it could.

Reprocessing

The risk of nuclear weapons spreading will increase spectacularly if there is, in the future, any large-scale reprocessing of spent reactor fuel elements. Currently, the world's nuclear power reactors are generating a total of about 150,000 MWe of electricity and producing about 35,000 kilograms of plutonium a year. By the Year 2000, the world's power reactors may be generating about 600,000 MWe and producing about 150,000 kilograms of plutonium a year.

If fast breeder reactors are developed and used commercially, they will require large amounts of plutonium (rather than uranium) for fuel and there will, therefore, be strong economic pressures for reprocessing the bulk of spent reactor fuel, so that it can be used again. Perhaps eight or so industrialized countries are likely to operate commercial reprocessing plants. But the nuclear-power reactors will be spread through 40 or more countries. Plutonium will therefore have to be transported in massive quantities by road, rail, air and sea on the world's transportation networks to and from the reprocessing plants. Plutonium may well be diverted from reprocessing plants by governments for military purposes, or even by individuals for terrorist or criminal purposes. All plants and nuclear transports will, therefore have to be specially protected against the unofficial diversion of even very small amounts of plutonium. The present system for safeguarding plutonium, developed by the IAEA, is based on accountancy and material control. Even using the best available and foreseeable technology they are not now, nor in the likely future, able to give a satisfactory assurance that significant quantities of plutonium have not been removed from a given reprocessing plant. It must be remembered that even if safeguards were 99.5 per cent accurate, large amounts of plutonium would still be unaccounted for. Specifically, if 150,000 kilograms of plutonium, the figure for the Year 2000, were involved, 750 kilograms of plutonium would be unaccounted for, enough to make a Nagasaki-type nuclear weapon each week.

Effective protection against the theft of

small amounts of plutonium from a reprocessing plant would involve the continuous observation of workers, on and off the job surveillance of numerous people and the use of an army of highly trained guards. It is very doubtful if the measures required for a satisfactory level of physical protection would be socially acceptable in any democratic society.

Conclusions

Unless barriers to the spread of nuclear weapons more effective than the existing ones are evolved, it is likely that the number of nuclear-weapon powers will increase. Because of the possibility of the clandestine production of nuclear weapons we do not certainly know which countries now have nuclear weapons and which do not. In any case, there are a number of countries in the Third World with significant nuclear-energy programmes, and this number will grow. These countries could rapidly construct nuclear weapons if they took the political decision to do so. For all international-political intents and purposes, therefore, these countries must already be regarded as virtual nuclear powers.

The danger of nuclear-weapon proliferation will considerably increase if the use of breeder reactors becomes widespread. In particular, the large-scale reprocessing of spent reactor fuel elements is likely to encourage the diversion of plutonium both by governments and by terrorists or criminals. Many nuclear physicists could design an effective nuclear weapon from information readily available in the open literature. (This was dramatically illustrated recently when a young American graduate student, as an exercise, designed a workable bomb using only publicly available information. His professor was surprised!) With the assistance of electronics specialists, metallurgists and experts on chemical high explosives, such a physicist could construct and assemble it. To put together a relatively crude but still very powerful nuclear explosion, a team of four or so people would be enough. The more countries or groups there are with access to nuclear weapons, the more likely is a nuclear war. The combination of these facts makes for a very uncertain future.

Frank Barnaby

Chapter 5

New War Technologies

In the past fifteen years the characteristics of major weapons and weapon carriers – tanks, combat aircraft, missiles and warships – have changed beyond all recognition, even though the new types of weapon sometimes *look* quite similar to their predecessors. The changes have been largely brought about by much increased accuracy in guiding weapons, mainly through the use of microelectronics; the development of new materials; more efficient fuels; greater engine efficiency; the development of better armour; improved resistance to electronic, optical and other counter-measures; greater adaptability of firing platforms; and small size and lower weight of weapons and weapon systems. In addition, technological improvements have taken place along the entire chain of the battlefield complex in which weapons are only one link – from the remote surveillance of borders to the identification and location of targets; from firing and controlling weapons to the assessment of the damage they do to enemy forces; and, if necessary, to remotely controlling repeated attacks in order to destroy the enemy totally.

These technological advances are the work of military scientists engaged in research and development (R and D). For many years now military scientists have not been significantly constrained by a shortage of money. In the past ten years, the USA, for example, spent about 130 billion dollars on military research and development, compared to 40 billion dollars on space research and development, and about 85 billion dollars on civilian research and development.[1] If one adds the R and D budget for space (which has many military applications) military activities account for fully two-thirds of government-financed research in the USA. The Soviets are spending as much on military research and development as the Americans. Globally, military R and D spending is running at about 60 billion dollars a year.

Equally staggering is the number of scientists working only on military research and development. Worldwide, this number is over 500,000, out of a total of about 2,300,000[2] scientists and engineers in research. In other words, about twenty per cent of the world's best scientists and engineers are working only at developing new weapons and their supporting technologies, or improving existing ones. If only physicists and engineering scientists, those at the forefront of technological innovation, are included, the percentage is much higher: some estimates show as many as 50 per cent of these people working on military R and D.

Few people today realize that the extensive use of science for military purposes is relatively new. Military men neither understood nor sympathized with the activities of scientists until World War Two. Even after World War Two, the resources given to military science dropped sharply again. But they started to climb around 1950, as the Cold War gained intensity, and have gone on climbing ever since.

The Americans are now spending about 25 billion dollars every year on military research and development, excluding the money spent on space research. In other words, the USA is spending annually roughly three times more (taking inflation into account) on military science than it did during the peak year of World War Two. The USSR appears to be matching the US effort in military science and

technology.

The USA and the USSR are by far the most active countries in military science, together accounting for about 85 per cent of the money spent world-wide on this activity. France, the United Kingdom, West Germany and China together account for another ten per cent. The rest of the world accounts for no more than five per cent of the money spent on military research and development. Of this group, the most significant spenders are Australia, Canada, India, Italy, Japan, the Netherlands and Sweden.

The Cruise Missile

The cruise missile is an excellent example of the way in which rapid technological advances have been incorporated into a weapons system. Cruise missiles are not rockets; they are, in fact, old weapons, dating back in principle to the German V-1, or 'buzz bomb', of World War Two. Soon after the war the USA and the USSR took up the cruise missile, and produced a variety of types – surface-to-surface, surface-to-air, and air-to-surface, for both short-range tactical and long-range strategic purposes. But during the early 1960s, American interest in cruise missiles waned in favour of ballistic missiles (which are rockets), at least for long-range applications. More recently, however, a

number of technological advances have encouraged cruise missile development. The most important by far was the extraordinarily swift miniaturization of computers in terms of their volume and weight for a given capacity of the data they can absorb and process. Also important was the availability of an accurate data base about the co-ordinates of potential targets. Very small but accurate missile-guidance systems could thus be developed. For example, the McDonnell Douglas Terrain Contour Matching (TERCOM) system, which

57

A cruise missile in flight. Tomahawk cruise missiles can be air-, ground- or sea-launched, with ranges either tactical (around 560 km) or strategic (around 2,500 km). This missile has not yet reached its low-altitude phase, during which it can fly – too low for radar detection – as low as 20 meters from the surface.

The launcher of a McDonnell Douglas Tomahawk missile, ready for action. As the McDonnell Douglas PR material points out, the mobility of the launcher 'offers unlimited launch locations, providing quick strike capabilities'. This seems to have little to do with nuclear deterrence.

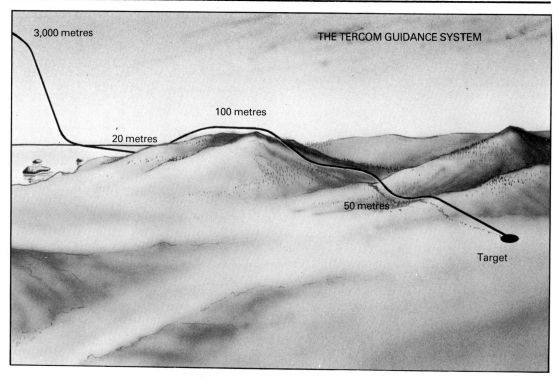

THE TERCOM GUIDANCE SYSTEM

3,000 metres

100 metres

20 metres

50 metres

Target

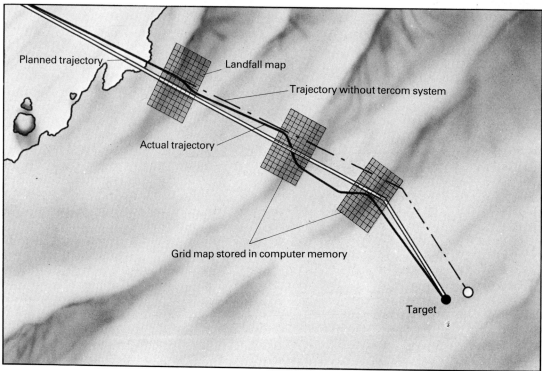

Planned trajectory

Landfall map

Trajectory without tercom system

Actual trajectory

Grid map stored in computer memory

Target

This is how terrain contour matching, usually abbreviated to TERCOM, works. Above, on nearing the end of its flight path near enemy territory, the cruise missile sinks to as low as 20 meters over sea, 50 meters over hills and 100 meters over mountains. Below, the missile computer compares the map-grid information with which it has been programmed with the readings of the on-board altimeter. If there are differences, it can redirect itself to the planned trajectory, with a terminal accuracy or CEP of 40 meters or less.
(Source: Scientific American, Feb. 1977.)

weighs only 37 kg, can guide a cruise missile to its target with a circular error of probability (CEP) of 40 meters or less. TERCOM uses a computer carried by the cruise missile to compare the terrain below the missile, which is scanned with a radar altimeter, with a pre-programmed flight path, which is fed into the missile's computer before its launch. Deviations from the planned flight are corrected automatically. From the very accurate maps that have become available using satellite mapping techniques, the positions of targets and contours of flight paths can be obtained with unprecedented accuracy. Targets could not be located accurately enough from earlier maps to make effective use of this sort of missile-guidance system, even if it had existed.

The development of relatively small jet engines and high-efficiency fuels was also crucial for the design of modern cruise missiles. For example, the Williams Research Corporation has produced a turbo-fan engine that is only 80 cm long and 31 cm wide, and only weighs 60 kilograms, yet it generates a thrust of about 275 kilograms.

Using these new technologies, the USA has developed a new generation of cruise missiles that can be launched from air, sea and ground platforms. Perhaps the most important characteristic of these missiles is that the ratio of the payload (the bomb) to the physical weight of the missiles themselves is relatively very high – typically about fifteen per cent compared with a fraction of one per cent for a typical ballistic missile. In other words, a quite small cruise missile can carry the same warhead as a ballistic missile more than fifteen times bigger.

Normally a cruise missile flies at sub-sonic speeds at very low altitudes, a couple of hundred meters above rough terrain and a few tens of meters up if the ground below is smooth. The missile also has a very small radar cross-section, which means that it is difficult to detect and destroy. By the time radars have spotted the missile, plotted its trajectory and instructed a surface-to-air missile to intercept it, the cruise missile has probably passed out of range.

The effective detection and destruction of cruise missiles, particularly if launched in large numbers, involves look-down radars operating with long-range interceptor aircraft and surface-to-air missiles.

Apart from their high accuracy and relative invulnerability, another factor in the popularity of cruise missiles is that they are quite cheap. In a production run of, say, 2,000 missiles, the unit cost (including development costs) is likely to be about one million dollars (much less than the cost of a modern main battle tank).

Cruise missiles have considerable potential as strategic nuclear-delivery systems for smaller countries. Britain and France, for example, are showing interest in these missiles as potential cheap replacements for their present strategic nuclear weapons as these become obsolete in the 1980s. Most industrialized countries (and possibly some Third World ones) are technically capable of producing cruise missiles themselves. But what is often lacking is a precise knowledge of the co-ordinates of potential targets and accurate information about the flight path that should be used to navigate as far as these co-ordinates while exploiting the full effectiveness of the missile's guidance system.

If cruise missiles do proliferate widely, they may turn out to be the most far-reaching military technological development ever made. Also, it is almost certain that improved versions of current cruise missiles will, in future, be developed in rapid succession. The Americans are already working on a supersonic version.

Airborne Warning and Control System Aircraft

AWACS is an exceedingly expensive piece of military high technology, incorporating the latest radar system and high-speed computers. The most recent American AWACS aircraft, the E-3A, cost one and a half billion dollars in research and development, and each aircraft costs about 100 million dollars to produce. This is about six times the cost of the most sophisticated US fighter.

According to current plans a fleet of 52 E-3As will eventually be built. The aircraft will be used for the defence of North America, Central Europe, and the Greenland-UK gap. The USSR also operates a fleet of Airborne Warning and Control System aircraft, based on the Tu-126 Moss, but Soviet AWACS aircraft are much less sophisticated than their American counterparts.

Many commentators regard AWACS as an absurdly expensive microelectronic white elephant, in that the aircraft would be a prime and vulnerable target in any war, likely to be lost soon after the war begins. Also, of course, Airborne Warning

and Control System aircraft would have to operate in an environment saturated with electronic countermeasures (ECM). Critics claim that AWACS radars are insufficiently effective against ECM.

AWACS enthusiasts argue that these airborne radar systems can resist ECM much better than current ground-based surveillance radars can, and that the aircraft would survive long enough in a hostile environment to fulfil a worthwhile role. They emphasize the value of an early-warning period against any surprise air attack, however short this period turns out to be.

AWACS aircraft have evolved from a line of previous early-warning aircraft. The first was the EC-121 Warning Star, which became operational in 1951. Warning Star was developed for high-altitude, long-endurance radar surveillance at distances of up to 3,500 kilometers from the American coast. The aircraft could patrol for twenty hours at an altitude of eight

A modern Hornet aircraft on the deck of an aircraft carrier.

kilometers. An aircrew of about 30 operated and maintained the nearly five tons of radar and other electronic equipment carried aboard.

Then came the E-1 Tracer (operational in 1960) and the E-2 Hawkeye (1964). Hawkeye, designed to detect the approach of hostile supersonic aircraft soon enough to ensure interception, is equipped with highly sophisticated early-warning search radars linked to a tracking and intercept computer which automatically provides digital target reports. A notable external feature of the aircraft is the 7.3-meter-diameter saucer-shaped rotodome fixed above the fuselage which carries the radar aerial.

A modern Airborne Warning and Control System Aircraft, like the E-3A, performs the functions of an airborne early-warning aircraft and, in addition, provides extensive command and control facilities for all friendly aircraft within its range – including interceptors, transport

computers and multi-purpose display units.

The E-3A is a modified Boeing 707. The liquid-cooled radar aerials are housed in a rotodome (a revolving dome) fixed over the fuselage. The aerials scan a range from ground level to stratospheric altitudes.

Because of the long patrolling times involved – up to about eleven hours, which may be extended to over twenty hours with air refuelling – the E-3A is provided with exceptionally accurate navigational systems. Typically, about a dozen AWACS specialists would be carried in each aircraft, in addition to the flight crew of four.

Modern Combat Aircraft

Developments in the use of materials, particularly alloys, and in electronics have vastly increased the performance of combat aircraft. The most advanced avionics are to be found in air-superiority fighters, aircraft designed to seek, find and

aircraft, reconnaissance aircraft and so on. The identification and tracking of hostile aircraft and the control of friendly aircraft – at long range, at high and low altitudes, in all weathers and over land or sea – are achieved by the use of highly sophisticated, beyond-the-horizon, look-down surveillance radars, high-speed

destroy any type of enemy aircraft, whatever the weather. More than half the cost of a modern combat aircraft goes into its electronics.

In the future there will be an increased use of rapid-response sensors, both for controlling the aircraft and for firing and controlling its weapons. These systems will

An American Airborne Warning and Control System Aircraft (AWACS) in action. Opponents of the AWACS say that it is immensely expensive and would be 'knocked out' in the early moments of any global war; supporters say that AWACS would last a little longer – and certainly long enough to affect the outcome of such a war.

A Hornet fighter being refuelled in midair. The Hornet (F/A-18) is a single-seat, twin-engined multi-mission aircraft. The standard Hornet carries two heat-seeking Sidewinder missiles on the wingtips, two radar-guided Advanced Sparrow missiles on the fuselage, and a nose-mounted M-61 20-mm gun carrying 570 rounds.

make the pilot increasingly redundant so that eventually remotely-piloted vehicles will be able to perform most of the tasks, including air-to-air combat, now performed by manned aircraft. Taking the pilot out of the aircraft will dramatically reduce costs. Not only is it extremely expensive to train pilots for advanced combat aircraft but the need to protect the pilot greatly adds to the cost of the plane.

It is so difficult simultaneously to fly and to fire the weapons of a modern combat aircraft that it is almost beyond the capability of one man. One possible solution which has been the subject of various experiments is to use some of the pilot's facilities other than his arms and legs (which are already occupied) to activate microelectronics systems. Such systems could, for example, be voice-activated. The new British combat aircraft, the Tornado, uses a built-in computer to help in flying the plane, but even this may

not be enough. The aircraft is said to be quite difficult to fly, let alone (at the same time) to fire and control its weapons. Eliminating the pilot altogether may ultimately be the only solution.

A modern combat aircraft's avionics typically include a light-weight radar system so that the aircraft can detect and track high-speed targets at great distances and at all altitudes down to tree-top level. The tracking information is normally fed into the aircraft's central computer for the accurate launching of missiles or the firing of an internal gun. For close-range combat, the radar automatically projects the target on a 'head-up display' (as in the F-16) which details all the necessary information, as symbols, on a glass screen positioned at the pilot's eye level. The pilot can thus be automatically provided with the data required to intercept and destroy an enemy aircraft without taking his eyes off the target. The head-up display also provides the pilot with

A flight of F-15 Eagles, airborne. The F-15 is a dual-role fighter capable of both air-to-air combat and air-to-ground missions. Its maximum speed is around Mach 2·5. It has been used extensively in the Middle East against its Soviet-built equivalents, and has proved its worth.

navigation and control information under all conditions and with details about the aircraft's performance so that he can detect any faults which develop in any of the aircraft's systems as soon as they occur. The drawback is that these head-up display units can become hopelessly complicated. To interpret the display information and to act upon it swiftly enough can put an intolerable strain on a pilot's reflexes.

An 'identification-friend-or-foe' system informs the pilot (in theory – see Chapter Eleven) if an aircraft which he has detected by eye or radar is a friend or foe. And an air-data computer and an attitude and heading reference set display information on the pitch, roll and magnetic heading of the aircraft. This, together with an inertial navigation set, enables the pilot to navigate with great accuracy anywhere in the world.

The United States is considering a so-called quick-reaction interceptor aircraft,

having speeds greater than Mach 3 (three times the speed of sound) and extremely rapid acceleration, for operations in conjunction with future air-defence weapons systems. Such an aircraft may have air-superiority and tactical strike roles in addition to the intercept role. Even faster aircraft with hypersonic (up to Mach 10) speeds are also under active consideration.

Air-to-Air Missiles

Air-to-air missiles, designed to shoot down enemy combat aircraft, are among the most sophisticated of all missiles. A typical air-superiority fighter would be armed with short- and medium-range air-to-air missiles. The US Sparrow is an example of an air-to-air missile for use in all weathers and environments. It uses a semi-active radar guidance system and carries a high-explosive warhead weighing about five kilograms. A solid-propellant rocket accelerates the missile to a speed of Mach 3 over a range of about 50 kilometers.

The avionics in the missile are miniaturized: the consequent reduction in the volume of avionics allows a larger solid-propellant motor to be installed. The missile also has good ECM capabilities, and is very reliable and manoeuvrable for

An artist's impression – from the Pentagon's Soviet Military Power *– of two Russian Su-25 ('Frogfoot') aircraft in action. Frogfoot gives close air support to ground forces, carries 4,000 kg of missiles and bombs, and has been deployed in Afghanistan. Less fast and sophisticated than its US counterparts, it may well be more reliable.*

This small research model is the American fighter of the future, the Grumman X-29A. Its forward-swept wings will offer higher manoeuvrability with virtually spin-proof characteristics, lower stall speeds and improved low-speed handling. But it will need a computer to help fly it.

short-range combat.

The very latest Sparrow air-to-air missiles combine radar and infra-red in their target-seeking system. Missiles with semi-active radar guidance require the target to be continuously 'illuminated'. The aircraft's radar transmits illuminating signals so that, after launch, the missile can home in on the reflections of these signals from the target. But because the aircraft's radar antenna has to be directed at the target until the missile hits it, only one target can be engaged at a time. Heat-seeking (infra-red) missiles, however, carry their own terminal guidance and need only be fired in the general direction of the target.

The High-Technology Arms Race

The Americans are striving to retain a technological superiority in as many weapons systems as possible, a superiority which the Soviets are seeking to eliminate. A fundamental American belief is that, provided sufficient resources are devoted to research, the nature of their political system is such as to encourage innovation more than the Soviet political system does. This may well be true. The comparatively open society of the

Top: The 'head-up' radar display on an F-15 aircraft provides the pilot with all he needs to know about the location of enemy planes. Unfortunately, such systems frequently provide a pilot with more information than he can possibly assimilate, so becoming largely useless.

Centre: The underside of a Tornado Air Defence Variant displays four Sky Flash missiles. Sky Flash is in full production by British Aerospace Dynamics Group for the Royal Air Force; it will arm RAF Tornado and Phantom Aircraft.

Bottom left: an Advanced Sparrow missile — suitable for use in all weathers and environments — launched from an F-15 Eagle. The Sparrow is an air-to-air missile capable of achieving velocities of about Mach 3 over a range of 50 kilometers.

Above: the cockpit of a Harrier-II, showing the various controls.

Americans enables them to maximize the skills that are available. (The same could be said of other nations of course – notably Israel.) It is true that the cost of weapons systems can be so high that the necessary funds are not always made available (as could be seen in the reluctance of Congress to approve the budget for developing the MX missile system). However, the major constraint remains the skills that can be called on, and here the Americans probably have an advantage.

Weaponry development, then, is a field of activity, and possibly the only one, in which the United States hopes to be able to keep permanently ahead of the USSR. Failure to do so would, so it is believed, bring military or political disaster. But such opinions, based on perceptions rather than facts, are by no means confined to Americans. Political leaders in general appear to believe that military technological superiority prevents potential adversaries from applying pressures and blackmail in international affairs, or brings victory in war. This may not necessarily be true. Military strength is not the only lever that can be used in influencing world affairs, or even the safety of a nation.

The struggle by both the USA and the USSR to preserve the tenuous balance of power is one of the most important causes of the arms race in both nuclear and conventional weapons. The arms race will undoubtedly continue until both sides cease attaching such enormous political importance to gaining and retaining technological superiority. Past arms races have sometimes led to wars, sometimes to economic collapse, and sometimes to both. There is no reason to believe that modern arms races are exceptions.

Official Western assessments credit the existing Soviet-deployed forces as having technological superiority in anti-ballistic missile systems, strategic air-defence interceptors, all aspects of civil and industrial strategic defence and recuperative planning, tactical anti-ship

missiles, surface attack ships (excluding carriers), anti-aircraft artillery systems, some armoured combat vehicles, medium- and high-altitude surface-to-air missile defences, surface-to-surface tactical missiles, and heavy-lift helicopters. Approximate technological parity is said to exist in deployed systems such as tanks and anti-tank weapons, satellite tracking systems, satellite navigation systems, and small arms. But the Americans still claim to retain a technological lead in intercontinental-ballistic-missile guidance and penetration aids, strategic bombers, strategic submarines and submarine-launched ballistic missiles, attack submarines, anti-submarine warfare sensors and patrol aircraft, satellite communications systems, airborne warning and control systems, airborne surveillance sensors, defence-suppression weapons and systems, deep-strike tactical aircraft, aircraft carriers, guided ordnance, air-to-air superiority weapons, man-portable air-defence systems, close-support helicopters, aircraft and aerial weapons, long-range logistic transports and artillery. This is a formidable list.

The dynamics of Superpower military technology can be illustrated by one example, the military use of high-energy lasers. Many others could be given. The rapid progress in the production of high-energy lasers (power outputs of a few hundred kilowatts can now be achieved) has stimulated great interest in the development of thermal laser weapons. Likely applications for the first generation of these revolutionary weapons, in combination with appropriate electronics, include ground-based air-defence against low-flying aircraft, missiles and remotely-piloted vehicles (RPVs) and also air-to-air combat. The idea is that the great heat of the laser will burn out critical parts of the vehicle being attacked. The range of military applications of high-energy lasers will undoubtedly increase as their power output increases, including, perhaps, the development of a space-based defence system against enemy ballistic missile warheads. (See Chapter Eight for full details.)

Military Communications Networks

Because of the great effort they have put into military research and development, the two Superpowers have developed military machines far outstripping those of other powers. There is an enormous gap between the USA and the USSR on the one hand, and their nearest rivals, such as the French, British and West Germans, on the other hand. This is dramatically illustrated by the US Worldwide Military Command and Control System. This is based on a truly vast network of information gathering systems, on land, at sea, in the air and in space. No smaller power could hope to undertake such a gigantic operation. The United States spends in excess of one billion dollars a year on the system, which employs about 90,000 people just to operate the communications and command centres.

The purpose of the system is to enable the United States National Command Authority (the President, the Secretary of Defense, and their authorized successors in the chain of command) to have operational control of the strategic forces at all levels of combat. This includes providing the means by which the National Command Authority can receive warning and intelligence of enemy actions in order to make its decisions; it is also through this sytem that it assigns appropriate military missions and directs the various military commands.

At the centre of the Worldwide System is the National Military Command System, which includes the command centres and the communications used by the National Command Authority. The main command centre is in the Pentagon but there is an alternate ground centre and also an airborne command post; the latter may be the safest place to be in the event of a nuclear war. In addition to this command system, four American Commanders-in-Chief (of the Strategic Air Command and of the European, Atlantic, and Pacific areas) have fixed and airborne command posts capable of communicating world-wide with the nuclear forces. The Commander-in-Chief of the Strategic Air Command keeps his command post continuously airborne.

The airborne command post is designed to allow National Command Authority staff to fight a nuclear war even after the fixed ground-based command centres and communications networks have been destroyed. The aircraft used are Boeing 747 airliners which have been modified to provide a conference room, a briefing room, a battle staff work area and a communications control centre. Three of these aircraft are in operation to provide airborne command, control and communications for the National Command Authority and the Commander-in-Chief of the Strategic Air Command. Three more are to be procured. The fleet is being modernized, in particular with two new communications systems, one at super-high frequency and one at very low frequency, and automatic data-processing equipment.

There are direct communications between the command aircraft, on the one hand, and the intercontinental ballistic missile wings and the aircraft relaying messages to strategic nuclear submarines, on the other hand.

World-wide communications links to strategic nuclear forces and tactical nuclear weapon storage sites are provided by a special satellite communications system. The system consists of ultra-high-frequency communications transponders on several communications satellites. Satellite terminals are installed at key points, including airborne and ground-based command posts, strategic bombers, reconnaissance aircraft and intercontinental-ballistic-missile launch-control centres.

The US Navy keeps an aircraft continuously airborne over the Atlantic to ensure that National Command Authority orders can be relayed to strategic nuclear submarines in the area, even if fixed

R FORCE

The upper photograph must be more or less unique: it shows a US F-4 Phantom-II aircraft flying nose-to-tail with a Russian Tupolev TU-95. In the lower photograph we see a TU-95 in action on its own.

ground-based transmitters have been destroyed in a nuclear war. A similar continuous-airborne system will soon operate over the Pacific. The aircraft are equipped with powerful very low-frequency transmitters for communication with submarines.

An early-warning satellite system is used with ground-based radar systems to provide the National Command Authority with early warning of any attack by intercontinental ballistic missiles or submarine-launched ballistic missiles. Ballistic Missile Early Warning System radar sites operate in Greenland, Alaska and England. Perimeter Acquisition Radars are in operation in the USA. Surveillance radars to confirm satellite warnings of submarine-launched ballistic missile attack are deployed along the American coast. These systems are being continuously improved as new electronics become available, in particular by the installation of new computers and new phased-array radars.

Over-The-Horizon-Backscatter radar is being tested to provide long-range surveillance of aircraft and warning of a bomber attack. And the Distant Early Warning Line radars are being improved, particularly to detect craft flying at low altitudes.

The Integrated Operational Nuclear Detection System is being developed to increase United States capability to detect, quickly locate and report nuclear explosions right around the world. The system will provide nuclear-damage-assessment information, both during and after any nuclear attack, for the National Command Authority. At the moment, these nuclear-detection sensors are carried on the early warning satellites.

The United States world-wide military communications system involves a network of bases, including among others stations in North West Cape, Australia, Diego Garcia in the Indian Ocean and Guam in the Pacific. There are also world-wide networks of radars – like the US Air Force Satellite Control System – to track,

control and interrogate US military satellites.

In addition to all of this breathtaking display of technological might there are command, control, communications and intelligence systems for tactical purposes which are used to support land, sea, marine and air forces, as well as theatre nuclear forces. These include a network of radar stations across the NATO countries in Europe to detect enemy aircraft; ground mobile-forces satellite communications involving hundreds of the various types of transportable terminals, ultra-high-frequency satellite communications with theatre nuclear forces, and so on.

The Defense Satellite Communications System, a super-high-frequency satellite communications system using seven satellites, links the continental United States with military forces abroad. Large

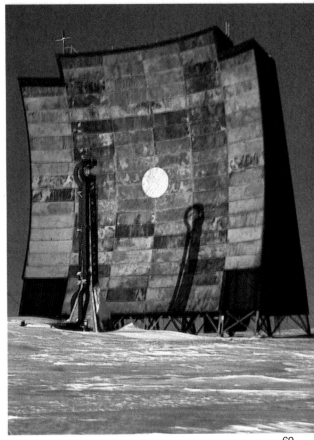

A distant early-warning system radar antenna in Canada. Such systems are of limited use: the time between their picking up approaching ICBMs and the arrival of the missiles themselves is too short for effective counter measure – military or civilian.

fixed and mobile terminals based overseas link in with the Worldwide Military Command and Control System and tactical systems.

The Defense Communications System provides American military forces with worldwide voice, data and teleprinter services. This is being made more flexible, so that it can be linked in with the systems of America's allies. New electronics are continuously being used to make the main radio links more secure from jamming, interception, electronic eavesdropping and other forms of interference.

Given the demands that are and will be made on modern military communications, it is hardly surprising that the Superpowers are investing large sums in them. The US Department of Defense, for example, is spending more than three billion dollars a year on computer software. Much effort is going into qualitatively improving the production of software (the weak link in many current computerized systems). There is also an active multi-million dollar programme to accelerate the introduction of advanced integrated circuit technology into military systems, and the relating of this to the problems of interoperability and software. In fact, the Department of Defense funds some of America's most advanced projects in the development of, for example, very high-speed integrated circuits. The aim is to produce silicon chips that are both faster and more reliable than those currently in use, in order to ensure that United States superiority in this area continues.

Also under continual and rapid development are technologies for survivable computer communications, secure message and information-transfer systems, crisis-management and command systems, and miniature computers. During a war, for example, the data coming in to command centre screens will be 'noisy' – difficult to make sense of. New software is being developed to allow command centre personnel to penetrate this 'noise' more quickly.

The vast sums of money and the huge range of skills involved in large-scale military command, control, communications and intelligence operations are awe-inspiring. Only Superpowers can readily afford the effort. Unfortunately, the technological jargon that surrounds this area of military development serves to make its operations a complete mystery to the man in the street who reads about it. In fact, the analogy of a spider's web is appropriate. Both Superpowers have constructed enormously complex networks designed to transmit the slightest tremor at any remote part of the web to the controlling intelligence at the centre. And to press the metaphor to its utmost, both Superpowers would prefer the role of spider to that of fly. The big question is always to decide whether what is caught in the web is dangerous to the spider.

Other Arms Races

Technological arms races are under way in *all* the world's regions. An indication of the extent of the participation in these strenuous races is the list of countries producing military aircraft. The industrialized countries doing so include Australia, Belgium, Canada, Czechoslovakia, Finland, France, the Federal Republic of Germany, Italy, Japan, the Netherlands, Poland, Romania, Spain, Sweden, Switzerland, the United Kingdom and Yugoslavia. Third World countries producing military aircraft include: Argentina, Brazil, China, Egypt, India, Indonesia, Israel, North Korea, South Korea, Pakistan, the Philippines, South Africa and Taiwan. Most of these countries – the exceptions are Czechoslovakia, Finland, the Netherlands, Poland, Romania, Spain, Switzerland, Indonesia, North Korea, South Korea, and the Philippines – also produce missiles.

Of the Third World countries listed, Argentina, Brazil, China, India, Israel and South Africa have significant defence industries and they export weapons.

By and large, these Third World countries along with the industrialized weapons-producers are developing, or have developed, a modern military technological base. But none can compete with the USA and the USSR in the range and sophistication of their equipment, nor can any keep up with the Superpowers in military research and development.

Many smaller countries acqquire their most sophisticated weapons through the international arms trade (see Chapter Twelve). But often these countries are unable effectively to operate the complex weapons they buy. Nor can they maintain them properly. About 40 Third World countries operate combat aircraft which rely for efficient operation on complex electronics. Many are unable to cope with this equipment.

The fact that only the Superpowers can produce and operate the necessary equipment for automating warfare and for the most up-to-date command, control, communications and intelligence systems means that some important types of warfare can now only be waged by these powers. The edge that this gives the Superpowers gives them, of course, a great deal of political influence around the world. One single American aircraft carrier packs a punch comparable to that of many countries' entire military arsenal. The appearance of such a ship off a smaller country's coast can obviously influence the actions of that country.

The gulf between the high-technological capabilities of the advanced countries and those of the others is steadily widening. This has obvious consequences for regional and world power balances. Of course the arms trade in low-technology weapons – Kalashnikov rifles, mortars and so on – is still extremely important in the Third World. But even here there has been a recent shift to the importing of weapons that are more sophisticated though still not comparable to the armouries of the industrialized nations. The low- and medium-technology arms trade is discussed in Chapter Twelve.

There are, of course, many who question whether the extraordinarily advanced technology being deployed by the military of the great powers will actually work effectively under battlefield conditions (See Chapter Eleven for more on this). Most of the middle-ranking officers who now plan military tactics are, it is pointed out, often technological enthusiasts with little or no real experience of war. They are inclined to introduce technological equipment with scant regard to its practicability under fire. It is significant that those generals who have had actual battle experience, now usually retired or with diminishing influence on the course of events, are often among the most severe critivs of the amount of high technology being introduced into weapon systems.

Frank Barnaby

References

1   Sivard, Ruth Leger, **World Military and Social Expenditures – 1978**, WMSE Publications, Leesburg, Virginia, 1978

2   Norman Colin, *Knowledge and Power: the Global Research and Development Budget*, Worldwatch Paper 31, July 1979

Also relevant to much of the material in this chapter is:
Barnaby, Frank, 'Microelectronics in War' in Friedrichs, G. and Schaft, A. (eds), **Microelectronics and Society: For Better or for Worse**, Pergamon Press, Oxford, 1982 pp 243-72

Chapter 6

The Battlefield of the Future

'On the battlefield of the future, enemy forces will be located, tracked and targeted almost instantaneously through the use of data links, computer assisted intelligence evaluation, and automated fire control. With first round kill probabilities approaching certainty, and with surveillance devices that can continually track the enemy, the need for large forces to fix the opposition physically will be less important.

'I see battlefields on which we can destroy anything we locate through instant communications and the almost instantaneous application of highly lethal firepower.'

This version of the automated battlefield was described as long ago as 1969 by General W.C. Westmoreland,[1] then Chief of Staff, US Army. The General based his statements on his experiences of new war technologies in the Vietnam war. Like most wars in the Third World, the Vietnam war was used enthusiastically by military scientists to test their new inventions under operational conditions.

The General predicted that 'no more than ten years should separate us from the automated battlefield'. The military scientists have not worked as efficiently as he hoped. They have not yet automated the battlefield. But they are getting close. If the General had given them another ten years he would probably have been right. On current evidence, we can expect the General's vision to be the reality of the early 1990s.

Just how automated future warfare will become is very difficult to foretell. But we can be sure that the battlefield of the future will use organizations and techniques radically different from those

FERRANTI **PACER MARK 2**

The new 'next-generation' Pacer Mark 2 muzzle-velocity measuring device is under 30 cm across. In the photograph on the right it is shown in position – in the centre of the picture, above the gun barrel.

political consequences as dramatic as did the industrial revolution. The post-industrial information society of the Year 2000 will differ from today's society almost as much as our society differs from pre-industrial agricultural society.

What is much less well known is that microelectronics is having as revolutionary an effect on military activities as it is on peaceful ones – more revolutionary in fact. Military scientists are continually pushing the technology forward and maximizing the applications of microelectronic advances. Consequently the biggest and fastest computers are military computers.

Automating Warfare

Over the past fifteen years or so giant steps have been made in automating warfare in land, sea and air combat. This is perhaps the most dynamic of all current military technologies. The development of new electronic offensive weapons, particularly guided missiles, inevitably stimulates the development of electronic countermeasures against them. In turn, electronic counter-counter-measures are developed, and so on. Military technological revolutions follow one another with such bewildering rapidity that no one person can hope to keep abreast of all the developments.

Most battles have four distinct stages. First, the enemy forces are located and

used by the military today. Warfare is being transformed, largely because of developments in microelectronics.

It is well known that the peaceful application of microelectronics is revolutionizing our society; the information revolution will have social and

The AN/TRC 80B tropospheric radio terminal set which provides the Pershing firing battery with communication to battalion headquarters.

identified. Second, a decision is made about how to deal with them. Third, appropriate weapons are chosen and fired at them. Finally, the damage done to them is assessed to find out if the sequence needs repeating.

These four operations are known collectively as command, control, communications and intelligence – often shortened to C31. The success of modern military operations depends on an efficient C31 system, as well as on effective weapons and supporting technology.

On the automated battlefield the location and identification of enemy forces would be done by remotely piloted

to their targets.

The damage done by the barrage would be assessed by reconnaissance devices – sensors, remotely piloted vehicles and perhaps satellites – and the information fed into the computers; the computers would decide whether or not it was necessary to fire more weapons and, if so, fire them and direct them to their targets. The whole sequence would be repeated until the enemy forces were destroyed. Computers can 'make decisions' very rapidly, if adequately programmed, and it is possible that this whole sequence might take place without any human intervention at all. Indeed, by the time human reflexes had reacted, the sequence

could be over or at least so far advanced as to be practically unstoppable!

Sensors
A sensor is a device used to detect the presence of matter or energy and locate it. The sensors on the automated battlefield may be sensitive among other things to light, sound, magnetic fields, pressure and infra-red radiation. They can transmit information about enemy forces by radio over long distances.

The most common types of battlefield sensor pick up seismic disturbances in the

vehicles, by sensors planted in the ground, and, if the country can afford a space programme, by reconnaissance satellites. The information collected by these devices would be transmitted through the military communications network back to the central computers. The computers would decide on the action to be taken against the enemy forces and then select appropriate weapons and direct them on

The new Martello radar system, developed by Marconi Radar Systems, and now in use by the RAF. Knowledge of the enemy's activities is crucial on the automated battlefield of the future.

ground caused by the movements of people and vehicles. They can be implanted on the battlefield by hand, but often they would be fired onto the battlefield by artillery or dropped by aircraft. They are usually buried in the ground with just an aerial visible. A typical seismic sensor can detect people at distances of up to 50 meters and vehicles at ten times this distance. The sensors remain active for many months.

A seismic sensor cannot normally distinguish between a light vehicle at a close distance and a heavier vehicle further away. Because of this limitation, seismic sensors are often used with acoustic sensors, which 'hear' sounds. A combination of seismic and acoustic sensors allows a more certain identification of enemy forces to be made. In fact, it would be normal to use a number of types of sensor in combination. The computers would then be able to analyse the signals from the sensors with a good chance of detecting and identifying a high proportion of enemy targets.

Microelectronics has made possible the development of very small sensors, even though the power supply for their transmitters is still strong enough to allow them to send signals over distances of several kilometers. Ground relay stations can be used to transmit sensor signals over much larger distances to the central computers. Relay equipment can also be carried in high-flying aircraft, which may be remotely controlled, or the information can be relayed via satellite.

In a present-day war human operators sitting in command-and-control posts away from, or flying over, the battlefield would monitor the computer analysis of the reconnaissance data and participate in the firing and controlling of appropriate weapons. But, in a future war, this phase of the battle may be completely automated.

The Weapons

The weapons used on the automated battlefield of the future will be mainly guided weapons – surface-to-surface missiles and guided bombs. These may be fitted with automatic homing devices so that, once launched, the missiles will seek out and destroy their targets without further external help. These are the so-called 'fire-and-forget' missiles.

As recent conflicts in the Middle East and the Falklands have shown, modern warfare relies more and more on missile warfare, in which armoured vehicles, aircraft and warships are platforms for firing missiles, and in which missiles are, in turn, used to destroy these platforms.

Existing anti-tank, anti-aircraft and anti-ship missiles are effective, but they have disadvantages in some environments. A main aim of current military technology is to use microelectronics to make more effective the use of missiles in fog, rain, and haze; when the battlefield is covered with smoke and dust; and against electronic countermeasures, including chaff (to confuse radars), jamming devices

The parachute-borne Ferranti HB-876 'Area Denial Sub-munition' is designed to prevent the repair of previously bombed airfields. Spring-loaded legs ensure that the sub-munition lands upright: the charge located in the top aims to destroy armoured repair vehicles on the ground, while charges in the side emit shrapnel aimed at soft targets – repair crew personnel and light vehicles.

and decoys.

Microelectronics are revolutionizing the guidance systems of missiles. In adverse weather and battlefield conditions, missile guidance will rely increasingly on sensors operating on frequencies in the far infrared and on radio frequences. There is also a strong interest how in millimeter-waves for missile guidance; millimeter-wave technology will almost certainly come to dominate in guidance systems for missiles. Millimeter-waves are able to penetrate the atmosphere even when it is polluted with a great deal of dust, smoke or fog. They will make 'smart' missiles smarter, in fact, 'ultra-smart'. These ultra-smart missiles will make tactical warfare possible in all weathers and all environments.

It is not possible in a short chapter to describe very many of the huge number of missile developments now under way. But we can get some impression from a brief description of a few of the developments

in anti-tank missiles.

A typical anti-tank missile now in operation is the American TOW (Tube-launched, Optically-tracked, Wire-guided).[2] TOW is used by many armies and is the most numerous of the guided missiles so far produced. Its popularity is based on its effectiveness as a tank destroyer and on its price. Each missile only costs about 8,000 dollars. It can

destroy with a high probability a main battle tank costing three million dollars or so, at a range of nearly four kilometers.

TOW is carried on a jeep, an armoured car or a helicopter. The missile is fired when the operator has an enemy tank in his viewer. He keeps his viewer on the moving enemy tank and the missile searches the line of sight and hits its target. Information from the viewer is transmitted to the missile by a trailing wire.

An optical sensor in the viewer measures the position of a light source carried on the missile, relative to the line of sight. Signals from the optical sensor are sent along the wire to operate control fins attached to the tail of the missile. The missile's warhead can penetrate the armour of all existing tanks.

A limitation of TOW is that it has to follow the line of sight (*see also* Chapter Eleven). The projectile can, therefore, hit its target only if the tank stays within the line of sight throughout the flight of the missile. TOW travels at a maximum speed of 1,000 kilometers per hour but still takes about fifteen seconds to travel three kilometers. There is a good chance that the tank will go behind cover during this time.

A more effective anti-armour system called the Assault Breaker is under development in the United States. The weapon is designed to engage in a short time many enemy armoured vehicles spread over a wide area. Radars carried in aircraft or in remotely piloted vehicles are used to seek out and track moving targets far inside enemy territory. When an enemy group of armoured vehicles is detected, a missile is launched from the ground and guided by the radars into the air above the tanks. Small sub-munitions are fired from the main missile to engage and destroy the enemy tanks. Each sub-munition scans the target area with a sensor which seeks out a tank and, when it has found one, guides the sub-munition downwards towards the turret of the tank. The sub-munition fires a high-speed

The TOW (Tube-launched, Optically-tracked, Wire-guided) anti-tank system here being tested by troops in the USA. One disadvantage to TOW is that the target tank must be kept in view of the sighting soldier from the moment of launch to the moment of impact, since he continues to direct the missile through its flight.

projectile into the turret. The turret is the weakest part of a tank. If it takes, on average, two sub-munitions to destroy a tank, each Assault Breaker missile could destroy ten tanks, a truly formidable weapon.

Tanks are certainly vulnerable to missiles. So are combat aircraft. Anti-aircraft missiles range from the very large, like the American Patriot missile, to the man-portable, like the British Blowpipe missile, which can intercept low-flying aircraft. The aim of an anti-aircraft system is to engage successfully a number of enemy aircraft simultaneously. Modern radars allow air defences to track many enemy aircraft and guide many surface-to-air missiles to their targets. The radar developed for the Patriot missile, for example, gives early warning of an air attack, tracks the enemy aircraft, fires the missile and guides it to its target.

At the right moment in an engagement with enemy aircraft, the computer, which handles the data from the radar and controls each interception, fires a Patriot missile. The radar continuously tracks both the target aircraft and the missile. The missile, which travels at nearly four times the speed of sound, carries a seeker receiver which is aimed at the target by the ground radar and which guides the missile to the target.

Patriot is a relatively large missile – 5.2 meters long, 40 cm in diameter, with a fin span of 90 cm. It has a launch weight of nearly 1,000 kilograms. The system requires a number of trucks to contain it and the electric power alone requires four gas-turbine generators. The only manned equipment is the control station – a vehicle carrying the control computer which handles the data from the radar and controls each interception. This vehicle also provides immediate fault detection and location for the whole system.

In contrast, the Blowpipe is a small missile – 1.4 meters long and 7.6 cm in diameter with a tail-fin spanning 27 cm. The missiles weigh only eleven kilograms. When the operator sees an enemy aircraft

he fires the missile out of its tubular container, after having identified the aircraft as hostile with an 'identification-friend-or-foe' (IFF) system. (These do not always work – see Chapter Eleven.) An infra-red sensor attached to the tubular container detects the flare of the missile and centres it on the line of sight. Blowpipe is guided to its target by command signals from a thumb controller clipped to the container. The missile, which carries a 2.2-kilogram shaped-charge warhead, is effective against low-flying aircraft over a range of about three kilometers.

An effective anti-aircraft system would consist of a judicious mixture of surface-to-air missiles and light anti-aircraft artillery – perhaps 20-mm Vulcan AA guns. These guns have very high rates of fire and, when operated with early-warning and control radars, are particularly effective against high-speed *low*-flying aircraft. Against modern *high*-flying aircraft travelling at high speeds, however, AA guns are not effective. Heavy AA guns have, therefore, been replaced by surface-to-air missiles which can reach great altitudes, change course in flight to out-manoeuvre jet aircraft and automatically home in on their targets.

Remotely Piloted Vehicles
Remotely piloted vehicles are unmanned aircraft guided by radio or pre-programmed computers. They may well put pilots out of business. We have already mentioned the use of RPVs for reconnaissance. They will also in a future war be used for air-to-air combat and for ground-attack missions.

Some RPVs now under development fly by recognizing the pattern of the landscape. The flight-path can be programmed or a TV camera in the RPV can transmit a picture back to an operator behind the lines. He can then decide whether to keep the RPV flying in a certain area or move it to another sector.

Because they carry no pilots, RPVs can be made very small and be submitted to accelerations high enough to injure a human if used in a piloted aircraft. Their small size gives them a very small radar cross-section. This makes them hard to detect and destroy, particularly when they are flown at high altitudes. The need to fly inside enemy territory can, in any case, be much reduced by the use of side-looking radars which can scan wide areas and be carried on RPVs flying along the border.

The utility of RPVs was demonstrated by the Israelis during the Lebanon war in 1982. They used both Scout RPVs, built by Israel Aircraft Industries, and Mastiff-2s, built by Tadiran, an Israeli company, for reconnaissance and other combat missions, such as targeting artillery fire. The Scout RPV carries a TV camera aimed and focused by a remote operator on the ground. The operators had no problem in observing vehicles on the streets of Beirut from the comfort of a home base, or in tracking helicopters in flight.

The Scout and the Mastiff-2 are small RPVs; in fact, they can be called mini-RPVs. They weigh a hundred or so kilograms and can carry a payload of about 25 kilograms at a maximum speed of about 150 kilometers per hour. Much larger RPVs are under development. These will carry several hundred kilograms of cameras, electronic intelligence equipment, radars, communications equipment and so on. They will be able to operate at very high altitudes, 25,000 meters or so; they will reach speeds of some 500 kilometers per hour and take off and land on a runway.

Remotely piloted vehicles will become cheap enough to make the use of a relatively large number feasible. On an automated battlefield, a large number of RPVs would be operated from computerized control centres.

Electronic Warfare

Electronics are playing a rapidly increasing role in virtually all military activies. On the automated battlefield, the 'electronic order of battle will be decisive'. The never-ending electronic race for countermeasures and then for counter-countermeasures has stimulated the development of a whole range of electronic-warfare equipment to gather and coordinate as much data as possible about the enemy's radar, command, control and communications systems.

It is in this area that a whole new military activity, known as electronic intelligence or Elint, has sprung up. Effective Elint uses world-wide land, sea, air and outer-space information-gathering operations. It is an enormous and exceedingly costly enterprise, using the most sophisticated electronic equipment. Large establishments are involved, like the British Communications Centre at Cheltenham, recently in the news because of the espionage activities of Geoffrey Prime. The knowledge gathered by Elint is used to develop appropriate devices and procedures for electronic countermeasures and electronic counter-countermeasures.

Effective Elint is extremely expensive. Only the great powers can afford it. The result is that the gulf is widened between the military technological capabilities of the advanced countries and those of other countries. Another example of the increasing disparity in ways of conducting tactical warfare is navigation. The United States is now deploying a satellite navigational system called Navstar, or the Global Positioning System, due to come into operation around 1985. Navstar will use 24 satellites to provide navigation of unprecedented accuracy for land, sea and airborne weapons systems. It will be possible to obtain continuous position fixes in all three dimensions to within ten meters or so, and to calculate velocities to within a few centimeters per second. Navstar will enable missiles to be navigated to their targets with great accuracy and will help synchronize activities on the automated battlefield. A country with access to such a system will have a considerable military advantage over one that does not.

Robot Wars

We do not yet know how far the ramifications of automated warfare will go. Will human beings always be involved in battles? Or will future battles be fought mainly with machines over evacuated territory? It is now possible to imagine a perfectly feasible system in which both sides during a future war evacuate a strip of territory on either side of the border. One side might send in automated tanks or aircraft. The other side might counter the invading forces with automated missiles. The defensive missiles might even be moved using robot troops.

This sort of scenario has always been extremely popular with science-fiction writers. For example, in his story 'Second Variety' (published as early as 1953) the late Philip K. Dick imagined the sad fate of one of the last human survivors on a battlefield occupied by self-replicating machines of a human-seeming appearance. In practice, however, it is difficult to imagine any military function that could be carried out more efficiently by a humanoid robot than by a machine that had no human appearance at all – an automated tank for example.

Although the 'battlefield without people' is feasible in theory, the military mind will certainly find it difficult to accept as a practical means of warfare. We seem to demand, as in some primeval ritual, that some human blood (rather than machine oil) is spilled on the battlefield to propitiate the wrathful gods of battle that still lurk in the collective unconscious – even though most of us would hope that the bloodshed was minimal.

It is interesting to ask how victory would be defined on an automated battlefield. Would the side that suffered the greatest losses of equipment be adjudged the winner? A more immediate question is, Since automated warfare will use munitions at an unprecedented rate, will it not put a great premium on having the economy on a permanent war footing? And would this not lead to the total militarization of society? Not much

thought has been given to these questions, partly because very few people are keeping abreast of the technology that is coming to make the automated battlefield a real possibility.

One much more optimistic point we can make, however, is that much of the technology we have discussed in this chapter favours the defence. Missiles that can destroy tanks, aircraft and warships are very much cheaper than the weapons they destroy. Each generation of offensive weapons is considerably more expensive than the last. Defensive weapons, on the other hand, are getting relatively cheaper.

A Future Military Policy for Smaller Nations?

Only the larger powers can readily afford the latest offensive weapons in numbers that are strategically significant. The smaller powers may well be forced to adopt a defensive deterrent policy based on relatively cheap anti-tank, anti-aircraft and anti-ship missiles. The object would be to make the military occupation of the

The use of remotely piloted vehicles (RPVs) may well put pilots out of business. During the Israeli invasion of the Lebanon in 1982 Mini RPVs were used extensively; the Scout Mini RPV shown here both on its launcher and in flight is typical.

country so expensive that a potential aggressor would be deterred from attacking in the first place.

We can now envisage a military policy in which recently emerging military technologies are used to set up a *non-nuclear, non-provocative defence*. In such a policy the size, armaments, logistics, training and doctrines of the armed forces are arranged so that they are seen to be just capable of a credible defence without reliance on nuclear weapons, but incapable of an offensive strategy. Many of the systems used in the automated battlefield could also be used in a non-nuclear non-provocative defence posture. If a number of European countries could be persuaded to do so, Europe, and the world, would become a much safer place. The danger of a nuclear war would be much reduced.

Details of such a feasible defensive deterrent for NATO have been described by a West German military officer, Norbert Hannig.[3] The concept involves a barrier zone, four kilometers wide, prepared along the East–West frontier. Sensors are placed in the ground in peacetime and minefields could be fired by artillery into the zone at very short notice.

The NATO defenders would be equipped with laser target-designators and three types of missile, operating on laser beams or guided by infra-red or radar sensors. The medium- and long-range missiles would be deployed out of range of the Soviet artillery. Short-range missiles and their supporting technology would operate from behind cover.

Hannig calculates that the defending forces could be equipped with 100,000 guided missiles within the West German military budget alone. The first wave of a Warsaw Pact attack cannot possibly offer more than 60,000 armoured targets (tanks and armoured cars). With current missile kill-probabilities, the defending NATO forces could be sure of destroying at least 40 per cent of the attacking armour, even on very conservative assumptions. Such losses are more than enough to stop any

offensive.

With Egbert Boeker, I have suggested[4] a somewhat different approach using a strip about 40 kilometers wide along the East–West border to stop an offensive. In an attack, the first ten to fifteen kilometers would come under very heavy enemy artillery fire. Only a small number of NATO troops would be deployed in this forward defence zone (even though experience in World Wars One and Two showed that troops can survive extremely heavy artillery bombardment and immediately fight off attacking forces).

Enemy forces approaching and entering the forward defence zone would be detected by a variety of ground sensors, RPVs and reconnaissance satellites. Invading enemy armoured forces would be destroyed by land mines and guided missiles, and aircraft by surface-to-air missiles, light AA guns and interceptor aircraft.

Small, highly mobile squads of troops would be used to destroy any enemy forces which survived bombardment by the guided-missile barrage. The troops, and the selection and firing of medium-range missiles, would be controlled by decentralized command and control centres. The maximum range of the missiles would be about 80 kilometers.

In summary, it is now possible to evolve a non-nuclear non-provocative defence policy in which appropriate military technologies are selected to provide a militarily credible *defensive* deterrent. In one feasible scheme, an electronic barrier would be established along the border of the area to be defended. Data provided by intelligence and surveillance would be fed back to computerized, but not fully automated, command and control centres which would select and control missile and artillery fire to destroy the attacking enemy forces. Reconnaissance by RPVs and sensors would be used to monitor the success of the defending fire.

If any enemy forces pressed the attack, the command and control centres would again select and fire appropriate weapons.

The sequence would be repeated as often as necessary. Any enemy forces that penetrated the forward zone of defence would be dealt with by small squads of highly mobile troops.

It must be emphasized that, *assuming rational leaders*, it is extremely unlikely that a war will be deliberately started in Europe, whether or not nuclear weapons are deployed in Europe. The danger is that a nuclear war will occur through accident, miscalculation or madness. In addition, as we have seen, the probability of nuclear war will sharply increase with the deployment in Europe of nuclear war-*fighting* weapons.

The choice is not between nuclear war and conventional war in Europe but between war and no war, and this will remain the case for the foreseeable future. A non-nuclear, non-provocative defence in Europe would greatly decrease the probability of *any* war in Europe. And this is vitally important because any war in Europe is likely to escalate to a strategic nuclear war between the Superpowers.

The criticism that a non-nuclear defence may turn out to be 'a technological fix to a political and strategic problem' should be seriously considered. The argument is that modern 'weaponry is forever going wrong, expensive to repair and enormously demanding in terms of maintenance time' simply because it is so sophisticated. This is true for offensive weapons almost across the board (see Chapter Eleven) and for highly centralized command and control systems. But it is simply not true for many defensive weapons and their supporting technologies. The key is to make sure that the defensive weapons are operated well within their design characteristics. If this is done, and realistic values are used for lethality, weapons can be chosen to provide a strong defensive deterrent. The key then is selection of weapons of the right quality, in appropriate quantities.

A realistic assessment of the performance of defensive weapons (enhanced by the experience of the Falklands war) leads to a preference for infra-red seekers for terminal guidance in anti-tank, anti-ship and anti-aircraft missiles until millimeter-wave sensors are available. One might also prefer to avoid radar seekers, and have a preference for single-role combat aircraft and for small diesel-powered submarines for naval defensive forces. Such an assessment would include the realization that the optimum defensive mix includes, in addition to missiles, such traditional weapons as land-mines, light anti-aircraft artillery and anti-tank cannons. Complex technology would never be used for its own sake but weapons would be chosen for a specific task and operated well within their capabilities.

When all is said and done, the crucial factors are the tactics, operational skills and motivation of the troops. Morale inevitably plays a crucial role. The success of a military policy will be determined by whether or not the armed forces understand their role and are convinced of its usefulness. Current NATO (and

81

NATO troops on the exercise 'Amber Express' in Denmark in September, 1981. Curiously enough, while the battlefield of the future is visualized as a wasteland populated largely by warring robots, the morale and motivation of the human combatants are as important as ever.

Warsaw Pact) strategies are so incredible
that the armed forces cannot be expected
to be motivated by them. Moreover, the
reliance on the threat to use nuclear
weapons soon after a war begins in
Europe involves preparing NATO troops
for actions which civilized societies regard
as unacceptable morally and of doubtful
legality. On the other hand, a conventional
defensive deterrent is totally consistent
with the universally recognized right of
self-defence and, therefore, is morally
acceptable and unambiguously legal. It is
also militarily credible. The armed forces –
indeed, society at large – would have no
difficulty in identifying with it.

Frank Barnaby

FUTURE MILITARY TECHNOLOGICAL ADVANCES

The atomic bomb dropped on Hiroshima
exploded with an explosive power equivalent
to that of about 13,000 tons of TNT. It
weighed about four tons, so the yield-to-
weight ratio was about 3,000. The warhead
deployed on the American Minuteman-III
intercontinental ballistic missile has an
explosive power equivalent to that of about
330,000 tons of TNT and weighs only one
tenth of a ton so that the yield-to-weight
ratio is about three million, close to the
theoretical limit.

The Hiroshima bomb was dropped from a
B-29 bomber with an accuracy that
depended on the eyesight of the bomb
aimer. On average this accuracy was so bad
as to make it difficult even to state the
circular error of probability (CEP). But a modern
intercontinental ballistic missile (ICBM) has a
CEP of about 200 meters over a range of
about 15,000 kilometers and CEPs of a few
tens of meters are foreseeable.

The improvements in nuclear warhead
design and accuracy indicate the incredible
progress made by military technology over
the past 30-odd years. In the next 30 years
we can expect technological revolutions in
the following:

High Technology Aspects of War
- anti-submarine warfare
- anti-ballistic missiles
- anti-satellite warfare
- electronic warfare
- environmental warfare
- psychological warfare
- the automated battlefield

High-Technology Military Systems
- air-defence systems
- navigational systems
- early-warning systems
- airborne warning and control
- command, control and communications
- radio communications
- reconnaissance
- intelligence

Specific Fields of Rapid Technological Advance
- lasers
- radar
- heavy particle beams
- chemical-explosive technology
- missile guidance

These military technological revolutions will
significantly affect:

(a) weapons of mass destruction – nuclear,
chemical and biological
(b) conventional weapons – armoured
vehicles, aircraft, warships, submarines,
missiles, artillery, bombs, anti-personnel
weapons, counter-insurgency weapons
and remotely-piloted vehicles
(c) military tactics and strategies – nuclear
and conventional, on land, sea and air

References

1 Speech given at Luncheon Association of
the US Army, Sheraton Park Hotel,
Washington DC, Oct. 14, 1969
2 Gunston, W., **The Encyclopedia of Rockets
and Missiles,** Salamander Books, London,
1979
3 Hannig, N., 'The Defense of Western
Europe with Conventional Weapons',
International Defense Review, Nov. 1981,
pp 1439-43
4 Barnaby, F. and Boeker, E., **Defence
without Offence: Non-Nuclear Defence for
Europe,** Peace Studies Paper no. 8,
Bradford University, 1982

Chapter 7

The Military Use of the Oceans

Growing concern about shortages of raw materials is concentrating attention on the natural resources of the oceans, and their possible exploitation and use. Not surprisingly also, more attention is being paid by states to the future role of the oceans in international affairs. Countries are looking to naval power to secure and defend their perceived national interests at sea. Inevitably, navies are expanding in almost all regions of the world. Naval arms races are becoming more intensive than ever before.

Traditionally, naval power has been used to influence international affairs, both globally and regionally. It has often been a tool for military action but has even more frequently been used for political coercion. Navies are seen as enhancing a country's status, and with today's interest in exploiting the oceans' resources, navies will be increasingly used to police and defend economic zones.

The Superpowers will continue to use their navies to extend their influence globally, and we must expect Superpower naval rivalry in the major oceans to intensify. The overwhelmingly important aspect of this rivalry is the activity related to strategic nuclear war. Strategic nuclear submarines carry large fractions of the American and Soviet nuclear arsenals. Both Superpowers as a consequence are also devoting major resources to developing effective anti-submarine warfare techniques. Success in these activities will considerably enhance perception of a first-strike capability. This is why future naval developments will have serious repercussions on international security.

Any survey of the world's navies will be dominated by the enormous naval forces of the USA and the USSR, but it will also show a very rapid build-up of light naval forces world-wide. In fact, the steep rise in the number and quality of light naval forces is a major factor in the global militarization of the oceans. A modern fast patrol boat, for example, can and does carry missiles of considerable fire-power. The acquisition of 'light' naval vessels, therefore, allows new and small navies to expand rapidly into relatively powerful ones.

The Soviet Navy
Each Superpower publishes its assessment of the other's military forces. According to *Soviet Military Power,*[1] a US publication, the Soviet Navy has two main missions – to protect the seaward approaches of the USSR and its allies, and to destroy NATO naval forces which could threaten Soviet military operations. The first mission requires naval craft which are larger in number, smaller in size, more designed for a single task and less capable in terms of weapons and endurance than the forces required for the second mission. The estimates given of Soviet naval strength support this view of Soviet naval missions.

The Soviet Navy's four fleets operate in the Atlantic; the Baltic; the Mediterranean; and the Pacific, the Indian Ocean and the South China Sea. The major surface combat vessels[2] include three V/STOL aircraft carriers (37,000 tons), two helicopter carriers, one nuclear-powered cruiser, 33 other cruisers and 69 destroyers. In addition, the Soviets operate 183 frigates. Of these warships, five carriers, 27 cruisers, 42 destroyers, and 77 frigates are armed with missiles. The USSR operates 62 modern strategic nuclear submarines, 105 nuclear-powered attack submarines and 168 diesel-powered attack submarines. The Soviet

DISPOSITION OF SOVIET AND US FLEETS

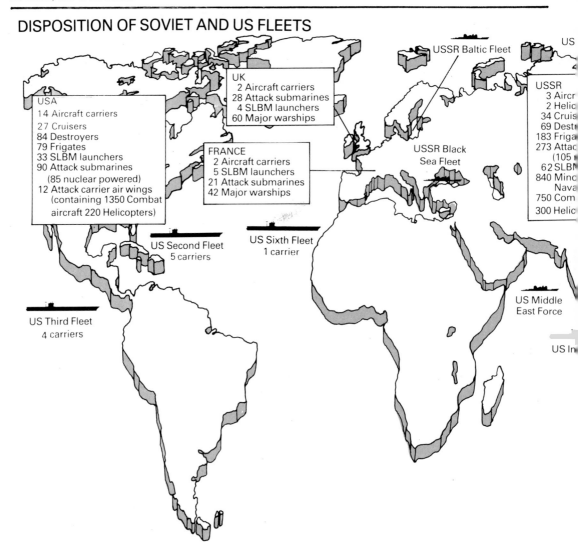

USSR Baltic Fleet

US

UK
2 Aircraft carriers
28 Attack submarines
4 SLBM launchers
60 Major warships

USA
14 Aircraft carriers
27 Cruisers
84 Destroyers
79 Frigates
33 SLBM launchers
90 Attack submarines
(85 nuclear powered)
12 Attack carrier air wings
(containing 1350 Combat
aircraft 220 Helicopters)

USSR
3 Aircr
2 Helic
34 Cruis
69 Destr
183 Friga
273 Attac
(105
62 SLBM
840 Minc
Nava
750 Com
300 Helic

FRANCE
2 Aircraft carriers
5 SLBM launchers
21 Attack submarines
42 Major warships

**USSR Black
Sea Fleet**

US Second Fleet
5 carriers

US Sixth Fleet
1 carrier

US Third Fleet
4 carriers

**US Middle
East Force**

US In

Navy also has about 840 minor surface ships including corvettes, fast attack craft, minelayers, minesweepers and amphibious ships. The Soviet Naval Air Force has some 750 combat aircraft and 300 helicopters.

The Soviets are still building seven classes of surface warships, five classes of submarines and four types of naval aircraft. These include a second nuclear-powered cruiser, and three classes of nuclear attack submarines. One of the nuclear submarines has a titanium hull which gives it a speed of 40 knots, the world's fastest. The Soviets are believed to be planning the construction of a large, nuclear-powered aircraft carrier, to enter service in the late 1980s.

The most modern aircraft being built for the Soviet Naval Air Force is the supersonic, variable-geometry-wing Backfire which is capable of carrying air-

The relative strengths of the US and Soviet navies. It is clear that the overall strength of NATO sea-going forces is some two and a half times greater than the Soviet equivalent.

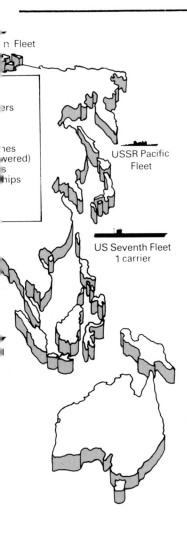

n Fleet

ers

ies
wered)
s
hips

USSR Pacific
Fleet

US Seventh Fleet
1 carrier

to-surface anti-ship cruise missiles with
speeds of about three times the speed of
sound.

The United States Navy

The Soviet assessment of US military
forces is published in *Whence the Threat
to Peace*.[3] The United States Navy, it says,
is assigned a special role not only in war
but in carrying out US global policies, as
an 'instrument for demonstrating force

and direct military intervention'. To carry
out its missions the US Navy has fourteen
aircraft carriers, 27 cruisers and 84
destroyers. In addition, the US Navy has
79 frigates. Of these warships, four aircraft
carriers and nine cruisers are nuclear-
powered. The aircraft carriers, the cruisers,
41 destroyers and 24 frigates carry
missiles. The USA operates 90 attack
submarines, 85 of them nuclear, and 33
strategic nuclear submarines. It also has
missile-carrying hydrofoils and
minesweepers, amphibious-warfare ships
and naval auxiliaries. The US Navy
operates twelve attack carrier air wings,
with about 1,350 combat aircraft and 220
helicopters. American fleets operate in the
Pacific, the Atlantic and the
Mediterranean; a naval task force is kept
in the Indian Ocean.

The Americans have built very large
surface warships. The biggest are the
91,400-ton Nimitz Class aircraft carriers.
The biggest Soviet surface warship is the
37,000-ton Kiev carrier. On the other
hand, the Soviet Typhoon strategic nuclear
submarine displaces about 25,000 tons
when submerged, significantly more than
the US Trident strategic nuclear
submarine, which displaces about 18,700
tons. (They are around the same length,
170 meters.)

If the navies of the European allies of
the USA and the USSR are added to those
of the Superpowers, NATO naval forces
have a significant numerical advantage
over Warsaw Pact naval forces for all
categories of major surface combatants
(frigates and above). Stockholm
International Peace Research Institute
(SIPRI) figures[4] show that the Western
superiority is greatest in the category of
aircraft and helicopter carriers (about
fifteen to one) and in the category of
frigates (about five to one). For all major
surface warships taken together it is about
two and a half to one. Warsaw Pact naval
forces, on the other hand, are numerically
superior in light naval forces (corvettes
and fast patrol boats) and in mine-warfare
forces.

The Warsaw Pact navies have more submarines than the NATO navies – about 100 more. A large difference also exists between NATO and the Warsaw Pact in the number of modern submarines carrying ballistic missiles that they operate: NATO has 42 and the Warsaw Pact has 62. But at any one time, only about fifteen per cent of the latter are out of port, compared with over 50 per cent of the NATO submarines.

As we have seen, naval forces operate large numbers of aircraft and helicopters. The two alliances operate between them more than 30 different types of fixed-wing naval aircraft, some in several versions, and about 20 types of helicopter. NATO naval air-power is considerably superior to that of the Warsaw Pact, especially in sea-based aircraft. The Soviets do, however, operate a fleet of land-based long- and medium-range bombers which are assigned a maritime role and armed with various types of anti-ship missiles. The Backfire bomber is becoming the mainstay of this bomber fleet.

The role of naval air-power is steadily becoming more important. The USSR is expanding its fleet of aircraft and helicopter carriers and almost all NATO countries are modernizing their naval air forces. We can expect that NATO's naval air superiority will, in general, be maintained and even increased.

Advances in Naval Technology

Although numbers of ships are usually used in assessing naval 'balances', a more important feature is the qualitative differences which determine the effectiveness of naval units in combat. In an assessment of naval technologies, SIPRI

An artist's impression – from the Pentagon's Soviet Military Power *– of a Kiev Class aircraft carrier in dry dock. The 37,000-ton Kiev carrier is significantly smaller than its US counterpart, the 91,400-ton Nimitz Class carrier.*

The variable-geometry wing Backfire aircraft of the Soviet Naval Air Force. This craft is capable of carrying air-to-surface anti-ship cruise missiles while travelling at a speed of about Mach 3.

Blackjack and Backfire Coverage from Soviet Bases
(2-Way Missions)

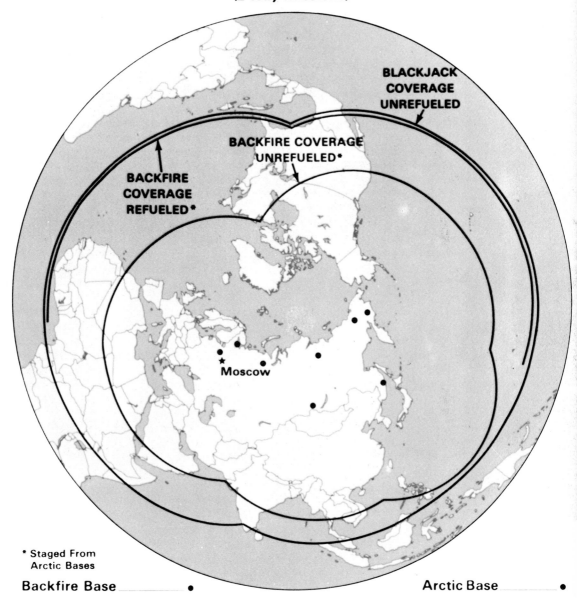

BLACKJACK
COVERAGE
UNREFUELED

BACKFIRE COVERAGE
UNREFUELED*

BACKFIRE
COVERAGE
REFUELED*

Moscow

* Staged From
  Arctic Bases

Backfire Base _____ ●

Arctic Base _____ ●

The ranges of the Soviet Backfire and Blackjack craft.
Assuming refuelling, the Backfire, which is becoming
the mainstay of the USSR's naval bomber fleet, can
reach every known nuclear power.

has shown that today's naval weapon systems are undergoing very rapid changes because of developments in electronics, propulsion plants, engines and construction materials. One particularly important use of naval technology is to offset the rapidly increasing costs of naval vessels.

The cost factor is limiting the size and number of naval vessels that even the richest industrialized countries can afford. The cost, for example, of a United States nuclear-powered aircraft carrier exceeds two billion dollars and a modern destroyer may cost about half a billion dollars. Even a frigate can cost nearly 200 million dollars. But a missile-armed fast patrol boat is only one-fifth as expensive as a missile frigate. Even though it is much smaller in size, the performance and fire power of a modern fast patrol boat has been increased to the former level of very much larger ships, such as destroyers. Fast patrol boats are rapidly evolving into heavily armed, multi-purpose warships – a trend shown by, for example, the French Combattante-III, the Israeli Reshef Class and the Swedish Spica-II.

Modern fast patrol boats operate all types of weapon systems – guns, torpedoes and missiles. Advances in automating light anti-aircraft guns and in surface-to-air missiles have now given fast patrol boats good defence against air attack. Fast patrol boats are a good example of how technology is used by designers to produce ships at less cost.

Another example of the naval exploitation of new technology is the increasing interest in ships mounted on hydrofoils. These vessels can operate at speeds of up to 70 knots, even in rough seas. And because the roll and pitch angles of these vessels are very small, their weapons can be operated with greater accuracy. Although current hydrofoils are small they are still powerful multi-purpose weapon platforms. For example the Italian PHM carries an automatic dual-purpose heavy gun, two ship-to-ship missiles and an electronic fire-control system, even though it displaces only 60 tons. The bigger Soviet Sarancha Class hydrofoil, with its 235-ton displacement, carries four ship-to-ship missiles, two surface-to-air missiles and a 23-mm six-barrelled gun.

88

An American aircraft carrier of the Nimitz Class. Carriers of the Nimitz Class are easily the largest surface warships ever built.

The USA plans to build hydrofoils of 1,000 or 2,000 tons displacement with ocean-going capabilities. Hydrofoils will greatly increase the potential of light naval forces, a fact recognized by, for example, the People's Republic of China which operates over 120 hydrofoils.

The main aim of a ship designer is to equip his ship with the most powerful weapons possible. Great care is taken to economize on space and weight by the use of special materials. For example, all-aluminium hulls have been developed for frigates, fast patrol boats and hydrofoils. Non-magnetic plastic hulls are used on minesweepers and a great effort is being made to develop better steels, particularly for submarine construction. The USSR has constructed a submarine-hull from titanium for deeper diving and faster speeds.

Naval Missiles

The most remarkable developments in naval weapons are in the guided missiles. New propulsion, fuel, guidance, launching and warhead technologies are revolutionizing anti-ship missiles. The success of the Exocet in the Falklands war dramatically brought home to ordinary people how vulnerable modern warships are in the face of anti-ship missiles. Many observers now believe that large warships are obsolete, except to symbolize military power abroad in peacetime and to threaten smaller countries.

Modern anti-ship missiles are exemplified by the US Harpoon and Tomahawk missiles. The Harpoon is already deployed in large numbers on surface ships, submarines and aircraft. The Tomahawk is in the final stages of development and testing. Both missiles can be fired from the standard torpedo tubes of submarines.

In its basic version, Harpoon is about 4.5 meters in length and weighs over 660 kg. It has a high-explosive warhead weighing 225 kg, of the blast-penetrating type, but it can also be fitted with a nuclear warhead. Harpoon has a range of

The Italian PHM hydrofoil, an example of the new range of smaller, less expensive combat vessels attracting the attention of many navies. Although it displaces only 60 tons, the PHM carries two ship-to-ship missiles, an electronic fire-control system and automatic dual-purpose heavy gun.

The launch of a US Harpoon missile. The range of Harpoon is around one hundred kilometers; when close to its target, the missile is directed by its active radar seeker to head skyward before dropping vertically down onto the foe.

about 100 km, which means it can reach targets well over the horizon. The location of the target is fed into an inertial platform before the missile is fired. The on-board computer-controlled inertial guidance system steers the missile towards the target even if it is directed at right angles to the correct direction.[5] A radar altimeter is used to fly the missile just above the surface of the sea. When it gets near its target an active radar seeker finds and locks on to the target. The seeker commands the missile to gain height to out-manoeuvre the target's defences and then dive down on to it from above. A solid-fuel boost motor accelerates Harpoon to a speed of about three-quarters of the speed of sound in less

tactical version of the air-launched cruise missile, is a very versatile weapon; it can be fitted with a high-explosive or nuclear warhead and fired from surface ships or submarines, as an anti-ship, anti-shore or anti-submarine weapon. Tomahawk is 6.1 meters long, has a diameter of 0.55 meters, weighs about 1,200 kg and can carry a 475-kg armour-piercing warhead. Like Harpoon it is first propelled by a solid-boost engine but uses a turbofan engine for cruising. The missile can be fired from a submerged submarine and has a range of up to 500 km, travelling at about 0.7 times the speed of sound. An advanced Harpoon system is used to guide Tomahawk, and it too skims about ten to fifteen meters above the surface of

than three seconds; the missile is then propelled by a turbojet engine. Once fired, Harpoon need have no contact with its parent ship. Information about targets at the extreme range is obtained using over-the-horizon radar and fed into the missile's computer before it is fired.

Harpoon is essentially a cruise missile. So is Tomahawk. Tomahawk, the naval

the sea.

The Soviet Navy operates a number of types of surface-to-surface anti-ship cruise missiles but probably none is able to fly at very low altitudes (to escape detection). Soviet naval bombers are often armed with air-to-surface anti-ship missiles. The Backfire bomber, for example, carries the AS-6, believed to be capable of 200-km

An artist's impression, from McDonnell Douglas, of the vertical launching of a Tomahawk cruise missile. The Tomahawk is a highly flexible system, and can be launched either from surface ships or from submarines.

range at high-altitude, supersonic and inertially-guided flight, and to use a radar-homing device to dive on to its target. Many other countries also operate anti-ship missiles – like the British Sea Skua, the French Exocet, the Norwegian Penguin, the French/Italian Otomat and so on.

Effective anti-ship missiles certainly give navies a considerable offensive capability. The threat from anti-ship missiles has stimulated efforts to develop a wide range of highly automatic, quick-reaction ship-defence systems and electronic countermeasures. An example of such a ship-defence system is the US Aegis which consists of a modern multi-function, phased-array radar for target detection

command guidance and a new digital on-board computer. They also include the British Sea Dart, which is designed to engage a number of low- and high-flying attacking aircraft and missiles at ranges of 30 km or so. The development of ever more sophisticated anti-ship missiles and systems to defend ships against them is stimulating an intensive Superpower naval arms race in which the quality of the weapons is becoming more important than the quantity.

Anti-Submarine Warfare
One component of the naval arms race is the effort being made by both Superpowers to develop effective anti-submarine warfare (ASW) techniques. If

and tracking, numbers of radars for target illumination, several computerized systems for control of different weapons (missiles and guns) and an automatic multi-purpose launcher. Quick-reaction missiles which may operate with this sophisticated fire-control system include the US Standard SM-2 ship-to-air missile, with a range of over 100 km, mid-course

strategic ASW succeeds in giving one side or the other the perception that it can greatly limit the damage the other side can wreak in a retaliatory strike with its submarine-launched ballistic missiles, then this perception may well contribute to the belief that a first nuclear strike may be effective. Of all naval developments those in strategic anti-submarine warfare are

A patrol ship of the Norwegian Navy carrying a Penguin missile. The Penguin is generally regarded as a highly effective anti-ship missile.

potentially the greatest threat to world security, in that they may significantly increase the probability of a nuclear world war.

The enormous effort being made by the Superpowers to improve ASW techniques to detect and destroy the other side's submarines will almost certainly lead, in time, to success. Even in the absence of a technological breakthrough – which cannot, of course, be discounted – steady progress in limiting the damage that can be created by enemy strategic nuclear submarines must be expected.

In ASW, detection is the critical element. Detection methods are being improved by increasing the sensitivity of sensors, improving the integration between various sensing systems and improving computer processing of data from sensors. Advances in micro-electronics are critical in all three areas.

All types of ASW sensors are being improved. The main categories of sensor are electronic radar-based, infra-red, laser-based and optical; acoustic (including active and passive sonar); and magnetic (in which the magnetic disturbance caused by the presence of a submarine is measured). Airborne, space-borne, ocean-surface and sea-bottom sensors are being increasingly integrated into detection systems and, therefore, working more effectively together. ASW aircraft, surface-ships, and hunter-killer submarines are also being forged into teams, where their functions are complementary. Each system has special characteristics and the integration of those that complement each other considerably improves the overall effectiveness.

American ASW activities are world-wide and continuous, involving a total system of extreme complexity and a network of foreign bases and facilities. A typical US ASW task force uses an ASW aircraft carrier carrying specialized aircraft, destroyers equipped with ASW helicopters, and nuclear-powered attack hunter-killer submarines. The task force works with long-range land-based aircraft

The twin-launcher of British Aerospace's Sea Dart GWS30 system. Sea Dart is effective against aircraft, other missiles and ships, as was proven in the conflict over the Falkland Islands (Malvinas) in 1982. As with the Exocet, this has improved Sea Dart's export-sales performance.

and receives information from unmanned surveillance systems, including sea-bottom arrays and space-based systems. The job of the task force is to hunt down single enemy strategic nuclear submarines. Once detected the submarine would be relatively easy to destroy.

Soviet ASW is based mainly on naval helicopter carriers and long-range, land-based aircraft. The Soviet helicopter carriers in service are mainly intended for fleet defence against submarine attack; this is tactical ASW. Soviet search helicopters carry very sophisticated electronic equipment to detect and track enemy submarines. Armed helicopters would drop weapons to destroy the enemy submarines. The USSR also operates a number of cruisers and destroyers for ASW activities.

The USSR uses several types of long-range aircraft, equipped with the most modern high-resolution radar and magnetic anomaly detection equipment to hunt down enemy strategic nuclear submarines. Soviet ASW activities tend to be much more short-range than those of the United States and they are largely confined to areas close to Soviet territory or Soviet fleets. As time goes on, though, one must expect the Soviets to extend the range of their ASW activities.

The most effective single ASW weapon system is the hunter-killer submarine – a nuclear submarine equipped with sonar and other ASW sensors, underwater-communication systems and a computer to analyse data from the sensors and to fire ASW weapons. The USA and the USSR each operate hunter-killer fleets a hundred or so boats strong.

Submarines can be destroyed with torpedoes, depth charges or missiles. A typical ASW weapon is the US Captor, or encapsulated torpedo, which is a torpedo inserted into a mine-casing to allow it to be stored in deep water for a long time. Captor has an acoustic detection system and a small computer which activates the launching mechanism when an enemy submarine is detected and identified in its

Top: A SH-2F multi-purpose system helicopter (lamps) armed with a Mk-46 torpedo and anti-submarine warfare magnetic anomaly detection gear lowered. Middle: A US Navy S-3A Viking, in flight with a Soviet Foxtrot-class patrol submarine underway below. Bottom: A practice Mk-46 torpedo is hoisted aboard the destroyer USS McKean, DD-784, during *Operation Valiant Heritage off the coast of southern California.*

vicinity. The weapon lies on the ocean bottom, waiting for a target for a long time if necessary, and is ideal for sealing off narrow straits to create an ASW barrier. The torpedo's sensor can distinguish between surface vessels and submarines and has a range of about 10 km. If it misses its target on the first attempt, it can turn and try again.

US hunter-killers carry the SUBROC ASW missile. This missile, equipped with a nuclear warhead, is launched from a torpedo tube, rises to the surface, flies as a missile over a range of about 50 km, re-enters the ocean near the enemy submarine and explodes as a nuclear depth charge. Other examples of ASW missiles include the Australian Ikara with its 20 km range, the Soviet SSN-14 with its 30 km range and the French Malafon with its 13 km range.

The British Navy has a sophisticated ASW capability and carries weapons with nuclear warheads. It is believed that the naval task force sent to the Falklands had

nuclear weapons on board, including ASW depth charges. British ships sunk during the war may have had nuclear weapons on board. The dispatch of nuclear weapons to the South Atlantic was against the spirit, if not the letter, of the Treaty of Tlatelolco, which was intended to make Latin America a nuclear-weapon-free zone.

Smaller Navies

There has been, over the past ten or so years, a sharp increase in the number of small naval vessels, displacing less than say 1,000 tons, operated by the navies of the smaller countries. Currently, about 50 countries (out of 122 with direct access to the sea) are operating a total of more than 5,500 patrol vessels. These vessels vary from missile and torpedo fast patrol boats to slow machine-gun-armed patrol boats. Some missile-carrying light naval vessels have considerable fire-power.

The proliferation of light naval forces in many Third World countries reflects the level of conflict there and is part of the

The launch of an Ikara long-range anti-submarine missile from the Brazilian frigate Defensora. *The Ikara, designed and manufactured in Australia for the Australian Department of Productivity, is guided into position over the sea and then drops a torpedo which homes in on the target submarine.*

general escalation of the global arms trade. An increasing number of countries are investing in patrol vessels of various kinds to protect their extended interests at sea. The extensions of territorial waters by certain countries and the establishment of New Economic Zones by the Law of the Sea Treaty mean that states are keen to secure their interests at sea using naval forces to police and defend these zones. Modern fast patrol boats are seen as the best vessels for the purpose because they have a strike potential sufficient to deter much larger naval forces. They are also relatively cheap. We must, therefore, expect the increase in light naval forces to continue.

Norway, Mexico, Peru, Brazil, Argentina, Japan and Indonesia are among the nations that have developed light naval forces to protect their extended interests at sea. This list will obviously grow. The establishment of New Economic Zones, together with the more traditional military conflicts and regional tensions, will be the main factors in generating and escalating world-wide naval arms races.

Conclusions
The military use of the oceans is intensifying with disturbing rapidity. In fact, ever more competitive naval arms races are leading to increased militarization of the oceans.

There exists a 'treaty on the prohibition of the emplacement of nuclear weapons and other weapons of mass destruction on the sea-bed and the ocean floor and in the sub-soil thereof', which entered into force in May 1972. The SALT-II treaty prohibits the development, testing or deployment by the USA and the USSR of fixed ballistic- or cruise-missile launchers for emplacement on the ocean floor, on the sea-bed, or on the beds of internal waters and inland waters, which move only in contact with the ocean floor, the sea-bed, or the beds of internal waters and inland waters, or missiles for such launchers. The SALT-II treaty has yet to be ratified by the US Senate but both the USSR and the USA say that they will stick to the requirements of the treaty. No treaty, however, *significantly* limits the naval activities of the great powers or controls the naval arms races.

The rising cost of warships and their increasing vulnerability are tending to reduce the acquisition of large warships in

95

A Soviet nuclear-missile submarine of the Delta-III Class, as depicted in the Pentagon's Soviet Military Power.

An Israeli Dvora mini missile patrol boat. This is a fast, highly manoeuvrable and low-cost alternative to submarines or destroyers in protecting coastal waters.

favour of smaller and cheaper vessels. But, because of the technological advances in ship construction and naval weapons, the fire-power of ships is not decreasing correspondingly. The naval arms race has, in fact, become a race for quality.

An increasing number of developing countries is participating in the global naval expansion. The expansion is being encouraged by the aggressive efforts being made by industrialized countries to export naval vessels and naval weapons.

The naval arms race is very expensive and absorbs vast sums of money and a great deal of skilled manpower. These are resources the world can ill afford to squander. Moreover, naval arms races are aggravating tensions in a number of regions. Most serious of all, the sea-based strategic nuclear forces of the Superpowers are being developed into nuclear-war fighting forces. If ASW techniques become effective they may give rise to perceptions of a first-strike capability. This Superpower naval activity is today's greatest threat to world security. The naval arms race may, if it is not controlled in time, be the major contributor to future world war.

Frank Barnaby

References

1. **Soviet Military Power**, Second Edition, US Government Printing Office, Washington, March 1983
2. **The Military Balance – 1982-1983**, The International Institute for Strategic Studies, London, 1982
3. **Whence the Threat to Peace**, Military Publishing House, Moscow, 1982
4. **World Armaments and Disarmament, SIPRI Yearbook 1979**, Taylor and Francis, London, 1979
5. Gunston, W., **Encyclopedia of Rockets and Missiles**, Salamander, London, 1979
6. **World Armaments and Disarmament, SIPRI Yearbook 1982**, Taylor and Francis, London, 1982
7. **Ambio**, Vol. XI, no. 2-3, 1982

Swedish ships and helicopters in the autumn of 1982 searching for a suspected Soviet spy submarine detected by the Musko Naval Base, some 65 kilometers south of Stockholm.

Chapter 8

War in Space

Space warfare sounds like the stuff of science fiction, and indeed no battles have yet been fought outside the atmosphere. Yet military hardware has been accumulating in orbit since the dawn of the space age. Space-battle scenarios are plotted in meticulous detail and deadly seriousness by generals in the Pentagon and the Kremlin. Today's military planners see space as a 'high ground', a vital part of the military equation. It provides a safe haven for spy satellites, whose untiring electronic eyes monitor the actions of potential enemies. Other satellites serve as pathways for military communications and beacons for military navigation. And because long-range ballistic missiles must pass through space on their way to their targets, military planners are considering ways to mount a nuclear defence in space.

Because military planners consider

1761-58

Warfare conducted from space used to be regarded as science fiction, as in the exciting movie This Island Earth, the 1954 equivalent of Star Wars. Here we see a space battle close to the alien planet Metaluna, which is being bombarded by laser-style beams from space and redirected meteors. Could this be tomorrow's fact?

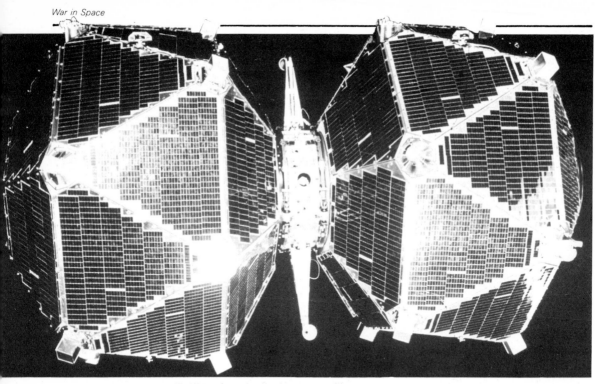

space so important, many technical details are classified, and that breeds uncertainty. Additional uncertainty comes from the fact that many proposed military systems exist only on paper, with their practical feasibility yet to be resolved. Military strategy is itself full of uncertainties. Although this chapter cannot pretend to tell you what *will* happen, it can outline the important possibilities.

Spy Satellites

The Soviet Union's successful orbiting of *Sputnik* in 1957 set an important precedent for military satellites: outer space was to be considered beyond the sovereign limits of nations on Earth. Satellites could pass over the skies of any country. The importance of that precedent became clear in 1960, when the Soviet Union shot down an American U-2 spy plane flying high above its territory. The shifting of surveillance functions from aircraft to satellites could put them in safe territory.

Today both the United States and the Soviet Union operate several different

types of spy satellites.[1] Probably the most vital are the early-warning satellites which continually watch for a missile launch or any other sign of the start of a nuclear attack. American satellites sit in geosynchronous orbit, 36,000 kilometers above ground, appearing to stay stationary over one point on the planet because their orbits take exactly one day. Soviet satellites have more complex orbits which keep them over the United States much but not all of the time. Signals from these satellites are transmitted around the globe to their operators, carrying – at least one hopes – the reassuring message that no attack is under way.

Other spy satellites collect other information. Many record images for analysis by intelligence agencies. Typically the images are encoded electronically and transmitted home via communications satellites, but some are still recorded photographically on film that is returned to the ground. These satellites occupy orbits only a couple of hundred kilometers above the ground, and are said to be able to resolve details as small as 15 to 30

The TRW Vela satellite, one of the many varieties of 'eyes in the sky' which survey our activities. Some 75 per cent of all the satellites launched are military; some may be able to distinguish surface features as small as 15 cm across.

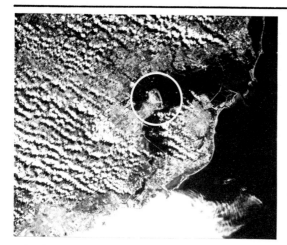

centimeters across. Separate ocean-surveillance satellites keep track of surface ships on the high seas using radar and other techniques. Other spy satellites eavesdrop on radio and microwave communications transmitted over ground or satellite links; increasing concern over such eavesdropping has helped stimulate interest in high-capacity networks of fibre-optic cables as alternatives to radio transmission links.

Military satellites do more than just spy. Some serve as communication links, others as navigation beacons. Geophysical satellites provide precise maps of terrain and measurements of gravitational fields that are vital in programming missiles to hit potential enemy targets (see Chapter Three). Oceanographic satellites collect data needed to help plot the paths of submarine-launched missiles, and to help figure out how to pinpoint enemy submarines, which currently (though maybe not for long – see Chapter Seven) can evade detection as long as they stay well submerged. Weather satellites keep military planners informed of weather conditions around the world.

All in all, roughly three-quarters of all satellites serve military functions, a total of 1,917 through the end of 1981. Over the past few years, the total of military launches has stabilized at about one hundred per year, with the Soviet Union accounting for about 85 per cent because its satellites are shorter-lived than their American counterparts.

Anti-Satellite Weapons

Military officials are uneasy about the unfriendly hardware overhead and are working on anti-satellite weapons. The Soviet Union's approach has been to develop 'killer' satellites. These weapons are launched into orbit like ordinary satellites, but once in space adjust their orbits to close in on the target satellite. As the weapon approaches the target satellite, a conventional (non-nuclear) bomb explodes, and debris from the explosion destroys the target. The Soviets have tested the system in space, and the United States considers that this system is 'operational' – that is, ready for use in case of war.[2]

The United States is developing an anti-satellite weapon of its own, a missile that would be launched into space from an F-15 jet flying in the upper atmosphere. The missile would home in on the target satellite and destroy it by detonating a conventional warhead. United States military officials do not consider their system 'operational' but hope to have it ready within the next few years.[3]

Military planners are wary of using nuclear explosions in space because they generate intense bursts of electromagnetic radiation.[4] These powerful electromagnetic pulse (EMP) effects could

Some idea of the high resolution believed to be possible from military-satellite surveillance photographs (the exact resolution is highly classified information) can be gained from looking at published civilian photographs, as in these taken from Skylab 4 over 100 miles up over Florida. The small circle marked on the left picture is blown up in the right picture to reveal an airfield, and for those with good vision, aircraft on the runways. It is rumoured that objects as small as a football can be photographed in good conditions from military satellites.

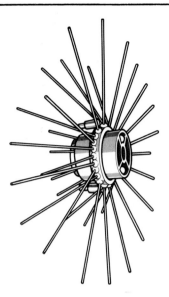

knock out not just the target satellite, but both friendly and hostile satellites hundreds or even thousands of kilometers away, and would also affect electronic and power systems on the ground. Thus the very potency of EMP effects is likely to limit their military use.

High-energy lasers could also attack satellites. Imaging surveillance satellites would be particularly vulnerable to blinding by laser beams because their function depends on devices which are inherently sensitive to light. Many other satellites rely on optical sensors to keep them aligned in the proper direction with respect to the Earth. Lasers could also attack the arrays of solar cells that power many satellites, although designers of military satellites have taken to using other power sources because of the vulnerability of solar cells. Only comparatively moderate laser-weapon powers would be needed to blind optical sensors. High-power lasers could deposit enough energy to throw off a satellite's thermal balance, heating some vital components to temperatures at which they would malfunction.

Anti-satellite lasers could be housed on the ground, flown in aircraft or orbited in satellites. Each approach has its

advantages and disadvantages. Present high-energy lasers are bulky laboratory-type devices which require the constant attention of highly trained specialists – just the type of equipment that *belongs* on the ground. Existing lasers in the United States and Soviet Union may even be powerful enough to knock out a low-orbit satellite overhead – if the atmosphere was not in the way. However, the atmosphere tends to bend or disperse high-energy laser beams, and a fixed ground-based laser can cover only a small fraction of the sky at the low altitude where most spy satellites orbit. If the laser could be squeezed into an aircraft, it would increase its mobility and could get above much of the atmosphere, but only at the cost of having to cope with aircraft vibrations and the air turbulence caused by the passage of the plane. The laser would have much better mobility and no atmospheric problems to overcome if it was in a satellite, but then it would have to be a very compact and efficient device which could operate reliably without maintenance or much fuel – a situation well beyond the state of the art.[5]

Military officials do not consider the problems of anti-satellite lasers to be insurmountable, but they are cautious. Despite some dire warnings which have appeared in the general press, especially since President Reagan's 'Star Wars' speech of March 23, 1983, the official assessment of the US Department of Defense is that prototype Soviet anti-satellite laser weapons would not be launched until the late 1980s or early 1990s, with an 'operational' system a few years later. Unofficial indications are that the United States is working on a comparable timetable.

Ballistic Missile Defence
There is an inherent appeal in the idea of defence against nuclear attack, but the task is a difficult one. Ground-based anti-ballistic missile (ABM) systems have serious limitations because massive radars are needed to track the fast-moving re-

The high-energy X-ray laser (see page 103) – if it could be built – would be a true superweapon. Here we see the proposed laser rods, of very dense material, arrayed around the central pumping mechanism – a small, compact nuclear bomb which emits X-rays. The rods are moveable, and each could be separately tracked on to an individual target. The idea is that many such laser rings could be put into orbit. A nuclear device has been successfully used to pump an X-ray laser by the Lawrence Livermore Lab., in 1980, but military observers are sceptical. The device would be quite small, with the rods no more than eight feet long.

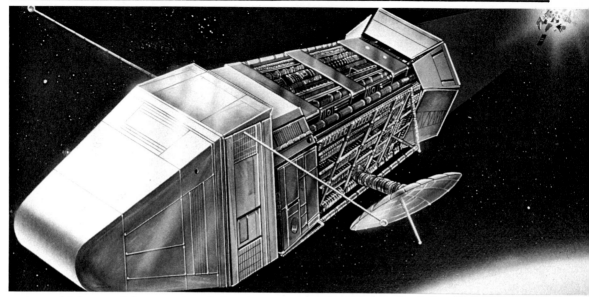

entry vehicles, and fast-moving defensive missiles are needed to hit them. Detonation of warheads before they could reach their targets might protect hardened military targets, but not vulnerable cities. With these problems in mind, in 1972 the United States and Soviet Union signed the ABM Treaty, which restricts deployment of such systems.

The treaty has not stopped both sides from working on new ideas, many involving space systems. In the United States, the favoured concept seems to be a 'layered' defence, in which attacking missiles would be made to run a gauntlet of defences. The first counterattack would come during the missiles' vulnerable boost phase, as they rose out of the atmosphere and before they could deploy their multiple re-entry vehicles (MIRVs). The re-entry vehicles (including any decoys) that survived could then be attacked during their flight through space. Finally, they would have to pass through an ABM counterattack as they approached protected targets. Military planners do not seem to believe in perfect defences, but they do talk about limiting losses to 'acceptable' levels.

Some analysts believe that fairly conventional technology can provide a space-based missile defence. A Washington-based group called High Frontier, aided by a collection of ex-generals and aerospace engineers, has urged construction of an array of nuclear-defence satellites, each of which would be equipped with non-nuclear 'kill vehicles'. Some of these satellites would be over the Soviet Union at all times, ready to counter a nuclear attack by destroying missiles during their boost phase. Other satellites in the system could attack surviving re-entry vehicles in mid-flight, while ground-based rockets would provide an extra layer of defence for critical targets. A report outlining the proposal says it could be built in a few years using 'off-the-shelf hardware' at a cost of around twenty billion dollars,[6] but other observers have questioned those estimates.[7]

A more futuristic-sounding proposal is to orbit a fleet of battle stations which would attack missiles with high-energy lasers during the boost phase. The most public advocate of this idea is US Senator Malcolm Wallop, a conservative Republican from Wyoming, who envisions some two dozen battle stations, each equipped with a five-million-watt infra-red laser powered by a chemical reaction, and a focusing mirror four meters in diameter.[8]

An artist's impression of an orbiting particle-beam weapon. The difficulty is that the acceleration of subatomic particles to extremely high velocities can only be achieved if the particles carry an electric charge. However, beams of charged particles can be bent by magnetic fields, so the beam would have to be rendered electrically neutral to be effective. Also, particle-beam accelerators are (so far) very heavy, and would be difficult to launch into orbit.

His proposals for a massive space-laser programme were shot down in Congress, but nonetheless the Pentagon is now spending well over one hundred million dollars a year to develop such systems.

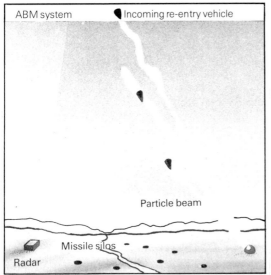

Such lasers would have to be much more powerful than anti-satellite lasers, and Pentagon timetables point toward the late 1990s. There are sceptics who doubt that the idea is feasible at all.

Another possibility is equipping a fleet of battle stations with particle-beam generators which could knock out enemy missiles. The system would start with negatively charged hydrogen atoms, accelerate them to high velocities, then strip off the extra electrons on the hydrogen to produce a neutral beam that would travel through space without being bent by magnetic fields. The defence establishment includes some particle-beam enthusiasts, but most observers believe that particle beams are at least a few years behind lasers. Even the Pentagon's official fact sheet on the particle-beam programme concedes that some important questions have to be answered before it is clear that particle-beam weapons would be useful against missiles.[9]

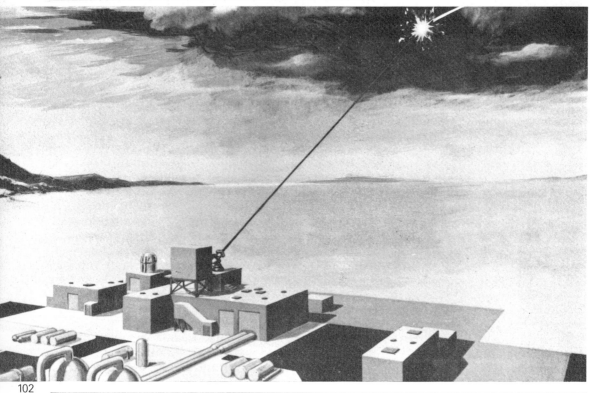

Above: it has been proposed that particle-beam weapons could be based on the ground as part of an ABM defence system. The multiple warheads of incoming enemy missiles would be tracked by radar as they approached the missile silos which would be their targets, and knocked out by particle-beam. Tracking would be very difficult: the missiles would travel more than a meter every thousandth of a second, and particle beams of this kind would only be effective in their terminal phase – the last couple of seconds. Below: a Pentagon artist's impression of a ground-based laser defence against incoming ICBMs. These might be more efficient than particle beams.

The most radical concept for space-based ballistic-missile defence is the X-ray laser, which first surfaced in unofficial reports in *Aviation Week and Space Technology*.[10] An X-ray laser battle station would consist of a ring containing about 50 laser rods surrounding a small nuclear bomb; detonation of the bomb would produce an intense burst of X-rays that would stimulate each of the laser rods to emit an extremely short and highly directional pulse of X-rays. In theory, the X-ray pulse could disable a missile during boost phase or a re-entry vehicle as it travelled through space (the atmosphere is essentially opaque to X-rays and would protect targets on the ground). Research into the concept has been sponsored by the Department of Energy in the United States, and advocated strongly by the controversial physicist Edward Teller, who is often considered the father of the American hydrogen bomb. However, the US Department of Defense and most other observers are sceptical of the idea.

The Future of Space Warfare

The prospects for new types of space weaponry are difficult to assess. Some laboratory-grade hardware exists, but actual weapon systems exist only in pencil-and-paper studies, which different analysts can make yield different results. Although advocates of new weapon systems have come up with optimistic conclusions, opponents have obtained very negative results.[11] In the United States, it is the Pentagon's attitude of 'let's try it and see if it works' that occupies the middle ground.

Efforts to assess the state of the art in laser and particle-beam weapons (other than X-ray lasers, which are a special case) are complicated by the fact that powerful lasers and particle-beam sources are fairly easy to build. The United States, for example, has operated a two-million-watt laser. The problem lies in getting the beam to the target, and in making sure that the beam does lethal damage. The difficulty is worst for defence against

An artist's impression of an orbiting laser battle station. These would be primarily defensive weapons, used to shoot down other satellites, or enemy missiles as they rose out of the atmosphere. Lasers are not very useful in air, where the beam becomes quickly dissipated.

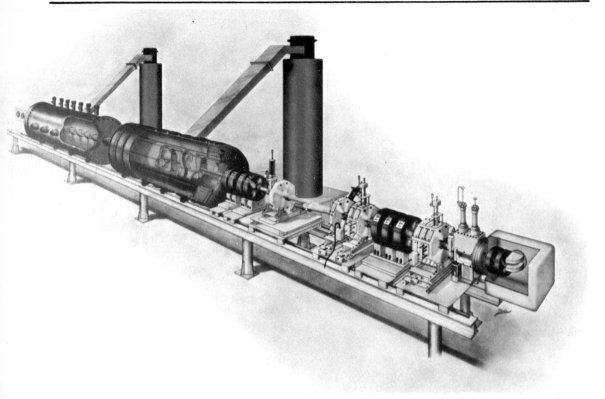

ballistic missiles, where a high-power beam may have to be pointed at a one-meter spot a few thousand kilometers away. Theoretical solutions to some of the problems exist, but translating them into hardware is another matter.

Successful development of anti-satellite weaponry – including lasers – seems a reasonable likelihood, although by no means a certainty. However, the roles of most military satellites would discourage attacks on them except in the case of war. Spy satellites may gather more intelligence information than the side observed would like, but as long as they are operating, the other side can be reassured that no nuclear attack is under way. In tense times, the destruction of a fleet of spy satellites – particularly early-warning types – could be taken as a sign of an impending nuclear attack, and perhaps as an excuse for launching a massive counterattack before the bombs could fall. Of course, once a nuclear war started both

Laser and particle-beam technology is not entirely theoretical. Above: the test stand, under construction, of the Neutral Particle Beam Program of the Los Alamos National Laboratory. This device will accelerate negatively charged ions to high velocities and then strip off the excess electrons responsible for the negative charge, allowing the generation of a beam of neutral particles which could travel undispersed over long distances in space. Below: MIRACL – a mid infra-red chemical laser in a laboratory. It does not look spectacular, but this is the kind of laser most likely to be used in space warfare. They would have to be less bulky than this, however.

sides would have much to gain and little to lose by knocking out the other's satellites.

Development of space-based missile defence is a much harder problem, but the impact of success could be much greater. Strategic policy relies (though this is changing – see Chapter Three) on a nuclear balance of terror, mutual assured destruction. The United States and the Soviet Union maintain nuclear arsenals large enough to devastate the other side even after sustaining a massive nuclear strike. Development of an effective nuclear defence would change the rules because this strategy is based on the assumption that there is no defence against ballistic missiles.

The change could be for better or for worse. If one side were far behind the other, it might be tempted to attack a satellite before a defence system in space made its missiles useless as bargaining chips. On the other hand, shifting to a balance of power based on defence rather than on the threat of attack might well be a positive step. Advocates argue that effective defence systems might devalue nuclear weapons enough to encourage the United States and the Soviet Union to become more serious about disarmament. There has even been a suggestion that a space defence system be entrusted to an international peace-keeping organization.[12]

In any case, neither success nor failure in developing nuclear defence systems will by itself put an end to the arms race. Military history has taught us that there is no such thing as the ultimate weapon. The best we can hope for is to buy enough time to deal with the international tensions that have produced the arms race.

Jeff Hecht

References

1 **For a popularized account, see Ritchie, David, Space War,** Atheneum, New York, 1982. For more details see Jasani, Bhupendra, ed., *Outer Space – A New Dimension of the Arms Race,* Taylor and Francis, London, 1982, particularly Appendix A for a tabulation of military satellites.

2 **Soviet Military Power 1983,** Government Printing Office, Washington, April 1983, p 67

3 Organization of the Joint Chiefs of Staff, **United States Military Posture for FY 1983,** p 77

4 Raloff, Janet, 'EMP, A Sleeping Electronic Dragon', **Science News,** 119, May 9, 1981, pp 300-302 and Raloff, Janey, 'EMP Defensive Strategies', **Science News,** 119, May 16, 1981, pp 314-35

5 For more detailed description of this and other uses of laser weapons, see Hecht, Jeff, **Beam Weapons,** Plenum, New York, forthcoming.

6 Graham, Daniel O., **High Frontier, A National Strategy,** High Frontier Inc., Washington, 1982

7 See, for example, Smith, Martha, 'Dr. Eberhardy Rechtin: C³ is the Heart of Any War in Space', (interview,) **Military Electronics/Countermeasures,** 8, 111, Nov. 1982, pp 9-20

8 Wallop, Malcolm, Opportunities and Imperatives of 'Ballistic Missile Defense', **Strategic Review,** Fall 1979, pp 13-21

9 Department of Defense, 'Fact Sheet: Particle Beam Technology Program', Washington, Feb. 1982.

10 Robinson, Clarence A. Jr, 'Advance Made on High-Energy Laser', **Aviation Week and Space Technology,** Feb. 23, 1981, pp 25-27

11 Parmentola, John and Tsipis, Kosta, 'Particle-Beam Weapons', **Scientific American,** 240, Apr. 1979, pp 54-65; Tsipis, Kosta, 'Laser Weapons', **Scientific American,** 245, Dec. 1981, pp 51-57

12 Nahin, Paul J., 'Orbital BMD and the Space Patrol', in Jasani, Bhupendra, ed., **Outer Space – A New Dimension of the Arms Race,** Taylor and Francis, London, 1982, pp 241-247

Chapter 9

Chemical and Biological Warfare

Most people find the thought of chemical and biological warfare particularly revolting, and with good reason. The history of the use of these weapons certainly produces a feeling of disgust.

During World War One, large amounts of chemical weapons involving at least 45 chemical agents were used by both sides, the most notorious of which were the lethal agents chlorine, phosgene and mustard gas. World War One chemical warfare used a total of more than one hundred million kilograms of chemicals to kill 100,000 people and to injure, often in a ghastly way, another million or so. Chemical weapons were also used by the Italians against the Ethiopians in 1935–36. Some seven hundred thousand kilograms of harassing and lethal agents were used.

Japan is known to have used chemical weapons against the Chinese between 1937 and 1945. During World War Two, Hitler's Germany gassed millions of Jews in the concentration camps.

The British were the first to use herbicides for military purposes, during their war against Malayan insurgents in the mid-1950s. This use was dwarfed by the Americans in Vietnam who between 1961 and 1975 used some 90 million kilograms of plant-killing (herbicidal) agents there to clear swathes of jungle, of which more later. Also, between 1964 and 1975, United States forces used about nine million kilograms of anti-personnel chemicals in Vietnam. In most cases this was CS gas – a form of tear gas that is also widely used in riot control, but at higher levels of concentration it can cause projectile vomiting and even (the Vietnamese alleged) death, although it is supposed to be non-lethal. About one third of this CS gas may have been in the form of CS2, which is much more stable,

and can render an area practically uninhabitable for 30 to 45 days.

In addition to these massive military uses of chemical weapons, military history is replete with stories of relatively minor outbreaks of chemical warfare.

Biological warfare also has a long history. Plague was used as a biological weapon in the fourteenth century. In the 1760s, the British spread smallpox during their wars against the Indians in Canada, using contaminated blankets. And in their war with China, the Japanese used plague

'Dressing the Wounded During a Gas Attack' – painting by Austin Osman Spare. During World War One, chemical weapons were responsible for the death of 100,000 people and the injury of about another million.

bacteria, in some cases spread by rats dropped on parachutes, against cities in North China. At least 700 people are known to have died. This story has been surprisingly little publicized, but the evidence seems quite good. The

Recent events have re-focused attention on chemical and biological weapons, which have so far been subject to much less public debate than nuclear weapons. The most dramatic of the recent events are the allegations by the United

allegations were initially made during the war, beginning in 1942, by the Head of the Chinese Red Cross and others. However, though the circumstantial evidence was strong, there was no direct evidence in the form of plague bacilli isolated from material known to have been dropped by the Japanese over the ten affected cities. Four years after the war a senior officer, a Japanese prisoner of war who had been captured by the Russians, testified that the Japanese *had* disseminated plague, using human fleas (*Pulex irritans*) as the carrier. This took place in central China where no previous plague epidemics had ever been recorded.

The grim experience of chemical warfare in World War One had one positive outcome – the negotiation of the 1925 Geneva Protocol prohibiting the use (but not the production and development) of asphyxiating, poisonous or other gases and of bacteriological methods of warfare. Most nations of the world have adopted the Protocol, although some 40 per cent of the parties (including the USA and the USSR) have reserved the right to use chemical weapons to retaliate in kind.

States Administration of the use by the USSR of chemical weapons in Afghanistan, but others include: the US allegation that Laos and Vietnam are using chemical weapons against the Hmong people in Laos; the US allegation that Kampuchea and Vietnam are using chemical weapons in Kampuchea; rumours that the USSR is significantly increasing its stocks of chemical munitions; the demand by NATO Commander General Rogers for the deployment of more chemical weapons in Europe; pressure by the Pentagon for the production of binary chemical weapons; and US claims that there was an accidental release of anthrax from a Soviet biological-weapons establishment at Sverdlovsk, with the implication that the USSR is conducting research into biological-warfare agents and may even be manufacturing them. All of this raises the prospect that the world may be on the verge of a new chemical arms race, with unpredictable but almost certainly far-reaching consequences.

Chemists and biologists are continually developing new materials with considerable potential for chemical and biological warfare. For example, a new generation of organophosphorus

The League of Nations addressed by Paul Painleve in 1925. Although the Geneva Protocol forbidding the use of gases and bacteria in warfare was signed in this year, some countries have yet to accept it in full.

French police using tear gas to break up a communist demonstration. Widely used in riot control at relatively low concentrations, tear gas was employed extensively at higher concentrations by the United States in Vietnam.

compounds, the bicyclophosphonates, of very high toxicity is under development. We can also foresee the development of a family of synthetic peptides with relatively low molecular weights and especially high lethality – maybe one hundred times greater than that of current nerve gases.

Chemical weapons

Of current developments in chemical-warfare agents, the most advanced is the development of binary nerve agents. A binary chemical weapon consists of two chemicals of relatively low toxicity. These are put separately into a chemical munition but they mix when, and only when, the munition reaches its target. The reaction produces a nerve gas which is normally lethal almost instantly. Sweating and vomiting are followed by paralysis, respiratory failure and death. A smaller, non-lethal dose can lead to long agony and permanent damage.

Because the two components of a binary chemical weapon are separately of relatively low toxicity, the weapon is much safer to handle and store than currently deployed chemical weapons. It is, however, still a dangerous weapon to handle because the components may have toxicities comparable with that of, say, strychnine when taken orally. One such binary component is methyl-phosphonyl difluoride, a potential binary component for the production of a nerve gas called sarin, or GB, which is already a constituent of some arsenals, although not in its safer, binary form.

One problem with binary chemical weapons is that their deployment would greatly complicate the negotiation of an international treaty to prohibit the production and stockpiling of chemical weapons – an urgently needed arms-control measure. Complications would arise in the verification of the provisions, because most of the separate components of binary weapons can have peaceful uses – for the preparation of pesticides, dye stuffs and pharmaceuticals – and, therefore, their production and stockpiling

for exclusively military purposes would be very difficult to prove.

Some components of binary chemical weapons, however, are not currently available commercially; the methyl-phosphonyl difluoride for sarin is an example. This is why the US Army has set up a production facility for binary weapons at Pine Bluff, Arkansas. Incidentally, Pine Bluff has a long history in chemical-warfare activities; it produced and stored mustard gas and lewisite in World War Two.

If binary agents are produced (and this will require the approval of the US President) they will probably be first deployed in 155-mm artillery shells. But there are also proposals for producing binary 8-inch artillery shells and 500-lb aircraft bombs using components which would produce the nerve gas VX. A request was before the US Congress (as of May 1983) for the budgeting of funds earmarked for binary nerve-gas production.

Only three countries – the USA, the USSR and France – are known to have chemical weapons in strategic quantities ready for military use. According to the British expert on chemical weapons, Julian Perry Robinson,[1] the USA probably has about 38,000 tons of chemical-warfare agents – about one half the lethal dermal agent mustard gas and the rest nerve gases (VX and sarin). This is enough to kill everyone in the world – it takes only one drop of nerve gas to kill – 4,000 times over. Robinson believes that about one eighth of the US arsenal has been located outside the USA – on Johnson Island in the Pacific and in West Germany. The stocks in West Germany are said to contain about 500 or 1,000 tons of nerve gas; and amounts similar to that are believed to be contained in the French arsenal.

There is no Western consensus on the size of the Soviet chemical arsenal, although US intelligence indicates that the USSR has not added to its chemical-weapon stocks since about 1970. The best

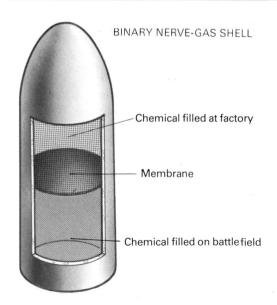

BINARY NERVE-GAS SHELL

Chemical filled at factory

Membrane

Chemical filled on battlefield

guess seems to be that NATO and the Warsaw Pact nations have comparable chemical-warfare capabilities.

Nevertheless, there have recently been official demands for the increase of NATO's chemical-warfare capabilities. Many NATO officers believe that the Soviets plan to use chemical weapons early in a war in Europe, against large-area targets such as airfields and against some population centres. Some of these officers want to modernize NATO's chemical arsenals (the USA has not produced nerve gases since 1969) by introducing binaries, to deter, so they say, Soviet use of chemical weapons. But NATO's arsenal (much of it in West Germany) already includes some three million sarin and VX artillery shells; thousands of sarin-filled aircraft bombs; thousands of VX 115-mm rockets; hundreds of thousands of VX land mines; and 1,500 2,000-lb aircraft spray tanks filled with VX. This is surely enough for any conceivable military purpose.

Recent claims by American and Australian Vietnam veterans, and indications among the Vietnamese population, that their exposure to defoliant agents has produced long-term health effects including skin lesions, and

birth defects among their children, bring home the unpredictability of exposure to toxic chemicals. We tend to forget how massive was the use of chemical-warfare agents in Vietnam. The Americans used some 90 million kilograms of anti-plant agents, of which about 60 per cent was the chemical Agent Orange, so called because of the colour-coding on the canisters in which it was stored. It inadvertently contained small quantities of dioxin. Some Vietnam veterans are convinced that they ingested some dioxin, and perhaps other contaminants, and that this poisoned them and produced genetic effects in their offspring. Dioxin is a nerve-affecting chemical – a chlorinated hydrocarbon – used in some pesticides, which can have disastrous effects on land which it has polluted. The best-known case was the lethal accidental release on July 10, 1976, of dioxin from the ICMESA chemical plant at Seveso, in northern Italy. Sheep which had been grazing on polluted land at nearby Desio died in 1980, four years later.

For a number of years now the US Administration has accused the Soviet Union and its allies of using chemical weapons in southeast Asia and Afghanistan. It is alleged that a new type of chemical weapon has been used based on mycotoxins, which are poisons produced naturally by fungi. They are well

Binary nerve gas shell. The membrane separating the two compartments shatters on impact, allowing the chemicals to mix and produce the deadly nerve agent.

So seriously is the threat of chemical warfare taken that NATO forces wear NBC protective clothing as a routine precaution on exercises.

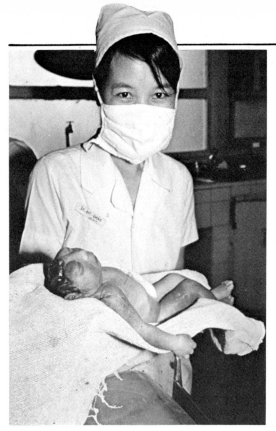

Thailand. The scientists concluded that the samples were fakes, consisting of yellow pollen grains from local rain forests. More recently some scientists have concluded that the yellow spots were bee faeces! In any case, the mycotoxin levels on the samples were so low as to have no military value. A United Nations expert group has also studied the evidence and could find no conclusive proof of the use

known to researchers. These toxins are said to be the agents in the 'yellow rain' reported by refugees from Laos and Kampuchea. In a typical attack described by, for example, Hmong people who had lived in the Laotian highlands an aircraft would release a cloud, often yellow in colour, which would descend on a village. The cloud seemed to consist of small particles which would fall like rain, hence the name 'yellow rain'. Those exposed to yellow rain were said to experience, very rapidly, symptoms like violent itching, vomiting, dizziness and distorted vision. Some would die within an hour from shock and massive bleeding from the stomach. This effect would indeed be characteristic of some fungus poisons.

The American allegations have, however, been seriously weakened by the analysis of samples by Australian and British scientists. The samples of leaves and pebbles said to have been contaminated with yellow rain were collected from refugees who had fled to

of mycotoxins.

If Soviet use of chemical weapons were established, it may be a breach of the 1925 Geneva Protocol mentioned above. And the use of mycotoxins may also be a violation of the 1972 Biological and Toxin Weapons Convention. The USA and the USSR have ratified the Geneva Protocol, but Afghanistan, Kampuchea, Laos and Vietnam have not done so. Nevertheless, the ban on the use of chemical weapons is usually considered a well-established customary international law, binding both on parties and on non-parties.

In the propaganda war of charge and countercharge, the Kabul regime in Afghanistan (a Soviet puppet regime) accused the USA of supplying the Afghan resistance forces with chemical-warfare agents. Three gas grenades, captured from rebels, were displayed to the press in Kabul. The grenades were marked 'CS', a tear gas. But CS grenades are readily available – many police forces have them – and the grenades almost certainly

This child owes its deformities to the effects of Agent Orange, a defoliant used by the United States in Vietnam. Agent Orange contained only small quantities of dioxin, but these were enough to have frequently disastrous effects.

Deformed fetuses in their jars bear mute testimony to the cost in human suffering of the use of Agent Orange. Modern warfare strikes even at the unborn.

reached Afghanistan via Iran.

Biological Weapons

The development, production and stockpiling of biological and toxin weapons is prohibited by the 1972 treaty, which has now been ratified by about 90 nations. Biological-warfare agents are disease-carrying substances and organisms. Possible agents include viruses, like yellow fever; rickettsiae, like typhus; bacteria, like plague; and fungi, like coccidioidomycosis.

There is a crucial difference between biological- and chemical-warfare agents. Whereas the military are very interested in chemical warfare and large chemical arsenals are deployed, they have never been greatly interested in biological weapons. Biological agents tend to die quickly, unless in an exactly suitable environment, and their spread is exceedingly difficult to control. (In ordinary civilian life epidemics – and these include epidemics of plague – come and go quite mysteriously. They quite often die out inexplicably, which is good luck for us, but bad news for any military organization that wants to use them.) Also, diseases do not take sides, and one's own troops might be stricken as well as the enemy's. The troops could perhaps be vaccinated first, but there would always be the chance that such a disease could ultimately strike one's own civilian population at home. The final, cynical argument against the military use of biological weapons is that they are often very slow to take effect.

Biological weapons do have one important similarity with chemical weapons, which is that small nations could produce them rather easily and cheaply in quantities which may, in their regions, be strategically significant. For this reason, many regard biological and chemical weapons as potential weapons of mass destruction for the smaller countries. The weapons are all the more dangerous because of the danger that they might proliferate.

In 1982, the USA accused the USSR of violating the Biological Weapon Convention. The allegations were based on reports of an epidemic of anthrax in Sverdlovsk, a city about 1,800 kilometers from Moscow, just over the Urals. According to some newspaper reports, the research laboratories of a Soviet factory making biological weapons exploded on April 3, 1979. The laboratories were said to be near the hamlet of Kashino, about 30 kilometers from Sverdlovsk. More than 1,000 people are said to have died from exposure to the bacteria.

But the evidence that the Soviet anthrax outbreak originated from biological-warfare agents is as weak as the evidence for yellow rain. Dr Vivian Wyatt, for example, says in a *New Scientist* article that 'the story of a germ-warfare disaster does not ring true. It is more likely that an epidemic resulted from intestinal anthrax. It is likely that weather conditions near Sverdlovsk favoured the formation of spores and that a greater number of

The object of the United States' use of Agent Orange in Vietnam: the defoliation of huge areas of the jungle in order to expose guerrillas attempting to shelter in it. The effects of such defoliants can last for years.

The production of some quantities of biological-warfare agents continues. And so does laboratory, and perhaps field testing, as well as relevant military training. (The British tested an anthrax weapon on deserted Gruinard Island in 1942; the island is still contaminated and off limits.) These activities are supposed to be just for defensive purposes. But defensive preparations are, at some stages of development, indistinguishable from offensive ones.

The treaty does not define the amounts of agents and toxins 'justifiable' for defensive purposes. It is, therefore, not possible to judge whether or not the production of a certain amount of a biological-warfare agent is lethal. Even if it were established that the Sverdlovsk incident was due to an escape of a biological-warfare agent it cannot be said that the treaty was violated. (The 1942 British experiment was, of course, a long time prior to the treaty.)

Under the treaty, research into the production of biological weapons is not banned. There may be some excuse for allowing research into biological agents for defensive purposes but there can be no such excuse for allowing research on biological *weapons*. These can only be offensive.

We are on the threshold of a new biotechnological age. Scientists are steadily moving towards an understanding of the fundamental processes of life, and genetic engineers are making available a vast range of new biological substances. We can be sure that other scientists, the military scientists, are looking hard at each new development for possible military applications. Much of the present work on recombinant DNA – which is developing very rapidly indeed – opens up the prospect of artificially created life forms. Among the easier to create would be bacteria specially tailored for military purposes, along with the production of vaccine to render chosen people immune to their effects. (It has been reported that there has been recent US military interest

animals than usual went down with anthrax. The most likely source of the epidemic is sausage from a pig.' Anthrax is still common in parts of the USSR and the epidemic may have come from an accident in a vaccine plant. We can only speculate.

But even if the killer outbreak of anthrax did come from a military laboratory it is unlikely that the Biological Weapon Convention was violated. There is a large loophole in the treaty. Development and production of biological weapons are banned but research into biological agents is not. The prohibitions in the treaty apply only to types and amounts of biological agents and toxins that have no justification for medical, protective or other peaceful purposes. The term 'protective' covers the development of protective masks and clothing, air and water filters, detection and warning devices and decontamination equipment.

A Hmong refugee in Thailand describing the effects of 'yellow rain' on the eyes and breast. In fact, it now seems that such descriptions may be fabrications: the evidence pointing to the use of yellow rain is poor.

in the creation by genetic engineering of a new influenza virus, which would debilitate enemy citizens and soldiers without killing them.) In the long term the creation of higher species of life may become possible, but this will raise issues – military and otherwise – well beyond the scope of this book. In any event, the Pentagon has shown itself interested in biotechnological research, and while biological warfare seems rather unlikely as things stand at the moment, the genetic engineers could change all that. Any industry with as much money invested in it as genetic engineering has is likely one day to have military spin-offs.

The military use of new chemical and biological knowledge can best be limited by an effective international treaty. The negotiation of a treaty banning the development, production and stockpiling of chemical weapons is an urgently needed arms-control and disarmament measure. And the Biological Weapon Convention should be made more effective, by closing the loopholes and unambiguously including any products of genetic engineering among the biological agents banned from military use.

Frank Barnaby

References

1   In Stockholm International Peace Research Institute, **Chemical Weapons: Destruction and Conversion**, Taylor and Francis, London, 1980

Further general information on the subject will be found in:

Evans, Grant, **The Yellow Rain Makers: Are Chemical Weapons Being Used in South East Asia?**, Verso, London, 1983
Seagrave, Sterling, **Yellow Rain: Chemical Warfare – the Deadliest Arms Race**, Abacus, London, 1982
Stockholm International Peace Research Institute, **The Problems of Chemical and Biological Warfare**, six vols, Alnqvist and Wiksell, Stockholm, 1971-5

Annually, members of the Royal Navy visit Gruinard Island to update the warning notices; aside from these visits, Gruinard is shunned. During World War Two, British scientists tested an anthrax weapon on the island. It may be decades before Gruinard is safe for visitors.

Chapter 10

How Much Damage Can Modern War Create?

The twentieth century has to date witnessed some sixteen wars that have each resulted in 300,000 fatalities or more. Three of these wars each had substantially more than three million fatalities, and one of them had around 50 million. Indeed, in the words of Arthur Koestler, it would appear to be true that 'The most persistent sound which reverberates through man's history is the beating of war drums'.[1] Koestler went on to note that 'Tribal wars, religious wars, civil wars, dynastic wars, national wars, revolutionary wars, colonial wars, wars of conquest and of liberation, wars to prevent and to end all wars, follow each other in a chain of compulsive repetitiveness as far as man can remember his past . . .' Unless we succeed in breaking this chain, we must, however,

bide our time in order to learn whether its next major link will be a nuclear or non-nuclear war. What is the character and extent of the damage that can be expected in either event?

Damage from Non-Nuclear War
In depicting damage from non-nuclear war it will be useful to consider thumbnail sketches of the most calamitous and ecologically damaging wars of recent centuries. These can provide a frame of reference not only for the non-nuclear wars of the future, but also for any possible nuclear ones.

The first is the Thirty Years' War of 1618–1648 in which the Protestant armies of (primarily) the German states and Sweden waged an ultimately successful war against the Catholic armies of the

114

An engraving by Jacques Courtois of fighting during the Thirty Years' War. During this series of wars, which were inspired partly by political and partly by religious reasons, some six million people died – about 40 per cent of the then population of Central Europe.

The interior of one of the Taku Forts immediately after its capture in August, 1860, during the Tai Ping Rebellion in China. This civil war saw the deaths of as many as 40 million people – perhaps seven per cent of the then population of China.

Holy Roman Empire, with most of the action occurring in central Europe. The theatres of action were ravaged during the course of this extraordinarily protracted and vicious war. The populations of the embroiled states were decimated, their agricultural fields widely devastated, and their towns and villages pillaged by the thousand. The loss of life during the war has been estimated to have been at least six million, representing 40 per cent of the population of central Europe at that time, and as much as 65 per cent of the total populations of several of the embroiled states. In what seems to have been the worst case, the population of the state of Bohemia (now a part of Czechoslovakia) was reduced by perhaps 75 per cent. All told, it took many generations and numerous decades for the wounds of this war eventually to heal.

For the next example we jump ahead two centuries and cross to the other side of the world. In the Chinese Rebellion of 1850–1864, the so-called Tai Ping (or Great Peace) movement was ultimately unsuccessful in its long-drawn-out attempt to overthrow the Manchu Dynasty. The Tai Ping forces pursued their rebellion with continuing violence of a high order and much pillaging. It was countered by the government forces with equal or greater terror and violence. Among other means, the Manchu forces employed large-scale scorched-earth tactics in order to starve the rebellious regions into submission. The final total number of war deaths on both sides is estimated to have been between twenty million and forty million, representing about seven per cent of China's total population at the time. The population particularly of the lower Yangtze River region – Anhwei Province plus portions of the surrounding provinces – was truly devastated and had still not regained its pre-war level a full century later.

The third example brings us into the present century and back to the Occident. World War One of 1914–1918 was again a large-scale cataclysm, especially so for Europe. There was great loss of life as a result of this terrible war, amounting to perhaps fifteen million or more. Some states were especially stricken. Thus, thirteen per cent of the population of Turkey was killed during the war, as was fully 24 per cent of that of Serbia (now a part of Yugoslavia). Moreover, this war introduced the horror of the large-scale employment of chemical warfare agents (see Chapter Nine). The more than one hundred million kilograms of chemicals expended by both sides resulted in some 100,000 fatalities and in ten times that many serious long-lasting injuries. The war also brought about enormous amounts of largely incidental devastation of agricultural and forest lands. Especially severe destruction of this kind occurred in France and Belgium, where there was hardly sufficient time for recovery to occur before the devastating onslaught two decades later of World War Two, which provides the fourth example.

World War Two of 1939–1945 was a great watershed in human history, almost literally deserving its appellation of 'world' war. World War Two became the first nuclear war, but only very briefly (and, by the standards of today, only very modestly) in the waning moments of its six agonizing years. A discussion of the nuclear portion of the war is left for the following section.

The catastrophic consequences of World War Two included a total of some 50 million fatalities, a number simply too huge for most of us to grasp in any visceral sense. To single out the several hardest hit states during this war, Germany lost at least nine per cent of its population; Yugoslavia eleven per cent; the USSR also eleven per cent (an enormous number in view of the size of the Soviet Union); and Poland fully eighteen per cent, nearly one individual out of every five. Among the survivors of World War Two, there were millions of people who became lifelong invalids, and there were millions of children who were orphaned. Many millions of people were displaced by the war, undergoing great physical and psychological hardships in finding new homelands. Moreover, certain ethnic groups – especially Jews and Gypsies – were viciously persecuted and to a substantial extent exterminated by Germany in those considerable regions of Europe under its control. On a global basis, the overall total of 50 million people killed during World War Two represented a premature death for perhaps one person in 70 (1.4 per cent) of all the people living on Earth during those six years.

World War Two resulted in enormous amounts of agricultural, forest and other ecological devastation, especially in its European and Pacific theatres. There was extraordinarily heavy use of high-explosive and incendiary munitions: more than 10,000 million kilograms by Germany, almost 8,000 million kilograms by the USA, and additional huge amounts by Japan, Britain and other participating states. There was much area bombing of urban and industrial regions, which caused the nearly total destruction of a number of German and Japanese cities. Many tropical Pacific Ocean island ecosystems were devastated. Some seventeen per cent of Dutch agricultural lands were destroyed through intentional hostile salt-water inundation, and a huge area of northern Norway was also systematically laid waste. European agricultural productivity was depressed by about 40 per cent by the depredations of World War Two and recovery from this setback took half a decade of intense efforts. Additionally there was, of course, profligate utilization of a broad array of natural resources by many nations.

For the final example of the damage that can be associated with non-nuclear war, we turn to the Second Indochina (Vietnam) War of 1961 – 1975. In this asymmetrical conflict, the USA expended immense amounts of high-explosive and incendiary munitions, all told more than 14,000 million kilograms. Total number of fatalities in Indochina by the end of the

war numbered almost two million people; in serious injuries to almost twice that number; and in population displacements totalling perhaps seventeen million, this last number representing one-third of the entire regional (Indochinese) population. The US strategy involved massive rural-area bombing as well as chemical and mechanical forest destruction; systematic large-scale crop destruction by a variety of mechanical, chemical and other techniques; and the destruction of untold thousands of towns, small villages, bridges, hospitals and so forth. As part of its general warfare programme, the USA directed unprecedented quantities of anti-plant chemical-warfare agents – more than 90 million kilograms – against forest and agricultural lands. In South Vietnam alone, these massive rural chemical and area-bombing efforts resulted in the total destruction of perhaps five per cent of the forest and in greater or lesser long-term damage to roughly half that nation's forest. These and related military activities also took some twenty per cent of the agricultural lands of South Vietnam out of

This photograph of Leuze Wood in November 1916 displays the almost incredible damage which the military could do even at that time. The number of lives lost in the 1914–18 war is estimated to have been perhaps more than fifteen million.

production during the war, and the pre-war output of food staples could not be matched until about four or five years after the war.

The Second Indochina War represents the culmination to date in a military progression that has been very evident all through the present century of an ever-greater ability to destroy large areas. This ability to disrupt ever-greater areas has been accomplished through the development of increasingly devastating weapons, better delivery systems and – most important – higher-capacity industrial bases and more efficient logistics. The staggeringly huge numbers of high-explosive fragmentation bombs dropped in Vietnam – of the order of twenty million – the blast munitions developed (both fuel-air explosive devices and concussion bombs capable of clearing perhaps one hectare at a time) are cases in point.

Non-nuclear war depends for its destructive fury primarily upon mechanical or incendiary means, including especially: high-speed projectiles; chemical explosive devices that hurl fragments or generate a blast wave; and devices that initiate fires. To this catalogue must be added the chemical-warfare agents that are destructive through their poisonous qualities. At least one or more of the world's major arsenals contain large stocks of lethal chemical-warfare agents that, if employed, would make the terrible impact of the chemical anti-personnel weapons employed in World War One appear trivial in retrospect.

To conclude this section on damage from non-nuclear war, it is abundantly evident that where the will, resources, industrial capacity and time exist, such warfare can wreak extraordinary levels of death and suffering, of material damage and of environmental disruption. It is additionally clear that human ingenuity and human motivation continually lead to advances in these so-called conventional military capabilities.

Damage from Nuclear War

The nuclear explosions of 1945 ushered in a new era; indeed, they formed the most important turning point in human history. In that year the awesome ability was achieved – and demonstrated twice over – to annihilate in one flash a city and its inhabitants with a single small weapon dropped from an aircraft. Since then a continuing stream of scientific and technological advances has enhanced the power of these devices many thousand-fold, has made a variety of ancillary improvements on them, and has developed accurate (and, in some instances, essentially invulnerable) delivery systems of intercontinental range. Today, several nations stockpile these efficient weapons of mass destruction for immediate use, overwhelmingly so the USA and USSR.

The bombs that obliterated Hiroshima and Nagasaki in 1945 had an explosive energy (or yield) equivalent, respectively, to about thirteen and 22 kilotons of TNT. The nuclear arsenals of today include a panoply of weapons some of which are smaller than those were ('tactical' weapons), some that are larger ('theatre' weapons), and still others that are far larger ('strategic' weapons). The total number of nuclear weapons ready for use today is not officially known, but it is

An aerial view of Hiroshima soon after the dropping of the atom bomb there on 6th August, 1945. The Hiroshima bomb was, of course, a comparatively modest device by the standards of the weapons available to the nuclear-weapon powers today.

widely assumed to be in the neighbourhood of 50,000; and these are said to have a combined yield of perhaps 15,000 megatons. Most of the smaller ones (the so-called atomic bombs) depend for their energy release upon the fission of atomic nuclei, whereas for the larger ones (the so-called hydrogen bombs) it is a combination of fission and fusion (as it also is for the so-called neutron bombs).

The actual effects of a future nuclear war are, of course, difficult to estimate because of the many major uncertainties involved. For example, we can only guess at how many bombs will be exchanged and what their types and yields will be. The impact of such a war will also depend heavily on the geographic locations of the detonations and on what proportions of them will be ground bursts as opposed to air bursts. Indeed, in order to multiply the degree of impact to any desired level one need merely increase the number of ground bursts.

Thus the next nuclear war could conceivably be as modest as – one is

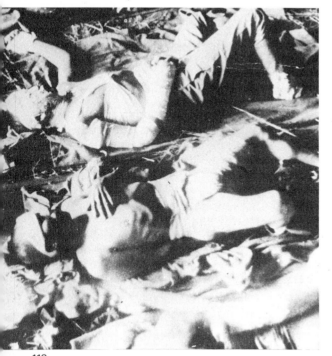

FALLOUT PATTERNS IN A PROJECTED NUCLEAR CONFLICT

almost tempted to say, as benign as – the last one, in which two small essentially fallout-free air bursts resulted in 200,000 immediate deaths, a further 200,000 latent deaths and an additional 200,000 physically and psychologically scarred survivors. At the other extreme, it could result in several hundred million immediate fatalities, perhaps as many latent ones again, the collapse of civilization as we know it and severe disruption of the natural environment. This latter possibility would be the outcome of an all-out war between the USA and the USSR which, it is commonly

Some of the victims of the Hiroshima blast – a photograph taken immediately after the explosion and later found in the files of a Hiroshima newspaper by an American soldier. People are believed still to be dying as a result of the Hiroshima and Nagasaki bombs.

The time in New York is 11 am in early June, 1985, in the scenario shown in the map above. Nuclear war has just broken out between the USA and the USSR. The total megatonnage used is 5,742. Targets are military (including missile silos), industrial and cities with a population over 100,000. The grey plumes show those areas which with average June winds will

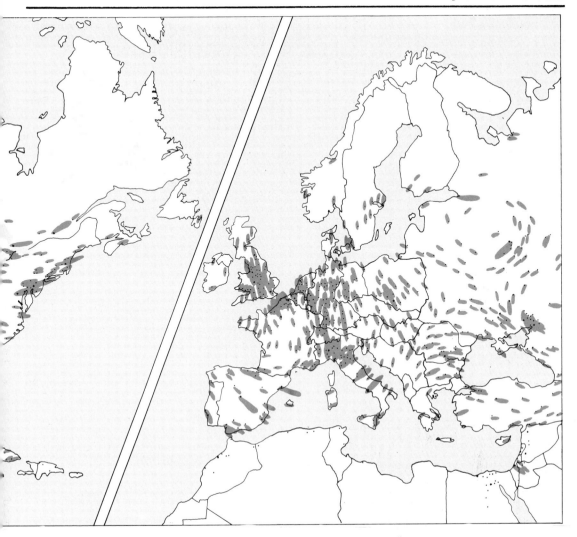

speculated, would involve thousands of bombs having a combined yield of the order of 10,000 megatons, and of which half would be detonated as ground bursts and the other half as air bursts.

Among the endless intermediate possibilities, one might envisage a 'small' or 'limited' war (one that – it is to be desperately hoped – would not escalate into an all-out war) in which only several hundred tactical or theatre weapons are employed. If such a war were to occur in a populated region such as central Europe – a not unlikely locale – it might result in five million to ten million immediate

fatalities, another similar number of latent fatalities, and yet again a similar number of severely injured and/or traumatized individuals. There would also be severe long-term disruption of the region's natural-resource base of agricultural lands, forests and so forth.

There are various forms of energy that are released by nuclear-bomb explosions, and we shall note the characteristics and extent of damage that each form causes. This will be followed by looking at some of the indirect or second-order effects of major concern to us in an evaluation of how much widespread long-term damage

receive more than 450 rad of radiation. Lethal fallout at this level will kill at least half the population. The fallout patterns would be very much worse if any nuclear reactors were hit (they are likely targets); in this case Europe would be almost entirely covered with fallout. In any event, as the map shows, because of its dense population and heavy industry Europe

would suffer the most. This grisly exercise was worked out for the Swedish environmental magazine Ambio *by a panel of scientific advisors.*

to expect from nuclear warfare. We do not need to devote much space to the immediate carnage and societal chaos that would result from a nuclear attack. They are very nearly self-evident. This chaos would include the difficulties experienced by the survivors within the directly afflicted region in meeting their immediate survival needs for water, food, clothing, shelter from the elements, protection from fallout, and medical services. Suffice it to say here that, in the days and weeks following an attack, access to these necessities would range from absent, or essentially so, to more or less available, depending upon the distance from the explosions and other vagaries of the local situation.

The energy releases of primary concern to us from the explosion of a nuclear bomb are in the forms of blast, of heat and of nuclear radiation. A nuclear bomb dissipates roughly half or more of its tremendous energy in the form of a shock or blast wave. It is this blast that is responsible for much of the immediate physical damage to humans, to their

artifacts and to nature. By way of example, a single one-megaton air burst would knock down virtually all of the trees over some 14,000 hectares (35,000 acres – about 54 square miles) as well as most man-made structures. It would, in addition, force thousands of tons of water vapour that are present in the lower atmosphere (troposphere) into the upper atmosphere (stratosphere). In contrast, a single one-megaton ground burst would blast out a huge crater, extending over perhaps twelve hectares (30 acres) and with a maximum depth of some 100 meters (330 feet). An estimated 50,000 tons of the rock and soil thus displaced would be hurled into the upper atmosphere as a fine dust. A single one-megaton underwater burst would lift tens of thousands of tons of water aerosol and vapour into the upper atmosphere.

A nuclear-bomb explosion dissipates roughly another third or more of its energy in the form of an intense thermal or heat wave. This heat would initiate fires over an immense area, the exact size depending, of course, upon the weather conditions at the time, the terrain, and the nature of the potential fuel – habitations, grain fields, forest land, prairie and so forth. Indeed, under certain terrain and fuel conditions the fires initiated would coalesce into a truly infernal firestorm. On a clear, dry summer day a single one-megaton air burst might well initiate wildfires throughout an area of more than 33,000 hectares (80,000 acres, or 130 square miles), and these would be likely to burn and spread for weeks. These fires would wreak havoc among the plants and animals surviving the blast and nuclear radiation. They would also inject immense amounts of smoke into the atmosphere. The surface disruption from blast and fire would in turn lead to massive site degradation of long duration (that is, of decades), this occurring as a result of soil erosion and of nutrient losses in solution, so-called nutrient dumping. Moreover, the exceedingly high temperatures momentarily generated by a single one-

A nuclear civil-defence exercise being carried out in Switzerland, one of the few nations in the world to take civil defence seriously. Sceptics claim that such measures are useless, since the devastation caused by all-out war would be so colossal that survival in northern Europe would be virtually impossible.

megaton air burst would result in the transformation of some 5,000 tons of the atmosphere into various oxides of nitrogen. These oxides of nitrogen would in turn produce a smog in the lower atmosphere and would degrade the ozone in the upper atmosphere, ozone being a molecule that forms a protective barrier for man and nature against excessive ultraviolet radiation.

A nuclear-bomb explosion dissipates the remaining ten per cent or so of its energy in the form of nuclear radiation, a portion of which is released as an initial burst and the remainder – in the form of radioactive fallout – much more slowly and widely. A single one-megaton ground burst would present a lethal dosage of nuclear radiation to all exposed humans and most other vertebrates – including, of course, our livestock – over about 36,000 hectares (90,000 acres – around 140 square miles).

As a highly sobering specific example, I cite the 'Bravo' test at Bikini on March 1, 1954. This single fifteen-megaton ground burst during the first four days deposited fallout lethal to exposed humans and livestock over an area of roughly two million hectares (five million acres – close to 8,000 square miles); that is, over an area approximately half the size of Switzerland. It is fortunate indeed that this huge area of deadly contamination spent itself largely over the trackless Pacific Ocean. However, it is most instructive to add here that although the nuclear test programme on Bikini ended more than a quarter of a century ago, the island remains uninhabitable despite intensive cleanup attempts; these, moreover, were cleanup attempts of a magnitude feasible only during time of peace.

While considering the extent of radioactive contamination it should also be pointed out that in a war some of the hundreds – how many no one could predict – of the existing nuclear-power reactors on land and at sea will inevitably be struck by conventional or nuclear weapons. The radioactive debris thereby dispersed will further extend the regions of death to flora and fauna and of uninhabitability to humans.

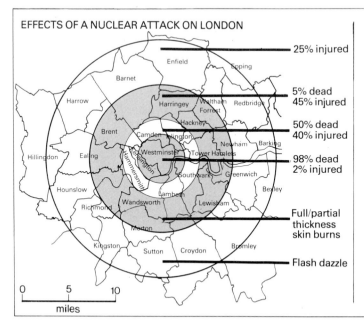

EFFECTS OF A NUCLEAR ATTACK ON LONDON

- 25% injured
- 5% dead / 45% injured
- 50% dead / 40% injured
- 98% dead / 2% injured
- Full/partial thickness skin burns
- Flash dazzle

0 5 10
miles

Casualties in attacks on the United Kingdom

	1980 'Square leg exercise'	'Counterforce' attack
No. of weapons	125	340
Explosive yield (Mt)	196.5	222
Burns deaths (millions)	2.5	3.1
Blast deaths (millions)	13	20.2
Fall out deaths (millions)	11.2	15.3
All deaths (millions)	26.7	38.6
Serious injury (millions)	6.8	4.3

Total population of UK (1981) 55.5 million

Left: some effects of a one-megaton nuclear airburst over the centre of London, those of the shock wave (which kills by pressure) and the burns and dazzle from the fireball. Fallout, whose effects are more variable and long-term, is here ignored. Right: estimates by Doctors Openshaw and Steadman of British deaths in two different kinds of attack: 'Square Leg' was a 1980 Home Defence exercise, in which presumed targets were military and urban; 'Counterforce' is based more directly on yields of actual Soviet weapons, targets industrial and military. The Home Office believes these figures, published by the British Medical Association, are exaggerated.

The several forms of intense energy released during a nuclear war that I have just summarized would leave large areas of appalling devastation to man and nature; even a single or small number of nuclear detonations would suffice. On the other hand, I now wish to raise the possibility that a large-scale exchange of nuclear weapons could result in widespread and long-term damage to the human environment of an even more substantial nature.

Among the potentially disastrous phenomena that we can conjecture would be those set in motion by the large-scale injection of fine particles of dust and frozen water into the upper atmosphere; by the generation of vast quantities of smoke and smog; and by the introduction of huge amounts of oxides of nitrogen into the ozone layer. The first of these – dust and water in the stratosphere – could have long-term adverse effects on our climate. The second – smoke and smog in the troposphere – could for a time (that is, for perhaps one or even two growing seasons) substantially lower the ability of plants to photosynthesize, thereby debilitating our agriculture and reducing the primary productivity of the Earth's ecosystems. The third and perhaps most worrisome – a depleted ozone layer – could permit damaging levels of ultraviolet radiation to reach the Earth's surface.

How much of the protective ozone layer would be destroyed by an all-out nuclear war or how long it would take for the ozone layer to return to its normal state of equilibrium are not at all certain. One authoritative study carried out several years ago by the US National Academy of Sciences suggested that of the order of half (30 per cent to 70 per cent) of the ozone would be destroyed and that substantial recovery would take up to a decade.[2] The uncertainties involved in such estimates are so intractable (both as regards the input data and the models) that it is not at this point fruitful to argue over the precise magnitude of this value. Using a 50 per cent depletion of the ozone of several years' duration as a reasonable possibility, we find that this will lead to a substantially increased fraction of solar ultraviolet radiation reaching the Earth's surface. In fact, this increase will be approximately three-fold in magnitude in the biologically active portion of the ultraviolet spectrum, namely in the wavelength range of approximately 280-380 nanometers, the so-called UV-B range. It must be added here, moreover, that this effect will in time become more or less world-wide, even if the war should be confined to portions of the northern hemisphere, owing to the world-wide lateral dispersion by diffusion of the ozone layer in the lower stratosphere.

The biological effects and ecological impact of enhanced UV-B radiation on humans, on plants, and on animals as well as on the various natural and artificial ecosystems of the world – oceanic, terrestrial and agricultural – could conceivably be devastating on a global basis. For example, the possibility cannot be excluded that for a number of years following a large-scale nuclear war people nowhere on Earth will be able to spend more than a few hours outdoors during the day without resorting to extraordinary protective measures. An immediate result of indiscretion could be ocular (corneal) impairment leading to temporary or permanent blindness (akin to snow blindness); and a delayed result could be a substantial increase in the frequency of skin cancers.

Agricultural endeavours during the first several years following a major nuclear exchange could be severely disrupted on a global basis by the enhanced UV-B radiation. And such damage would compound the already considerable problems resulting from radioactive contamination (to which crops, for example, are generally more sensitive than their weed competitors and their fungal and insect pests); from the smoke and smog pall (which would reduce productivity both directly and perhaps via adverse climatic changes); and from the paucity of farm workers, implements, fuel, fertilizers and pesticides (herbicides, fungicides, insecticides). Some crops – among them sugar beets, tomatoes, beans, peas and perhaps maize (corn) – turn out to be especially sensitive to enhanced UV-B radiation. Moreover, livestock could be expected to develop debilitating corneal and perhaps skin lesions.

The more natural terrestrial ecosystems could also be substantially disrupted on a global basis by enhanced UV-B radiation. This can be seen in the extrapolation from the limited available information that perhaps as many as one-fifth of the world's terrestrial plant species might succumb directly or indirectly to such an assault and an additional fraction of them would have their photosynthesis and growth impaired. And these debilitations, of course, again add to those of nuclear radiation from fallout (especially so in the case of the relatively sensitive conifer ecosystems of the world); of smoke and smog; and so forth. Such drastic perturbations among the primary producers of the world's ecosystems would, in turn, exert a substantial impact on the wildlife depending upon them for food and shelter. Some of the animal life might also be injured directly by the enhanced UV-B radiation. This is so, of course, because in most instances the newly created damaging levels of UV-B would not be directly detectable by the animals and this would therefore preclude evasive actions. Thus, for example, unavoidable damage to the cornea would reduce the efficiency of hawks, eagles and much other wildlife in their hunting or foraging abilities.

Even the great oceanic ecosystems could be greatly disturbed on a world-wide basis. Marine plankton live close to the surface of the ocean and if they were killed off to a substantial extent, the oceanic food chain would be largely broken. The fish stocks which depend upon this chain would as a result be placed in jeopardy. Since, as we have

noted, the ozone effect is more or less a global one (and adds to that of the pall of smoke and smog) repopulation might take a number of years, and would thus be unlikely to be rapid enough to save a major fraction of the many plankton-dependent species. The restoration of fish stocks throughout the world – both commercial and otherwise – might thus in turn take many years to occur.

In concluding this section on damage from nuclear war, it is important to stress once again that the several diverse impacts discussed separately above would, of course, occur simultaneously and, by reinforcing each other, would be likely to have combined effects substantially greater than simple addition of the separately occurring effects might suggest. Synergism of this kind is most difficult to predict. Moreover, any single major environmental perturbation could result in entirely unforeseen ecological ramifications. In more specific human terms, the long-term effects of large-scale nuclear war would be devastating owing not only to the overpowering combination of a disrupted agricultural enterprise and debilitated environment, but also to a largely destroyed industrial and manufacturing base and to largely disabled transportation and communications systems. Moreover, the inevitable uprooting of populations, the unavailability of potable water supplies, the breakdown of sanitation systems and the loss of public health services will greatly enhance the spread of disease.

Conclusion
It appears that warfare, whether old-fashioned or modern, results in a level of damage that is in large part proportional to the objectives, the will, and the tenacity of the parties to the conflict. Improvements in weaponry have followed one upon the other throughout the long sweep of human history. So far, this has not led through time to any discernible increase in the damage brought about by warfare, only in the efficiency with which

it is perpetrated. The chain of wars to which Arthur Koestler referred has been forged out of a seemingly limitless number of small links that are all too frequently punctuated by larger links and every so often by huge ones. At last, however, with the advent of nuclear weapons and their delivery systems we must come to grips with a truly *qualitative* change in this tragically monotonous litany.

Some would have us consider nuclear weapons as merely the current step in our continuing progression of ever more efficient means of warfare. It is true that nuclear weapons can be scaled down in their potency – potency, that is, in terms of their blast effect – to approach that of today's largest conventional weapons. There is, of course, also much precedent in warfare for the obliteration of entire cities, from Carthage in the Third Punic War to Lidice in World War Two and any number of others during the intervening two thousand years as well as before and after. And, as already outlined, various of the more vicious and protracted non-nuclear wars of the past have in time resulted in levels of carnage comparable to what might be expected from a 'limited' nuclear war.

But one of the horrors of nuclear weapons is the relative speed, ease and multiplicity with which large-scale annihilation can now be accomplished. Moreover, the horror of this instant obliteration is made even worse by the long-term, if not essentially permanent, legacy of widespread environmental, societal and medical damage and debilitation with which the survivors will have to cope. Not so long ago, John Stuart Mill was able to point out that countries had the capacity for recovering rapidly from the ravages of war because their land and its permanent improvements remained essentially undestroyed.[3] It is clear that Mill would not be able to maintain the same grounds for optimism today. Finally, the ultimate horror of nuclear weapons is that, in the last analysis, they threaten the very integrity of our civilization, if not the survival of our species.

To summarize: warfare represents man's most persistent pastime, from antiquity to the present. Indeed, it is probably safe to suggest that there has never been a day without war in the history of mankind. Until 1945, the human character flaw which has permitted this cruel indulgence was of little consequence to the progress of our civilization or may even have contributed to its continued advancement, at least insofar as this shows itself in the advancement of science and technology. Now, however, we – or at least the nuclear powers among us – leave Koestler's chain intact at the peril of destroying our society if not ourselves.

Arthur H. Westing

References
1   Koestler, Arthur, **Janus: A Summing Up**, Hutchinson, London, 1978
2   Nier, A.O.C. et al., **Long-Term World-Wide Effects of Multiple Nuclear-Weapons Detonations**, National Academy of Sciences, Washington, 1975
3   Mill, J.S., **Principles of Political Economy: with Some of Their Applications to Social Philosophy**, 1871
The following are useful general references:
      Committee for the Compilation of Materials on Damage Caused by the Atomic Bombs in Hiroshima and Nagasaki, **Hiroshima and Nagasaki: the Physical, Medical, and Social Effects of the Atomic Bombings**, Basic Books, New York, 1981
      Galtung, J., **Environment, Development and Military Activity: Towards Alternative Security Doctrines**, Universitetsforlaget, Oslo, 1982
      Iklé, F.C., **Social Impact of Bomb Destruction**, University of Oklahoma Press, Norman, Oklahoma, 1958
      Westing, A.H., **Weapons of Mass Destruction and the Environment**, Taylor and Francis, London, 1977
      Westing, A.H., **Warfare in a Fragile World: Military Impact on the Human Environment**, Taylor and Francis, London, 1980
      Westing, A.H. and Lumsden, M., **Threat of Modern Warfare to Man and his Environment: An Annotated Bibliography**, UNESCO, Reports and Papers in the Social Sciences No. 40, Paris, 1979

Chapter 11

The Economics of Warfare

Calculated in terms of current US dollars, the world as a whole spent some 4,860 billion dollars on the military in the twenty years between 1961 and 1980. Corrected for inflation and stated in terms of 1979 US dollars, that figure would be 7,770 billion dollars (constant-dollars). In 1982 alone, world military expenditures were on the order of 600 billion dollars. Continued growth at the trend rate of these past two decades would result in additional world military expenditures of the order of 15,000 billion dollars (current US dollars) in the next two decades.[1]

These are truly astronomical sums, so far from the daily realities of our lives as to be incomprehensible. It is only by analogy that we have even the roughest grasp of the order of magnitude of these figures. A printing press capable of printing a hundred-dollar bill every second, run continuously, day and night, for seven days a week would require nearly two centuries to print a sum equivalent to 1982 world military spending. At normal reading speed, that machine would have printed some 3,000 to 4,000 dollars in the time it has taken to read these past two paragraphs.

Though the United States and the USSR clearly dominate world military expenditures, this particular economic phenomenon is not the sole preserve of the two Superpowers, nor for that matter of the more developed world as a whole. In 1979, the United States and USSR combined accounted for nearly 50 per cent of the total; the rest of the more developed countries combined for slightly more than an additional 25 per cent, with the remaining 25 per cent spent by the group of less developed nations.

From 1961 to 1980, even after adjustment for inflation, world military expenditures increased by nearly two-thirds, a spectacular enough expansion. But military expenditures of the Third World grew far more rapidly over those two decades. In 1961, less than ten per cent of the constant-dollar world military expenditure was accounted for by the less developed countries; by 1980, the Third World's share of the total was over twenty per cent. Not only did the size of the 'pie' grow dramatically, but the size of the Third World's slice, in relative terms, had more than doubled. Furthermore, this phenomenon of world militarization is extremely widespread, with only some twenty of the 141 nations of the world for which data are available spending less than one per cent of their Gross National Product (GNP) – the national income – on the military.

As in all arms races, the world-wide expansion of military expenditures that has followed in the four decades since the most destructive war in human history is propelled by its own internal logic. The most powerful nations of the world at the end of World War Two, determined to avoid a repetition of the terrible devastation of that war, embarked on what sociologist C. Wright Mills referred to as a 'bombs for peace' programme. Once again the major nations of the world fell into the trap of believing the often quoted dictum that 'if you want peace, prepare for war', despite massive historical evidence to the contrary. It is difficult to find arms races that have not ended in war. Yet pushing this fact aside and ignoring the relatively recent and painful lessons of World War One, the world's most powerful nations embarked upon the most massive arms race in human history.

The 'logic' of this arms race is quite

ANNUAL MILITARY SPENDING (1982) COUNTRY BY COUNTRY
(Figures are for 1982 unless otherwise stated.
Only countries that spent more than one billion dollars –
at 1980 exchange rates – are listed, but totals include
all nations for which figures are available.)

WORLD MILITARY SPENDING

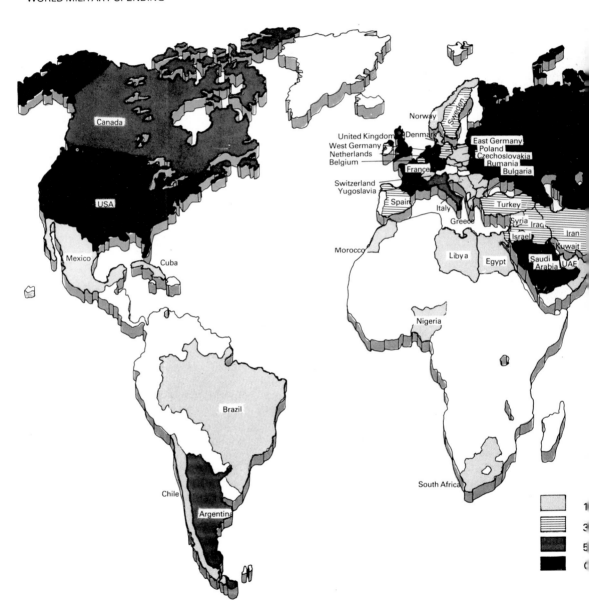

World spending on the arms race.

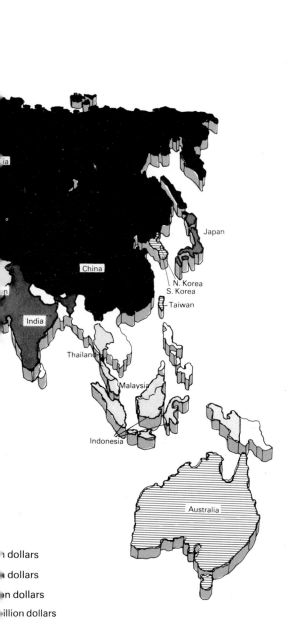

NATO Countries	(millions of dollars)
Canada	5,117
USA	169,691
Belgium	3,727
Denmark	1,625 (1981)
France	27,177
West Germany	26,990
Greece	2,656
Italy	10,265
Netherlands	5,318
Norway	1,731
Turkey	3,355
United Kingdom	27,163
Total	285,747

Warsaw Pact Countries

Bulgaria	1,093 (1981)
Czechoslovakia	2,473 (1981)
East Germany	4,130
Poland	2,673 (1981)
Rumania	1,342
USSR	135,500
Total	148,280

Other Europe

Spain	4,335
Sweden	3,702
Switzerland	2,122
Yugoslavia	2,671
Total	15,078

Middle East

Egypt	1,875 (1981)
Iran	4,995 (1980)
Iraq	3,850 (1981)
Israel	4,257
Kuwait	1,430 (1981)
Oman	1,679
Saudi Arabia	25,772
Syria	1,699
UAE	1,707 (1980)
Total	53,300

South Asia

India	5,344
Pakistan	1,679
Total	7,376

Far East

Indonesia	1,875
Japan	10,410
N. Korea	3,757
S. Korea	4,331
Malaysia	1,871
Taiwan	3,022
Thailand	1,338
China	39,400
Total	70,650

(Excluding Kampuchea and Vietnam; figures not available.)

Oceania

Australia	4,169
Total	4,617

Africa

Libya	2,820 (1979)
Morocco	1,228
Nigeria	1,438
South Africa	2,754
Total (approx)	14,000

Central America

Cuba	1,200
Mexico	1,005
Total	3,126

South America

Argentina	9,795
Brazil	1,531
Chile	1,762
Total	16,570

World Total   618,744

Figures in millions of dollars.

The arms race is expensive, and it is spreading now to Third-World nations. Even when the map is restricted to showing only those nations that spend more than one billion dollars annually on the military — as this map is — over 50 countries are included. The 1982 total — approximately 618 billion dollars (or the equivalent) staggers the imagination. Spending on this scale has very radical economic effects, many of them unhappy.

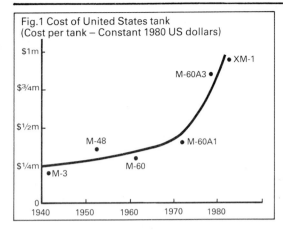

Fig.1 Cost of United States tank
(Cost per tank – Constant 1980 US dollars)

straightforward. The increase in the perceived or projected military capability of one nation makes the threat it poses to its opponent seem greater, creating pressure on the opponent to expand its own military capability. This in turn escalates the first nation's perception of the threat posed by the second nation's forces, thereby creating pressure on the first nation to increase its military capabilities. The vested interests, internal to each nation, that benefit from war preparation create additional pressure to support this reciprocating arms-race mechanism, often by projecting increased enemy threats – in effect, exaggerating them – to create a climate of increased anxiety conducive to public support for a promised 'national security' achievable through increased military strength. This process has been further enhanced, chiefly in the Third World, by the external pressure and sometimes the seductive security promises of more developed countries seeking to enhance their political influence and economic position through enlargement of their international arms sales. This factor, feeding into the usual arms-race mechanism between conflicting states, has undoubtedly played a large part in generating the remarkable growth of Third World military expenditures.

This arms-race process has been and continues to be driven by a species of what C. Wright Mills described as 'crackpot realism', that is the tendency to become '... so rigidly focused on the next step ... [as to] become creatures of whatever the main drift ... brings.'[2] Each step seems rational, in fact critical to maintaining or increasing security when weighing military strength against that of the opponent. However, four decades of this process have brought a 'main drift' not of improved or even stable security, but of increased danger on all sides. They have also taken a serious and increasingly severe economic toll.

This chapter will explore some aspects of the economic meaning of the arms race.

Expensive Weapons

Particularly in the West where the strategy has been to offset the allegedly greater number of weapons in the Eastern Bloc with higher quality, more sophisticated, more 'capable' weaponry, the pressure of the arms race has resulted in sharp increases in complexity that have caused a very great rise in the cost of weapons.

Fig.1: Comparison of unit costs for US tank production.

A modern tank, the XM1. It can be seen from the accompanying diagram that the unit cost of the average tank has increased by roughly a factor of four, in real terms, over the last four decades.

The pattern of unit-cost escalation common to weapons and related systems in general is illustrated by the pattern for three particular important classes of equipment in United States military forces. Figure 1 shows the cost trend for a major category of Army equipment, the tank, and Figure 2 gives comparable data for a major category of Air Force and Navy equipment, the fighter plane. Note that Figures 1 and 2 are adjusted for inflation and normalized for a constant production quantity so as to remove consideration of differences in the scale of output. By these data, the unit cost of a US Army tank has about quadrupled (in constant-dollars) over the past four decades; while the constant-dollar cost of a fighter plane has been multiplied 15 to 25 times. To take another major category of equipment (Figure 3) – an aircraft subsystem, air-to-air radars: during the ten years from 1962 to 1971 their cost rose tenfold. Over the quarter century following World War Two, the cost of avionics (aircraft electronics) rose from about 3,000 dollars to about two and a half million dollars per fighter

plane, and the cost of engines from 40,000 dollars to about two million dollars.[3]

These spectacular increases in purchase price are not the whole story, for the growth-complexity has vastly increased the cost of operating and maintaining weapons, and has also sharply reduced their reliability. It is interesting to note that even where this problem is explicitly taken into account and the weapon's original design incorporates features that are intended to reduce maintenance costs and increase aircraft 'readiness', the increased complexity tends to override these factors. For example, consider the F-15.[4]

The very complex avionics of the F-15 fighter aircraft were designed on a modular basis for easy maintenance. The plane has built-in test equipment on board that tells the pilot or crew chief if failure has occurred in a particular module. It is a simple matter to pull out the offending module and take it to the Avionics Intermediate Shop (AIS) for repair. Meanwhile another similar module is removed from inventory and plugged back into the aircraft, making it ready for flight once more. Flight line maintenance is thus greatly facilitated. The module itself consists of sub-modules, solid-state electronic circuit cards that are checked out at the AIS by computer in a lengthy, complicated procedure. When a defective card is found, it is replaced from supply and the defective card must be sent off-base to a depot for repair. On paper, this system seems like simplicity itself.

In fiscal year 1980, the AIS test computers broke down about twenty per cent of the time (down from 50 per cent during the fiscal year 1979). When the AIS computers break down, they can be very difficult and expensive to fix. Furthermore, one computer can only test one module at a time, with an average check-out time of three and a half hours – sometimes taking as long as eight and a half hours. After all of this lengthy procedure, the computer is often unable to find anything

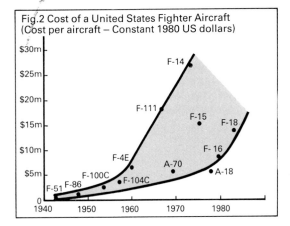

Fig.2 Cost of a United States Fighter Aircraft
(Cost per aircraft – Constant 1980 US dollars)

wrong with the module, which is then returned to supply, all that time and effort having been for nothing. During the period December 1979 to June 1980 the median monthly rate of these occurrences (the computer's inability to discover any problem) was 28 per cent. In summary, the F-15's operation and maintenance costs are quite high, despite the simplicity on paper of its maintenance.

Unreliable Weapons

Complexity of weapons not only affects their direct costs but also their reliability. The more complex a weapons system is, the more likely it is to fail. Even if each part is made much more reliable, the weapon as a whole will become much less reliable if the number of parts increases sufficiently. The data in Table 1 give striking evidence in support of this phenomenon, considering reliability measures for a series of United States Air Force and Navy (and Marine Corps) fighter aircraft, arranged by general degree of complexity. High-complexity aircraft have a remarkable failure rate, being fully capable of performing their assigned missions from only 34 per cent (F-111-D) to 63 per cent (F-111-F) of the time, with breakdowns of one sort or another occurring every twelve minutes (F-111-D) to 30 minutes (F-15) of flying time! (Everybody remembers the abortive rescue mission mounted by the United

States to rescue the US hostages in Iran, which failed partly because of helicopter breakdown.)

Given the marked drawbacks in cost, maintainability and reliability of increasingly complex weapons, it is natural to ask why there continues to be such a drive toward the so-called technological sophistication that breeds this complexity.

The answer is the belief that the performance of weapons systems is of the utmost importance. The perception that even small improvements in weapons capability can give rise to decisive advantage in battle is widespread. Combined with the perceived need to offset the greater *number* of weapons an opponent might have, this constitutes a powerful force pressing towards complexity.

There are, however, serious flaws in this approach even in military terms. For one thing, it is almost irrelevant what the performance capability of a weapon is if, for one reason or another, it is out of commission much of the time. For another thing, this extremely costly capability is far

Fig.2: Comparison of unit costs for US fighter aircraft production.

An F-15 fighter aircraft in steep bank, showing two AIM-7 missiles on each fuselage and AIM-9 missiles on each wing. The F-15 is both cheaper and more reliable than the naval F-14A fighter, but even then, maintenance costs are very high –a great deal higher than those of earlier fighters.

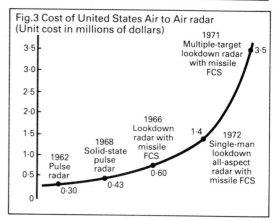

Fig.3 Cost of United States Air to Air radar
(Unit cost in millions of dollars)

1971 Multiple-target lookdown radar with missile FCS — 3·5

1966 Lookdown radar with missile FCS

1972 Single-man lookdown all-aspect radar with missile FCS — 1·4

1968 Solid-state pulse radar

1962 Pulse radar — 0·30

0·43

0·60

too often more relevant to the special conditions of 'friendly' tests than to the realities of battle. For example, according to F.C. Spinney, a Pentagon analyst, the most complex front-line air-to-air missile in the US inventory, at least as of late 1980, was the AIM-54 Phoenix missile. At that time it had never been tested in a multiple-firing mode against a mass air attack with electronic jamming – a realistic battle situation for which it was specifically designed to be capable.[4]

Two other examples are worth citing. Modern complex avionics and armament such as that embodied in the F-15 fighter plane, give these aircraft the capability not only of detecting but also of destroying other aircraft that are beyond visual range. In one-on-one tests this works well, since the pilot has no difficulty identifying the radar blip as an 'enemy' aircraft. But in the reality of massed air battles, the pilot must be able to see the other aircraft detected before attempting to destroy them in order to determine whether they are 'friendly' or 'hostile'. Electronic, so-called non-cooperative 'IFF' ('identification-

friend-or-foe') systems have defied adequate development for years. Thus the very expensive and complex 'beyond visual range' capability would be rendered virtually useless in any realistic air engagement.

Consider also the TOW missile, a wire-guided anti-tank missile (*see also* Chapter Six). In theory, a soldier stands and fires the missile at a distant tank, keeping the optical sight on the launcher aligned with the tank for at least ten seconds during the missile's flight to ensure a 'kill' despite evasive manoeuvres by the tank. As James Fallows[5] reports, '"To fire the TOW, you've got to stand there practically naked", a Marine Officer told me at Camp Pendleton. "A soldier's just not going to do that." ... Tom Kelly, a combat veteran of Vietnam says, "Soldiers will throw a weapon away if they don't have faith in it. The soldier is the guy making the ultimate decision on weapon systems..."' Under such conditions, the theoretical capability

Above: the diagram shows the escalating costs of the air-to-air radar systems used to identify enemy planes and missiles. Below: the sophisticated TOW missile can be used by soldiers in the field, but it leaves them vulnerable. It is safer when used tank-mounted, as here. For manual operation see picture page 76.

Aircraft Model	Level of Complexity	NMC%	MFHBF	Maint/ Sortie	MMH/ Sortie	Workload
(Air Force)						
A-10	Low	32.6	1.2	1.6	18.4	20.9
A-7D	Medium	38.6	0.9	1.9	23.8	20.3
F-4E	Medium	34.1	0.4	3.6	38.0	28.7
F-15	High	44.3	0.5	2.8	33.6	23.5
F-111-F	High	36.9	0.3	9.2	74.7	26.5
F-111-D	High	65.9	0.2	10.2	98.4	30.5
(Navy and Marine Corps)						
A-4M	Low	27.7	0.7	2.4	28.5	41.0
AV-A8	Low (?)	39.7	0.4	3.0	43.5	51.8
A-7E	Medium	36.7	0.4	3.7	53.0	60.6
F-4J	Medium	34.2	0.3	5.9	82.7	77.4
A-6E	High	39.3	0.3	4.8	71.3	67.9
F-14A	High	47.1	0.3	6.0	97.8	74.5

**TABLE 1.   COMPLEXITY VERSUS
RELIABILITY AND
MAINTAINABILITY OF UNITED
STATES FIGHTER AIRCRAFT**

Notes: 'NMC' describes what percentage
of the planes are 'not mission
capable' at any given moment —
that is, not fully ready for combat
because of repairs, parts
shortages, etc. 'MFHBF' stands
for 'mean flight hours between
failure', or how often breakdowns
of one sort or another occur. The
'Maint/Sortie' column lists how
many 'maintenance events', or
repairs, are necessary each time
the plane flies. 'MMH/Sortie'
means 'maintenance man-hours
per sortie' — how much
maintenance work must be done
per flight. 'Workload' combines a
number of figures (how often
each plane flies per month, how
much maintenance work it
requires per flight, how many
planes each repairman must
handle) to determine the monthly
load of maintenance hours per
worker.

Source: Spinney, F.C., **Defense Facts of
Life**, US Department of Defense
Staff Paper, Dec. 5, 1980

*The F-14A fighter aircraft is a great plane when it
works, but (see table above) it averages only eighteen
minutes between various kinds of system breakdown,
which adds considerably to the running expenses of
the US Navy.*

of a weapons system is simply an illusion.

Giant-Killers, Going Cheap

One more issue with respect to the weapons of modern conventional warfare remains to be discussed – that of cost effectiveness. In recent years a number of weapons have been developed that appear to be quite cheap relative to the weapons they are capable of destroying. This raises questions as to the point of continuing to build the enormously expensive weapons that are their targets. The 1982 war between Britain and Argentina over control of the Falkland Islands (the Malvinas) brought this issue sharply to public consciousness.

More than half of the 114 aircraft and ten ships lost by both sides during the conflict were put out of action by so-called 'smart' precision-guided weapons. Of these incidents, the most notable was the destruction of the 150-million-dollar (in 1982 US dollar-equivalent) British destroyer, HMS *Sheffield*, by a French-built Exocet missile costing at most a few hundred thousand dollars. The missile, fired from a distance of roughly 30 kilometers, travelled just above the water, colliding with the *Sheffield* amidships,

The F-14 Tomcat fighter aircraft. As can be seen from the accompanying diagram, over the last four decades the unit cost of fighter aircraft has multiplied by a factor of anywhere from fifteen to twenty-five times.

The American F-111-D. Its complexity is such that individual craft are capable of operation only just over one-third of the time. On average, each time the craft flies, about ten repairs are required before it is fit for operation again.

about two meters above the waterline.[6] Tables 2 and 3 give relevant data for a range of modern-day anti-ship warships and missiles, respectively. The cost comparisons are quite striking.

During the Falklands conflict, the Argentines fired only six Exocet missiles, four of which hit targets, resulting in the destruction of two ships and the severe damaging of a third. This 67 per cent success rate is impressive. It is easy to jump to the conclusion that such precision-guided weapons have rendered warships militarily obsolete on the basis of this observation alone. But some care should be taken here.

Recent reports indicate that the *Sheffield*'s radar did detect the incoming Exocet missile but that the ship's computers were programmed to identify the Exocet as a 'friendly' missile and so no alarm was sounded. (This might remind us of the earlier discussion of the aircraft 'identification-friend-or-foe' problem.) British naval officers argue that the *Sheffield* did not have *sufficient* air cover and was not armed with the Sea Wolf anti-missile missile designed specifically to

SHIP	YEAR DEPLOYED	DISPLACEMENT (TONS)	CREW	GUNS	MISSILES
RESHEF Class (Israel)	1973	450	45	2 76 mm 2 20 mm	5 Gabriel 4 Harpoon
SHEFFIELD (Britain)	1976	4,000	270	1 115 mm 2 20 mm	20 Sea Dart
TICONDEROGA (US)	1983	9,000	330	2 127 mm 2 20 mm	68 Standard 8 Harpoon 20 Asroc
INVINCIBLE (Britain)	1980	20,000	1,300	0	22 Sea Dart
NEW JERSEY (US)	1943 (Reactivated) 1983	58,000	1,600	9 406 mm 12 127 mm 4 20 mm	16 Harpoon 32 Tomahawk
NIMITZ Class	1975	91,000	6,300	3 20 mm	24 Sea Sparrow

TABLE 2. REPRESENTATIVE WARSHIPS

Notes: The USS **Ticonderoga** is the first of seventeen advanced fleet-defence cruisers planned for the US Navy. 'Jump jet' aircraft carriers such as the **Invincible** have replaced large-deck carriers in the British fleet. The battleship USS **New Jersey**, which was built during World War Two, was reactivated earlier this year. The Reagan Administration currently plans to build at least two more large aircraft carriers of the Nimitz Class.

Source: Walker, P.F., 'Smart Weapons in Naval Warfare', **Scientific American**, May 1983

AIRCRAFT	ESTIMATED COST (1982 US DOLLARS)
0	$50 million
1 Helicopter	$150 million
1 Helicopter	$1 billion
5+ Planes 9 Helicopters	$525 million
4 Helicopters	$326 million (Modernization only)
80+ Planes 10+ Helicopters	$3.5 billion

The type-42 destroyer HMS Sheffield *ablaze in the South Atlantic during the 1982 Falklands conflict. An air-launched Exocet missile penetrated the ship, the explosion killing 20 of the crew. Thanks to brave rescue efforts, the remaining 261 survived.*

counter such missiles as the Exocet. US naval personnel have argued that had the *Sheffield* been part of a flotilla providing adequate air cover and fitted with the variety of defensive and offensive weapons that similar US Navy ships carry, the Exocet missile would not have succeeded.

These arguments in defence of the warship's continuing viability may be correct. Then again they may not. It is always easy to say such things, but it is quite a different matter to prove them in any realistic test rather than by 'paper' arguments and computer simulations. And even if they are correct, such arguments may be quite beside the point. The military mission of a warship or for that matter of a flotilla of warships is not to protect itself, but to constitute a net capability for attacking the opponent. It is not clear that they are any longer capable, cost-effectively, of doing this.

For example, the United States now deploys about 500 subsidiary warships of various sizes around thirteen large-deck aircraft carriers. A Nimitz Class nuclear-powered aircraft carrier carries a total of roughly one hundred aircraft of various types: fighters, bombers, surveillance and anti-submarine aircraft, rescue helicopters and utility helicopters. What is striking is that roughly 70 per cent of the aircraft are intended to defend the fleet. A large number of other ships in the task forces, including cruisers, destroyers, submarines and supply ships, are also intended for defence or maintenance of the fleet. Thus only a small part of the capability of these very expensive fleets, and in particular these extraordinarily expensive large aircraft carriers, is available for attacking the opponent. In addition, small, relatively cheap precision-guided weapons may increasingly be able to destroy these highly costly ships.

However, the carrier-centred flotilla has a number of strong supporters, including the Secretary of the United States Navy.

The following (abbreviated) exchange, which took place between Senator

ANTISHIP MISSILE	YEAR DEPLOYED	RANGE (KILOMETERS)	SPEED (MACH NO.)	TYPE OF WARHEAD	ESTIMATED COST (1982 US DOLLARS)
Exocet AM-39 (France)	1979	50+	0.93	Non-nuclear	Few hundred thousand
Gabriel MK-III (Israel)	1979	60+	0.73	Non-nuclear	$400,000
Harpoon RGM-84A (US)	1977	90	0.90	Nuclear or Non-nuclear	$1 Million
Tomahawk BGM-109 (US)	1982	450	0.74	Nuclear or Non-nuclear	$3 Million
Styx SS-N-2C (USSR)	1965?	80	0.90	Non-nuclear	?
Kitchen AS-4 (USSR)	1962	300+	2.0+	Nuclear or Non-nuclear	?

TABLE 3. REPRESENTATIVE ANTI-SHIP MISSILES

Notes: Missiles such as the Exocet are designed to be launched from planes, helicopters and land-based installations; the particular model shown here, the air-launched Exocet AM-39, is the one that destroyed the *Sheffield*. The Russian ship-to-ship missile referred to as the Styx was used by the Egyptian Navy in 1967 to sink the Israeli destroyer *Elath*. The large Russian missile AS-4 is carried by the Backfire bomber. Mach numbers are multiples of the speed of sound.

Source: Walker, P.F., 'Smart Weapons in Naval Warfare', **Scientific American**, May 1983, p54

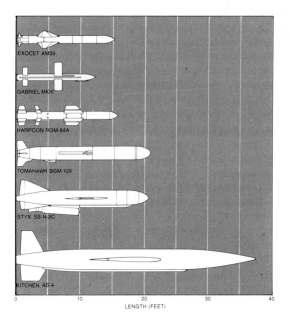

William Proxmire and just-retired Admiral Hyman G. Rickover ('Father' of the Nuclear Navy) during testimony before the Joint Economic Committee of the US Congress, further strengthens this point. *Senator Proxmire:* 'Now the Defense Department's fiscal year 1983 budget requests funding for two nuclear-powered aircraft carriers at a construction cost of about six billion dollars. It doesn't include the cost of the planes which is considerably more than six billion dollars. In fact, more than twice that. Considering the capability of the Soviet submarines,

The table compares performances of representative anti-ship missiles, and the picture illustrates them. (Source: Scientific American *May 1983.)*

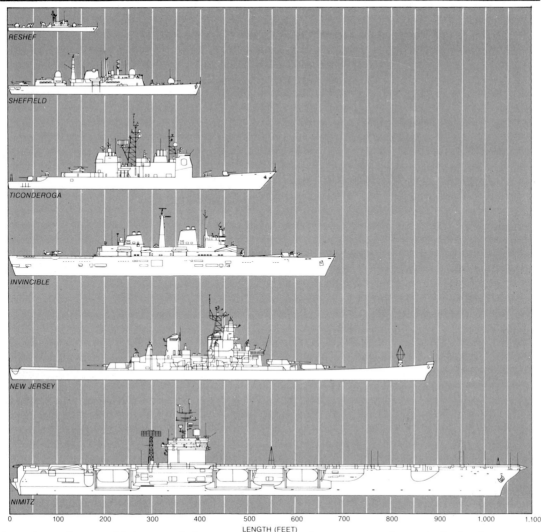

RESHEF

SHEFFIELD

TICONDEROGA

INVINCIBLE

NEW JERSEY

NIMITZ

| 0 | 100 | 200 | 300 | 400 | 500 | 600 | 700 | 800 | 900 | 1,000 | 1,100 |

LENGTH (FEET)

how long do you think one of these aircraft carriers would last in the case of an all-out war?'

Admiral Rickover: 'About two days.'

Senator Proxmire: 'About two days?'

Admiral Rickover: '. . . If you use ballistic missiles it does not make any difference whether or not you have carriers.'

In the past decade, the devastation of tanks by precision-guided weapons in confrontations in the Middle East also calls their continued military cost effectiveness into serious question, particularly as the technology of smart weapons improves. In general, it is likely that large, expensive, relatively slow-manoeuvring military weapons systems are becoming increasingly obsolete.

The Economic Impact of Military Expenditure on Society

Ultimately, the degree of material well-being generated by any economy depends not only on its ability to fully employ the productive resources (labour, capital, materials, energy, etc.) available to it, but also on its ability to employ them in ways that contribute to the standard of living in society at large. The production of ordinary *consumer* goods and services,

The six warships pictured are those described in the table on pages 134-5. (Source: Scientific American May 1983.)

such as food, clothing, housecleaning and barbering, clearly adds directly to the material living standard. The production of *producer* goods and associated services, such as industrial machinery, rail transportation systems, factory buildings and supporting engineering consulting services also contributes to our standard of living, but through a less direct route. This class of goods and services expands an economy's ability to produce, and by so doing enhances the supply of consumer-oriented output in the future. Hence it contributes not to the present, but to the future standard of living.

Military-oriented production, however, falls into a wholly different category. It does not add to the supply of consumer goods or to the supply of producer goods, and so contributes to neither the present nor the future material standard of living. Resources put to this use can then be said to have been diverted away from contributing to society. They are not adding to material well-being.

When idle resources are put to work, whether or not that work is useful, unemployment will be reduced, income will be distributed and at least the short-run appearance of prosperity will be achieved. But if those resources have been used unproductively, they will in the long term be a drain on society. Because resources are being wasted, things which need doing will not be done, and so the economy and the wider society will suffer.

The issue of the use to which resources are put is so fundamental, and so overriding in its impact on the ability of an economy to function efficiently, that economic systems as distinct as those of capitalism and communism experience similar problems when resources are diverted. This is particularly true over the long run.

During the half decade or so of heavy World War Two military spending (in the United States, for example) neglect of the renewal of various types of civilian-oriented equipment and facilities, such as railroads, mass-transit systems and

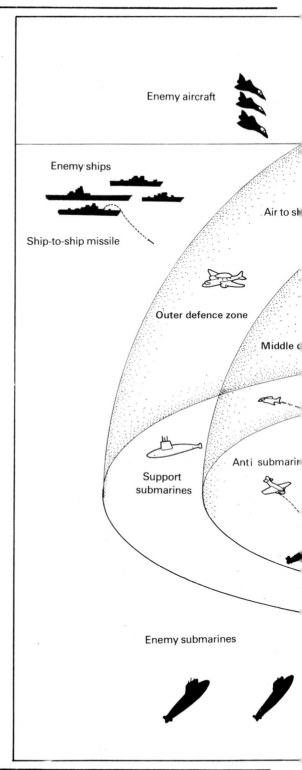

Enemy aircraft

Enemy ships

Air to sh

Ship-to-ship missile

Outer defence zone

Middle

Support submarines

Anti submarin

Enemy submarines

The problem with naval fleets of surface ships, as was shown by the Falklands dispute, is that they are vulnerable to attack. The illustration shows the concept of Zone Defence, in which up to two thirds of the aircraft carried on the carrier (centre) are used for defence, leaving only 30 or so for offence. In the outer zone attacking submarines, surface ships and aircraft

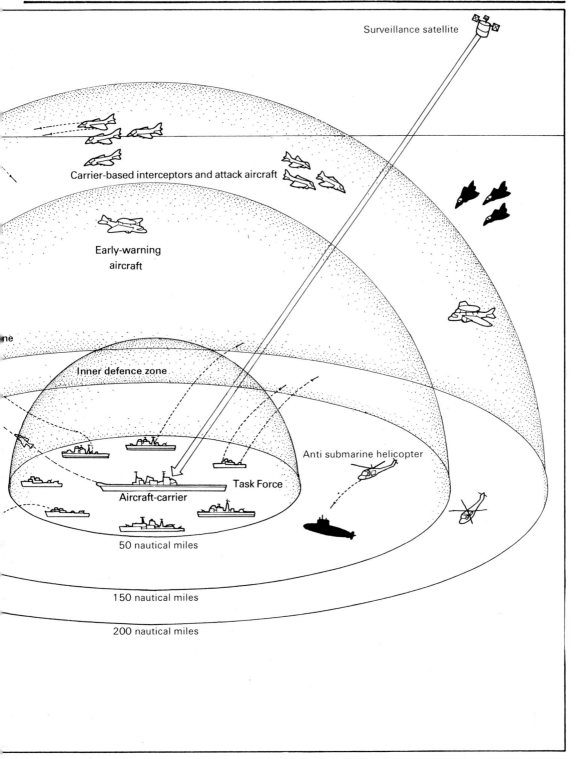

Surveillance satellite

Carrier-based interceptors and attack aircraft

Early-warning
aircraft

Inner defence zone

Anti submarine helicopter

Task Force

Aircraft-carrier

50 nautical miles

150 nautical miles

200 nautical miles

are identified by satellite and early-warning aircraft;
they are intercepted by carrier-based fighters and
antisubmarine-warfare aircraft and submarines. In the
middle zone the main defence is with missiles. In the
inner zone defence is with rapid-fire guns and anti-
missile missiles. In practice the three zones overlap
considerably. The main problem is the inner zone

defence; if there are too many missiles the system
could easily break down. Does such a cumbersome,
expensive, defence-oriented system as this really
make sense? The Americans operate thirteen such
carrier groups.

industrial equipment, and neglect of civilian technological development, did not create major problems. Such capital equipment is long-lived, and big technological leads do not disappear

the USSR, the damage has surfaced mainly as chronic problems of supplying a sufficient quantity and quality of consumer goods and services.

It is easier for a communist economic

overnight. But as the substantial diversion of productive resources stretched from half a decade to more than three decades, severe stresses did occur.

Neither capitalist nor socialist economies are capable of overriding the negative effects of persistently high military spending. Differences in economic systems and circumstances, however, can and do influence the way in which economic distress surfaces.

The United States and the USSR car be seen as case studies of the mechanism; by which persistently high levels of militaɪy expenditure generate severe economic damage. The economic damage done in part by the military burden in the US has surfaced mainly in the form of simultaneously high inflation and high unemployment, largely created by deteriorating productivity. In contrast, in

President Ronald Reagan in the Oval Office immediately prior to his celebrated 'Star Wars' address of March 1983, in which he threatened enormous increases in the scale of US military expenditure. In the background is a photograph of a Cuban airfield.

A Nimitz-class nuclear-powered aircraft carrier of the US fleet, at 3.5 billion dollars (excluding aircraft) the most expensive warship afloat. In the event of an all-out war, the survival time of ships like this is estimated to be about two days.

system than for a capitalist economic system to prevent unemployment and cope with inflation. Present-day capitalist economies must rely on the voluntary actions of individuals seeking private economic gain (with more or less government intervention) to provide employment, while also relying on such private decisions (along with the impersonal mechanism of competition and governmental control of the money supply) to mitigate inflation. A communist economy, on the other hand, features direct government control of jobs and prices (though the latter are subject to external influence through rising import costs). But incentive problems, along with clumsy information systems and ponderous bureaucracies, tend to make an adequate supply of goods and coordination of supply with demand more difficult for a communist economy than for one operated on capitalist principles.

Here we will concentrate on the United States context, not because the damage is greater there or more easily understood, but simply because the relative availability of data is presently so much greater than for the USSR. Some of the analysis,

however, fits the Soviet situation too.

Military Production and Inflation

Military goods do not produce economic value in the sense of a contribution to the material standard of living, but their production does require valuable economic resources. For this reason, they impose a real cost on society. This cost is best measured not purely in terms of money, but rather in terms of the sacrifice of the economically and socially useful goods and services that could have been produced with these resources.

Now, in market economies the money that flows from governments to producers of military goods in exchange for their products is spent by the firms primarily on producer goods and by their work forces primarily on consumer goods. Thus these funds, injected into the economy by the government, call forth an increased demand for consumer and producer goods without a corresponding increase in the supply of either consumer or producer goods. This situation of too many dollars chasing after too few goods is a classic economic prescription for inflation. For example, during nearly all of the latter part of the 1960s, when the United States' involvement in the Vietnam War was intensifying, the unemployment rate was under four per cent. But military spending was not offset, and between 1965 and 1969 the rate of inflation in the US more than tripled.

The Military and the Scientists

Since the beginning of World War Two, and with substantially more force since the latter half of the 1950s, the United States has channelled a large fraction of the nation's engineering and scientific resources into military-related research.

Any estimate of the fraction of the nation's total engineering and scientific talent engaged in military-related research is quite a bit more tortuous a task than it should be. It is not possible here to disentangle all the available data and make a fully accurate, up-to-date estimate of the pre-emption of engineering and scientific talent by the military sector. However, it is possible to produce reasonable and fairly conservative rough estimates by manipulating some of the published data.

According to data for 1982 provided in the Defense Economic Impact Modeling System (DEIMS) of the US Department of Defense, only about fourteen per cent of the nation's engineers and scientists are included in so-called 'defense-induced' employment.[8] However, the methodology used in DEIMS excludes from the 'defense-induced' category all employment related to arms exports; nuclear-weapons research, design, testing and production programmes (all of which are located outside the Department of Defense's budget); and the military-oriented part of the space programme. Perhaps even more significantly, the methodology assumes that the percentage of the workforce in any given industry made up of engineers and scientists is the same in the military-serving part of the industry as in the civilian-oriented part. Yet it is clear that the technological intensity of the labour force in military-oriented segments of industry is far greater. It is not unknown for military-industrial operations to employ one engineer or scientist for every production worker, as for example in the Rockwell Industries' B-1 bomber plant in the late 1970s. Such ratios of technologists to production workers are unsupportable in civilian-oriented industry. Conservatively assuming a 50 per cent greater intensity of technologists in the workforce of military-oriented segments of industry, and making a rough correction for all of the military-oriented activity completely excluded by the DEIMS methodology, yields an estimate of the fraction of the nation's engineers and scientists engaged in this form of activity of at least 30 per cent. Approaching the problem from another angle, using National Science Foundation data for three military-oriented categories of industry, yields a figure of just under 33

per cent.

Though it is inappropriate to rely too heavily on the accuracy of estimates so crudely developed, it would appear likely that a great many of the engineering and scientific personnel in the United States have been devoting their talents to the development of military-oriented technology. It is unlikely that the fraction would be substantially less than one-third. In all probability, it is far higher, since the calculations referred to above take very conservative estimates. It is important to remember that the pre-emption of technological resources has been maintained at this magnitude for two or three decades or more.

Now, the kind of new technological knowledge that will ultimately emerge from any given research or development project will not be wholly predictable in advance. By definition, the researchers are engaged in a quest for new knowledge, and such exploration of the unknown and untried must always involve uncertainty. However, even while not wholly determinate, the kind of new technical knowledge developed is strongly conditioned by the nature of the problems being studied and the type of solutions being sought. Since one-third or more of the United States' engineers and scientists have been seeking military-oriented solutions to military-oriented problems for the past several decades, it should be no surprise that the development of military technology has proceeded at a rapid pace in the US – or that the development of civilian-oriented technology has slowed down somewhat.

The much vaunted 'spin-off' or 'spill-over' argument that military-oriented technological development produces massive improvements in areas of civilian application makes very little conceptual sense. More to the point, it is massively contradicted by straightforward empirical observation. Of course, some transferability of technical knowledge between military and civilian application would be expected (in both directions), but conceptually it is difficult to see how directing attention to one area of technical research would routinely produce an *efficient* generation of knowledge pertaining to a completely different area.

On the empirical side, a 1974 report of a committee of the National Academy of Engineering[9] stated: 'With a few exceptions the vast technology developed by Federally funded programmes since World War Two has not resulted in widespread products, processes and services that have made an impact on the nation's economic growth, industrial productivity, employment gains and foreign trade.' The seventh annual report of the National Science Board,[10] the governing body of the National Science Foundation, expressed concern over the serious erosion of the United States' predominance in science and technology. Some of the empirical indicators behind this concern were detailed. For example, the report describes the relative production of a total of 492 major innovations by the United States, the United Kingdom, Japan, West Germany and France over the twenty-year period from 1953 to 1973: 'The US lead ... declined steadily from the late 1950s to the mid-1960s, falling from 82 to 55 per cent of the innovations. The slight upturn in later years represents a relative rather than an absolute gain, and results primarily from a decline in the proportion of innovations produced in the United Kingdom, rather than an increase in the number of US innovations.'

More recently, the NSF's *Science Indicators: 1978* (National Science Board, 1979) points to a continuation of these downtrends: 'US patenting has decreased abroad as well as at home ... From 1966 to 1976, US patenting activity abroad declined almost 30 per cent in ten industrialized countries ... The decline in US patenting abroad could be attributable to a number of factors, including ... a relative decline in the US inventive activity ... '

The relatively poor showing of the US is even more remarkable considering that these data do not specifically exclude military-related technology and hence are biased in favour of the US. It is interesting to note that in these comparisons, Japan and West Germany did quite well. 'Since 1963, inventors from West Germany have received the largest number of foreign-origin US patents (83,220). In fact, among US foreign-origin patents, West Germany was first in 11 of the 15 major product fields and second in the remaining four ... Japan ranks second in the total number of US patents granted to foreign investors between 1963 and 1977 (61,510). Japan has the largest number of foreign patents in three product groups ... and is second in an additional five categories ... Since 1970, Japan has dramatically increased its patent activity by over 100 per cent in every product field except the two areas in which it already had a large concentration of patents.'

Not so coincidentally, these two countries spend on defence and space only about four per cent (Japan, 1961–1975) and twenty per cent (West Germany, 1961–1967) of overall government R and D expenditures, as opposed to a US average of about 70 per cent (1961–1977).

If the transferability of invention and innovation between the military and civilian worlds was and is actually low, then the decades-long diversion of at least a third of the engineers and scientists in the US to military-related work would predictably have produced precisely the sort of civilian technological deterioration that has in fact been experienced.

Military Spending and Lowered Productivity

It is widely recognized that civilian technological progress is the keystone of improvement in productivity and economic growth. Accordingly, as the development of civilian technology became increasingly retarded in the US, productivity growth began to collapse. From 1947 to 1967, output per labour-hour grew at an average annual rate of 3.4 per cent in the non-agricultural business sector of the US, according to the Council of Economic Advisors. From 1967 to 1977, that average rate of growth dropped off dramatically to 1.9 per cent per year. From 1977 to 1981, the rate of growth became a rate of decline, with productivity dropping slightly at an annual average of 0.1 per cent. The deterioration of productivity growth has been accelerating.

The improvement of productivity plays a crucial role in the countering of inflationary pressures, for it is sustained productivity growth that offsets the effects of rising output costs. In the absence of strong productivity improvement, rising costs of labour, fuels and so on will be translated into rising product prices. As this occurs over a whole series of industries, a self-reinforcing rise in the general level of prices, or 'inflation', occurs.

As the prices of US-produced goods rose higher and higher, the nation's industry became less and less competitive internationally. Overseas markets were lost and the US export position weakened. Domestic markets were lost to foreign production and the US import position worsened. The progressive loss of markets induced cutbacks in US-based production with high unemployment rates as a result. And this problem was exacerbated by the flight of US-owned production facilities to cheap-labour havens abroad, as one logical response to the inability to offset higher costs in the US because of the productivity failure. It is thus pre-eminently the declining competitiveness of US industry resulting from decreasing productivity growth that has generated unemployment even in the face of high product demand.

Productivity growth thus is 'the economic linchpin of the 1980s', as the Joint Economic Committee of Congress described it in its mid-1979 analysis of prospects for the economy. Its warning that, as the *New York Times* put it, 'The average American is likely to see his standard of living drastically reduced in the 1980s unless productivity growth is accelerated' is precisely correct.

Although numerous other factors come into play, this analysis of the situation in the United States is very relevant to the situation in the United Kingdom, where the productivity problem is worse. In the UK also a great deal of government R and D spending is concentrated in the defence industries, and there is no doubt that this has damaged British civilian technological development, because of the diversion of resources and especially because of the diversion of skilled personnel.

The Economic Impact of Military Spending in the Soviet Union

The Soviet economy is basically an economy of priorities and the priorities become most serious in terms of supply. Supply is perhaps the main problem for both national central planners and managers of individual enterprises in the USSR.

Under conditions of chronic aggregate shortages, the priorities used in the allocation of productive resources become especially critical to the functioning of the economy. Every industry in the Soviet Union has a different priority or ranking associated with it that determines, in effect, where it stands in the line of industries waiting for needed supplies of productive resources of all sorts (engineers and scientists, production workers, materials, fuels, equipment and so on). Military industries, and the portions of other industries that support them, are at the head of every line.

The top priority accorded to military industries shrinks the resource base of the entire civilian economy. They receive inputs of the highest quality in ample supply, leaving all of the civilian industries to vie for what's left.

The impact of Soviet military industry on the USSR civilian economy goes beyond the direct diversion of resources into the military sector. There is what could be called a 'contingency diversion' that also hampers efficiency. Civilian production facilities and even civilian products have sometimes been designed so as to allow ready convertibility to military-oriented production – for example, tractors that have been designed with caterpillar treads rather than wheels to facilitate the switching of production to tank-type vehicles. Practices of this sort can easily result in sub-optimal production adding to the distortion of the civilian economy.

One more point about the operation of military industry in the USSR: the head of a large Soviet military enterprise will typically also be a ranking official in the Communist Party and a high-ranking uniformed military officer. Such an individual holds a position of simultaneously high economic, political and military authority, and will accordingly be a major force in society, particularly in the region where the enterprise is located. This is especially true should the enterprise be located in a smaller or more remote city.

As indicated earlier, the basic causal nexus through which military spending continues to damage the Soviet economy is similar to that which operates in the United States. By directly diverting productive resources from the civilian economy, the military sector drains civilian industry rendering it less capable of providing goods and services (that would improve the standard of living) of decent quality cost-effectively and in sufficient numbers.

In the case of the United States, much emphasis was laid on the pre-emption of engineering and scientific talent into military-related activity; the same, of course, is also true in the USSR. But it is probably true that the drain of other resources is somewhat more of a problem in the USSR, partly because the economy is younger and not as large, and partly because the resource base itself is smaller.

The economic damage done by the military burden in the United States surfaces in the form of simultaneous high inflation and high unemployment, through the intervening variable of deteriorating productivity. In contrast, in the USSR the damage surfaces mainly in the form of chronic problems of supplying sufficient quantity and quality of goods and services – particularly consumer goods.

It is important to understand, then, that a centrally planned socialist economy is no more and no less able to override the negative economic effects of military spending than a market economy. The impact of resource diversion remains the overriding consideration. The only way to redevelop any economy severely stressed by the burden of military spending is to rechannel resources back into productive civilian activity. Nothing short of this redirection can succeed in undoing the long-term damage generated by maintaining high levels of military spending over long periods of time.

Conclusions

For some time now many people have argued that the development and proliferation of nuclear weapons have rendered warfare obsolete as a means of settling international conflict. Others have argued that the growing economic interdependency of the world's nations has made even general conventional warfare counterproductive and hence foolish. It is a clear implication of the analysis in this chapter that not only the prosecution of war but also the preparation for war have become increasingly untenable.

The growing sophistication of weapons systems has resulted in strikingly higher costs and strikingly lower reliability. This has often been used as an argument for building weapons in greater numbers and, still more paradoxically, for attempting an even greater technological sophistication to overcome these problems. And, of course, as more and more weapons of greater perceived capability are acquired by a nation's potential opponents, the pressures for further qualitative improvement and quantitative expansion

of our forces grow. Thus we have, all of us, become entrapped in a treadmill of militarism.

The economic drain of diverting large amounts of key productive resources from those activities which enhance the population's material well-being to economically unproductive military activity takes a growing toll among the nations of the world. Neither market economies nor planned economies are immune to either the short-term, or more importantly the long-term damage this diversion of resources produces. Furthermore the damage is cumulative and hence would grow even if levels of military expenditure were held constant. In fact, levels of military spending have grown in rather spectacular fashion ever since World War Two. Thus, while there may be transitory improvements in the world economic situation, the long-term prognosis is not bright for those of the world's nations that insist on continuing to participate in the ongoing international arms race.

If a nation as well developed, economically strong and rich in resources as the United States can be as severely damaged economically as it has been by persistently high levels of military spending, it is quite clear that the rapid expansion of military expenditures among Third World nations is a cause for concern. The United States was, after all, the only major industrial nation to emerge from World War Two essentially unscathed. Yet in less than four decades, the military burden it has carried has done what the war did not do – severely damaged the ability of its economy to function. The US today is less and less able to compete with the developed nations which have not maintained large militaries. How much greater, then, is the damage likely to be to those nations struggling to develop, if they persist in burdening their much weaker economies by continuing to divert critical resources to the preparation for and prosecution of war?

There is, of course, a way out. Whether more developed or less developed, the world's nations can shed the terrible economic burden of the international arms race and shed it before it leads to either irreversible economic debilitation or catastrophic war. It will take a great effort of will and a deep political commitment to do so, but it will not

The familiar dour row of faces of the Soviet top brass during a military parade – in this case part of the 'Odra-Nysa' joint exercises. Before them they see the massive military might which is wrecking the Soviet economy.

require universal goodwill or deep trust among nations. It simply requires a commitment to pursue, develop and utilize other means toward national and international security and the settlement or at least management of the inevitable conflicts among nations. This has become the single most effective policy for the improvement of world economic conditions. There is little question that it can be done. But will it?

Lloyd J. Dumas

References

1   Several of the following figures are calculated or taken from data in Sivard, R.L., **World Military and Social Expenditures – 1982**, World Priorities, Leesburg, Virginia, 1982
2   Mills, C.W., **The Causes of World War III**, Secker and Warburg, London, 1959, p89
3   Sprey, P.M., Defense Department analyst, testimony before the Senate Armed Services Committee (Dec. 8, 1971), cited in Fallows, J., **National Defense**, Random House, New York, 1981, p251
4   Spinney, F.C., **Defense Facts of Life**, US Department of Defense Staff Paper, Dec. 5, 1980
5   Fallows, J., **National Defense**, Random House, New York, 1981, p23
6   Walker, P.F., 'Smart Weapons in Naval Warfare', **Scientific American**, May 1983, p54
7   Rickover, Adm. H.G., **Economics of Defense Policy**, Hearing Before the Joint Economic Committee of the Congress of the United States, 97th Congress, Second Session, Part I, Jan. 28, 1982, US Government Printing Office, Washington, 1982, pp 43-44
8   Department of Defense, **Defense Economic Impact Modeling System**, [Occupation of Industry Model, Table 3, Estimates of Industrial Employment by Occupation (Engineers and Scientists)], Department of Defense, Washington, 1983
9   National Academy of Engineering Committee on Technology Transfer and Utilization, 'Technology Transfer and Utilization, Recommendations for Reducing the Emphasis and Correcting the Imbalance', National Academy, Washington, 1974
10 National Science Board, National Science Foundation, **Science Indicators: 1974**, US Government Printing Office, Washington, 1976

Chapter 12

The Arms Trade

Of the 650 billion dollars spent each year by the world's military, roughly 160 billion dollars goes on buying weapons. This makes weapons production and sales the world's second biggest industry, after oil. About 40 billion dollars' worth of these weapons are traded annually in the international arms markets.

Recent events, like the wars in the Falkland Islands and the Lebanon, have focused attention yet again on the morality of the global arms trade. They have shown how aggressively arms salesmen, often civil servants from the industrialized countries, ply their wares abroad; they also show that the arms trade is out of political control, and has been for some time. The fact that the Superpower arms race fuels regional arms races can hardly be questioned. Whether or not these arms races lead directly to wars is not known. But we can say that once a conflict begins, sophisticated weapons considerably increase the level of violence. Also, the weapons sold abroad often *are* the most sophisticated. There are many instances of advanced weapons being sold to foreign customers even

The devastating array of sophisticated weaponry on display at the world's international arms fairs shows only too clearly that the machinery of death and destruction is available to the highest bidder.

before they are put into the arsenals of the supplier.

Almost all of the 150 or so wars since World War Two have been fought with weapons imported from the advanced countries. Are the arms exporters not at least partly responsible for the tens of

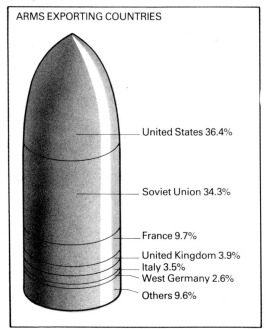

ARMS EXPORTING COUNTRIES

United States 36.4%

Soviet Union 34.3%

France 9.7%

United Kingdom 3.9%
Italy 3.5%
West Germany 2.6%
Others 9.6%

missiles – sold abroad go to Third World countries. Within the Third World the Middle East is by far the most active importing region. Between 1979 and 1982, for example, about 45 per cent of the major weapons transferred to the Third World went to the Middle East.

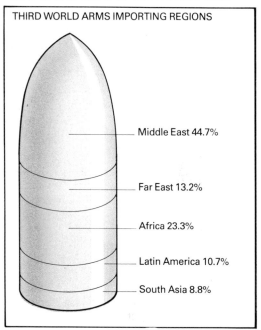

THIRD WORLD ARMS IMPORTING REGIONS

Middle East 44.7%

Far East 13.2%

Africa 23.3%

Latin America 10.7%

South Asia 8.8%

millions of deaths and serious injuries caused in these wars?

What Countries Trade in Arms?

The USA and the USSR are the biggest arms traders. Together they supply some 70 per cent of the weapons exported to the Third World. France comes next, accounting for twelve per cent, then Italy with five per cent and the United Kingdom with four per cent. The top five arms exporters have captured between them over 90 per cent of the global arms trade.

Most weapons sold abroad go to the Third World. According to figures published by the Stockholm International Peace Research Institute (SIPRI), nearly 65 per cent of the major weapons – armoured vehicles, aircraft, warships and

About 25 per cent went to Africa; about 20 per cent went to Asia; and 10 per cent went to Latin America. The top ten Third World major-weapon importing countries were, in rank order: Libya, Saudi Arabia, Iraq, Syria, Israel, India, South Yemen, Egypt, Vietnam and Morocco. These accounted for about 60 per cent of the major weapons transferred to the Third World.

The motives for selling arms vary. The Superpowers do so to gain political or economic influence in Third World regions or to acquire military bases abroad. The smaller suppliers believe that selling weapons helps their economies, particularly in times of recession. Also important are the economies of scale to be had from long production runs. By selling arms abroad countries reduce the

149

There are some surprises in arms-trade figures. Latin America is quite a long way down the list of importers, not far above India and Pakistan (South Asia). The figures, (calculated on a slightly different basis from those in the text) are for 1978-82. The four-year period conceals the fact that Italy outsold the UK in 1982.

aerospatiale
long range missiles

EXOCET

FOR SEA POWER

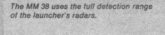
The MM 38 uses the full detection range of the launcher's radars.

The AM 39 can be launched at all altitudes.

MM 40 has an over-the-horizon capability.

☐ They can be:
- Surface-launched (MM 38 - MM 40) from ships of all tonnages, or from fixed or mobile coastal batteries.
- Air-launched (AM 39) from helicopters, strike aircraft or maritime patrol aircraft.
- Sub-launched (SM 39) (under development).

☐ They have basically the same principle of operation and the same maintenance equipment.

☐ They are FIRE AND FORGET and SEA SKIMMING, which makes them practically INVULNERABLE to all enemy defences.

☐ They provide SUPERIORITY in anti-surface warfare to those countries which adopt them, owing to their range, speed, accuracy and killing power.

27 countries have chosen the EXOCET.

More than 2.000 EXOCET missiles have been ordered.

aerospatiale
Division engins tactiques : 2-18, rue Béranger – 92320 Châtillon – France
In the United States:
aerospatiale, Inc. 1101, Fifteenth Street, N.W. Washington, D.C. 20005

cost of those same weapons for their own armed forces. Also, countries want to recover the enormous research and development costs involved in modern weapons design and construction. And, of course, commercial firms apply considerable political pressure on governments to persuade them to grant export licences for this lucrative trade.

Andrew J. Pierre, in his book *The Global Politics of Arms Sales* (1982), stresses the political impact of the arms trade. 'Arms sales', he says, 'are a barometer of politics among nations.' As alliances, the use of

An advertisement from the French Aerospatiale for Exocet missiles. The proven effectiveness of these and other missiles in the 1982 Falklands conflict has provided useful marketing material for their manufacturers in the international sales arena.

foreign bases and the credibility of the threat of direct action all decline, arms sales, he believes, acquire a new significance in world affairs – a significance likely to increase in the foreseeable future. Pierre draws this conclusion for several reasons: because arms transfers will be a major element in increasing East-West competition in the Third World; because the rise of regional powers will stimulate large arms purchases; and because the spread of nuclear weapons to new countries will, by creating a more fragmented world in which local military power will often be of greater importance within the Third World, increase rather than decrease the incentives to acquire conventional weapons.

The motives for buying arms also vary. Some countries do so because they have real, or perceived, security needs. Arms are seen to be needed for internal and external conflicts in which force may be required. A vicious circle may then be established. When one country acquires modern weapons a neighbour may feel provoked to do the same thing, and an arms race begins.

In some Third World countries the political leaders are military men who want the most sophisticated weapons because they are the most glamorous. Other governments need the political support of senior military officers, and they believe that they can get this support by satisfying the military demands for the most modern weapons. Some Third World countries have a sublime faith in the superiority of technology, particularly military technology, and they feel most secure when their arsenals contain the most sophisticated weapons.

On the other hand, some large arms deals may have little to do with security or any other military matter. Many people suspect that the very expensive weapons which are, for example, bought by Saudi Arabia are purely a medium for the re-cycling of petro-dollars. Other Third World countries buy large quantities of arms abroad in the probably false belief (see Chapter Eleven) that high military spending in some way assists domestic civilian development. For this reason, some countries have developed significant weapon-producing industries.

The Boomerang Effect

The global arms trade is not only of doubtful morality; it can also be unwise. Weapons which are sold to other countries may then be used against the supplier. For example, the United Kingdom sold many major weapons and much military equipment to Argentina. It then went to war with Argentina. Many of the 250 British servicemen killed in the Falklands war were killed by British weapons. HMS *Ardent*, for example, was sunk by Aermacchi MB339A jet aircraft; 24 of the crew of 170 were killed and 30 injured. The Aermacchis are powered by Rolls Royce engines, as are the four frigates being sold by West Germany to Argentina. Many parts of the Exocet missiles are British made.

The eminent American economist Ruth Sivard in her *World Military and Social Expenditure – 1980* (World Priorities, Leesburg, Virginia, 1980) gives many examples of how the large military investments made by the great powers in Third World countries have boomeranged. Egypt received four billion dollars in Soviet military aid before switching to the United States as its main arms supplier. Some of the Soviet arms supplied to Egypt were used against the Soviets in Afghanistan by the rebels. Nicaragua depended for years on US military aid before the rebellion which ousted Somoza in 1979; it now receives arms originating from the Soviet bloc. Mozambique received communist arms aid after 1975 but in 1980 started turning to the West for military assistance. The Shah of Iran was America's best arms customer; he was toppled from power in a revolution which used 300,000 weapons taken from the Shah's arsenal. The United States is now using the Berbera military base in Somalia, constructed by the USSR before Somali-

Soviet relations soured in 1977. The Soviets are now using the naval facilities at Cam Ranh Bay and Danang in Vietnam; they were built by the Americans.

Overseas Troops

Despite the danger of the Boomerang Effect, we must expect the Superpowers to continue using the arms trade to exert influence in Third World countries, maintaining military bases abroad, sailing their navies into all the oceans, stationing troops in other countries and making use of proxy forces. It has all become part and parcel of Superpower behaviour.

For example, according to *The Military Balance – 1982-1983*, published by the International Institute for 'Strategic Studies (London, 1982), the USSR has forces in Afghanistan, Algeria, Angola, Congo, Cuba, Ethiopia, Iraq, Kampuchea, Laos, Libya, Mali, Mauritania, Mozambique, Syria, Vietnam and North and South Yemen. The numbers of military personnel range from about 100,000 in Afghanistan to only 100 in Mali. Excluding Afghanistan, the total significantly exceeds 1,000 in Cuba (2,800), Ethiopia (1,350), Iraq (2,000), Libya (1,800), Syria (2,500), Vietnam (5,000) and South Yemen (1,500). In some cases the personnel are military advisers or technicians teaching locals how to operate and maintain Soviet major weapons. Cuban troops are often regarded as Soviet proxies. Cuba has some 18,000 troops in Angola, 13,000 in Ethiopia and a few hundred in each of Congo, Mozambique and South Yemen.

Unlike the USA, which has extensive military bases in places like Diego Garcia in the Indian Ocean and Guam in the Pacific, the USSR does not maintain military bases of its own outside the Warsaw Pact area. But the Soviets do have the use of some naval facilities. The main ones are Cam Ranh Bay and Danang in Vietnam, Najin in North Korea, and Socotra, Aden, and Dhalak Island in the Indian Ocean. They also have access to some anchorages, mainly in the Indian Ocean, and some limited port facilities.

The USSR has military ties with Afghanistan, Angola, Cuba, Ethiopia, Iraq, Libya, Syria, Vietnam and South Yemen, and could presumably use bases in these countries in a time of great crisis. It has also, in military manoeuvres, shown a capability to deploy its forces over a wide area – through Benghazi and Tobruk in Libya, Latakia in Syria and Aden in South Yemen, for example.

The United States is also building up forces that could be used for rapid deployment into the Third World. The purpose is to intervene militarily in areas 'far from our shores', particularly in the Middle East/Persian Gulf area to protect Western oil supplies. Currently, about 200,000 personnel, including support units, are earmarked for the rapid-deployment force. Heavy equipment and

Afghan rebels continue to defy the Soviet forces occupying their country, sometimes with weapons originally supplied by the Soviets. But, as this picture shows, much of their weaponry is antique and pitifully inadequate. There is still a large market for the low-technology arms trade among the world's poorer armies and guerilla groups.

The late Shah of Iran taking part in a military parade. The United States invested huge quantities of weaponry in supporting the Shah's regime; those very weapons were used in the revolution which ousted him from power. Another example of the 'boomerang effect'.

The rapid-deployment force is supposed to be highly mobile, but there is scepticism about this. Some experts calculate that with current capabilities it would take fourteen days to airlift one army brigade and its equipment from the United States to the Persian Gulf. To do so would require many round trips by each of 130 large transport aircraft. The rapid-deployment force could hardly take an enemy by surprise.

Apart from their base in Diego Garcia, the Americans are establishing other military facilities in the Gulf region including: the use of the port and air base at Bahrain; the use of the port and air base at Berbera in Somalia; the use of the port and some naval facilities at Mombasa in Kenya; the use of the air base on Masirah Island in Oman; the use of the Egyptian military base and air base at Ras Banas; and access to the French military and naval facilities at Djibouti. It can be assumed that Israel would also make facilities available if the rapid-deployment force were ever used.

The United States has promised military and economic aid in return for the use of some of these facilities. For example, in return for the use of the air base at Berbera and naval facilities at Mogadishu, the US government is giving Somalia five million dollars in economic aid and 40 million dollars' worth of military equipment.

Both Superpowers hold manoeuvres to test their deployment forces. The United States, for example, held joint manoeuvres in November 1981 with Egypt and Oman. The USSR did rather better at about the same time in joint manoeuvres with Libyan, Syrian and South Yemeni troops, also in the Middle East. About 7,500 Soviet troops were air-lifted into the region from bases in Tashkent. The Soviets have the advantage over the Americans that heavy equipment can be picked up from arms dumps at Tobruk and Benghazi in Libya.

Great power rivalry in the Persian Gulf and Indian Ocean regions is intensifying

supplies for the force are stored in pre-positioned ships. The long-term plan is to have twelve ships scattered throughout the world. Four of them would carry the equipment for a Marine brigade – about 1,200 vehicles, 36 artillery guns, 100 amphibian tractors and 53 tanks. The Marines would be airlifted to meet the ships which would sail from the nearest location. The Marines would take two days' supply with them and the ships would bring in another 30 days' supplies.

Seven ships have been chartered as an interim measure. They are anchored off Diego Garcia Island in the Indian Ocean, some 3,500 kilometers from the Persian Gulf. The fleet carries enough supplies to keep a 12,000-man strong Marine brigade going for two weeks or so, and enough ammunition for several fighter squadrons.

A group of the 18,000 or so Cuban troops sent by Fidel Castro to assist the MPLA in its swiftly successful bid to gain control of Angola after the granting of independence from Portugal in 1975. The Cubans are often described as being merely Soviet forces under another guise.

alarmingly. Some states in the region are being caught up in this rivalry, particularly through the provision of military facilities for one side or the other. It is likely that others will come under pressure to do likewise.

Weapons Producers
When World War Two ended, only five countries – Canada, Sweden, the United States, the USSR and the United Kingdom – had the capacity to develop and produce major weapons. Today, 54 countries produce these weapons, and 23 of them are in the Third World or outside NATO and the Warsaw Pact. If small arms are included, the number of weapon-producing countries is much larger. In 30 years, then, the number of arms producers in the world has increased tenfold, and there is no sign of any slowing down.

Some Third World countries have established sizeable weapon industries in an effort to become self-sufficient in armaments. The drive for independence in weaponry is stimulated by the increasing tendency on the part of the great powers to manipulate arms supplies for political, economic or military reasons. Countries like South Africa and Taiwan find it so difficult to buy military equipment that they must produce their own. Countries

like Israel do not like to depend on others, even if they have dependable suppliers.

Status is another motive for countries establishing arms industries. Argentina, Brazil and India are examples of countries which believe that economic advantage is to be had from arms industries, including cheaper weapons, the saving of scarce foreign currencies and the creation of jobs.

The emphasis these days is for weapon-producing nations to reserve the greatest thrust of their arms-sales programmes for selling major weapons and high-technology equipment. Such sales help to subsidize the production of these same weapons for their own forces. As we have suggested above, for a variety of motives (including status) there has been a recent shift in even quite small Third World countries to buying weapons of greater sophistication (though nothing like as sophisticated as those in the arsenals of the great powers). Sometimes the technology of these weapons goes beyond what an objective observer might recommend as necessary for the preservation of a small country's security.

Nevertheless, it is worth remembering that the trade in traditional small arms – rifles, grenades and so on – along with light armoured trucks, mortars, etc. remains influential. Many of the 150 or so armed conflicts that have taken place since World War Two have been fought with low-technology conventional weapons. The majority of actual war deaths are still caused by what many nations might regard as obsolete equipment – rifles, machine guns, grenades, revolvers and so on. (The light Kalashnikov Russian rifle is among the cheapest and most popular weapons in use around the world, notably in Africa.) Indeed, in some conflicts people are still killed by knives, clubs, machetes and bayonets. The bloody fighting in Guatemala does not use much equipment more sophisticated than light counter-insurgency aircraft.

In 1981 both the USA and the USSR held manoeuvres for their rapid-deployment forces in the Middle East. This is part of the American operation, 'Bright Star'. Men of the 101st Airborne Division unload a Black Hawk helicopter from a C-5A transport aircraft in the desert. Rapid deployment could help protect oil supplies.

Third World arms industries are still very small compared with those of the industrialized countries. The top seven industrialized arms producers – the United States, the USSR, France, the United Kingdom, Italy, West Germany and Sweden – make nearly 600 types of major weapons (about 230 types of aircraft, 70 types of armoured vehicles, 150 missiles and 150 warships). However, the top seven Third World arms producers (China, Brazil, Argentina, Israel, India, Taiwan and South Africa) do make some 140 types of major weapons (about 65 aircraft, 15 armoured vehicles, 30 missiles and 30 warships).

The most sophisticated major weapon built in the Third World is Israel's Kfir-C2, a fighter-bomber capable of speeds in excess of twice the speed of sound. The Kfir is based on the French Mirage–5. The theft of the plans (which were said to weigh about two tons) of this French aircraft from a Swiss firm that was building it under licence was a brilliant coup for the Israeli secret service. Most of the other aircraft produced in Third World countries are trainers or transports or counter-insurgency aircraft.

So far, the missiles produced in the Third World have been mostly anti-tank or air-to-air missiles. China, however, produces a wide range of missiles, including intercontinental ballistic missiles. Israel has produced an advanced surface-to-surface missile called the Jericho that is thought to be capable of carrying a nuclear warhead. Israel also produces advanced ship-to-ship missiles.

All the top seven Third World arms producers except Taiwan make aircraft, warships and missiles. Taiwan makes aircraft and missiles only. China has a very versatile arms industry. It produces seven types of missiles and ten types of warships. Most of these weapons are indigenously designed and are mainly Chinese versions of Soviet weapons.

South Africa produces three types of aircraft, one armoured vehicle, a missile and a warship, all under licences issued by France, Israel or Italy. Apart from China, South Africa is the most self-sufficient of all Third World countries in armaments.

There are sixteen Third World countries that produce warships – a surprisingly large number. A total of about 40 types are produced, mainly patrol boats and support ships, although Argentina, Brazil and India produce frigates and destroyers under licence from Britain. The world-wide rapid increase in light naval forces is the main stimulus for Third World naval ship-building.

Although much Third World arms production is done under licences issued by the rich countries, the amount of indigenous design and production is steadily increasing. Brazil, for example, produces a tank, the twenty-ton X1-A2, that is armed with a 90-mm cannon and two machine guns. It is built and designed indigenously, an off-shoot from the domestic automobile industry. Nevertheless, it will be a long time before Third World countries can free themselves to any significant extent from dependence on the technology of the developed countries. Even Israel requires some such assistance – the engines for the Kfir aircraft are American.

Israel is, however, an object lesson in what a small country can achieve in arms

Small arms on display at an American arms fair. It is often forgotten that low-technology weaponry still plays an influential part in many of the armed conflicts currently in progress around the world.

production. The list of arms produced in Israel is indeed impressive. The armoured vehicles in production include the Merkava main battle tank, two types of reconnaissance armoured cars, the Shoet armoured personnel carrier and the Soltam self-propelled gun. Apart from the Kfir, other major weapons manufactured include Reshef Class missile patrol boats, Gabriel ship-to-ship missiles and Shafir air-to-air missiles. Israel also produces a range of smaller weapons like the Uzi machine gun, the Galil assault rifle and the M-71 155-mm field gun, and much military equipment including military electronics, avionics, communications systems, mine-detection devices, anti-guerrilla detection systems and fire-control systems. In some weapons – including small arms, bombs and some guided missiles – the Israelis are virtually self-sufficient. Across the board, Israel makes about half of its weapons.

Arms Traders from the Third World

The Israeli arms industry, which employs about 20,000 workers (fifteen per cent of the industrial workforce) exports over one billion dollars' worth of military equipment annually – 1.2 billion dollars in 1980 according to the *Financial Times* (Nov. 12, 1981). Israeli arms exports are increasing continuously. But Israel is by no means the only Third World country in the global arms trade. On the contrary, the Third World share of this trade is steadily increasing.

Third World arms producers are following the pattern established by the industrialized arms producers. Arms industries are started gradually. First imported weapons are overhauled and maintained. Then some weapons, or parts of weapons, are made under licence. With this experience, new types of weapons may then be designed and produced by the domestic industry. Normally, however, parts of the indigenous weapons are bought abroad or produced under licence.

The design of weapons requires substantial research and development. Recovery of some of the cost of this activity is a major reason why arms producers are anxious to sell their products abroad. Third World countries

The arming of an Israeli Kfir-C2, the most sophisticated major weapon produced by any Third World country. The plans for this fighter-bomber are said to have been stolen from the Swiss firm manufacturing the French Mirage-5, on which aircraft the Kfir-C2 is closely based, by the Israeli Secret Service.

are no exceptions to this general rule.

From data published by SIPRI, the main source of information about the arms trade, it is clear that Third World arms exporters can be put into two groups. The first group is those with significant domestic arms industries, particularly Argentina, Brazil, India, Israel and South Africa, which export weapons they design themselves or produce under licence; the second group is those, like Egypt, Libya and Saudi Arabia, which re-export arms that have been bought from the industrialized countries. Between 1979 and 1981, according to SIPRI figures, the three largest Third World major-weapon exporting countries (Brazil, Israel and Libya in rank order) accounted for 80 per cent of total Third World exports. The next three biggest exporters (South Korea, Egypt and Saudi Arabia) account for another fifteen per cent. Third World countries also export large quantities of small arms.

The success of Brazilian arms salesmen can be seen in a quote from the 1982 SIPRI *Yearbook*: 'The Engesa company reportedly sells about 1,000 armoured vehicles a year to 32 countries, mostly on arms-for-oil terms to OPEC members in Africa and the Middle East. Brazilian rifles and machine guns are in service in Angola and the Congo. The Avibras company sells, among other things, air-to-ground missiles to Iraq, and Embraer markets a wide range of aircraft including jet trainers, counter-insurgency aircraft and transports. In 1981 Brazil started deliveries of the Xingu trainer/light transport jet to the French Air Force.'

The Brazilian-French deal was exceptional. Arms produced in the Third World are normally sold to other Third World countries. They are in fact often more suitable for these customers' requirements, and are usually seen to be better value for money. Even so, the Third World share of the global arms trade in major weapons is still relatively small, about 2.5 per cent of the total.

Government Encouragement of Arms Sales

It must be emphasized that arms sales are almost all approved by governments. The purely private dealers – the hard-faced men of popular mythology – account for a very small fraction of the business. Usually, as most recently shown by the Mitterand government in France, attitudes to arms sales are independent of which party is in power. Many people might have assumed that the previous Giscard d'Estaing government's policy of selling arms to almost anybody would be altered when a socialist government came to power. In fact the Mitterand government is just as aggressive in its arms salesmanship – or more so, according to some observers.

The United Kingdom gives another example of the same familiar pattern. Successive British governments have tried hard to maintain Britain's share of the arms market. In 1966, Denis Healey, then Labour's Defence Secretary, set up the Defence Sales Organization, instructing it 'to ensure that this country does not fail to secure its rightful share of this valuable commercial market'. Denis Healey was worried by the decline of British arms sales abroad. Just after World War Two the arms market was essentially monopolized by the United States and the United Kingdom. But by 1966, the UK had lost much of its share to the USA, the USSR and France. West Germany and Italy were beginning to compete successfully as well. To try to stop the decline an arms super-salesman was appointed by the government to head the Defence Sales Organization. The organization now employs about 400 civil servants and about twenty members of the armed forces. Prime Minister Margaret Thatcher has ordered the Defence Sales Organization to step up its efforts. The present level of British arms exports, she has said, is 'a handy sum but not enough'.

Many people believe that Britain, like most other arms exporters, should be more particular about countries to which it sells arms. In 1980, for example, the

British government lifted the embargo banning arms sales to Chile, an embargo which had been in force since 1974. Yet Chile has a very bad record for human rights. Arbitrary detentions, torture sometimes leading to death and political killings have become features of Chilean life. In 1982, Britain sold the Chilean Navy a destroyer, even though the Chilean Navy has used ships as prisons and torture centres.

Conclusions

High military expenditures, the global arms trade and the spread of weapon-production are militarizing the planet. The arms trade in particular encourages Third World countries to waste scarce financial resources on sophisticated modern arms. These arms require many skilled scientific and technical people to operate and maintain them. But it is just these skills, now diverted, which poor countries need for their civilian development. Arms sales, therefore, seriously undermine development.

The arms trade also reduces employment in the countries that supply the weapons, curiously enough. Money spent in areas like transport, housing, education, building construction and health creates far more jobs than the same money spent on the military. US figures show that for the investment (one billion dollars) which employs 80,000 people in the arms business, 140,000 jobs could be created in the health service, or 190,000 jobs in education, or 100,000 jobs in construction or 90,000 jobs in manufacturing. This is another aspect of the military impact on the civilian economy that was discussed in Chapter Eleven.

A leading British politician has described the arms trade as 'the most bestial development in modern times, and second only in obscenity to the nuclear arms race itself'. But, once in power, politicians seem to do nothing about the arms trade. Unless public opinion is mobilized against it, the global arms trade will go on, making massive profits for the few but also making wars (which affect the many) considerably more violent and more likely.

Frank Barnaby

Chapter 13

War Games and Military Planning

A favourite way of looking into the military future is by means of war games. Analysts tell us that war games must never be used to *predict* what will be the outcome of a given situation; that they are merely a useful device for broadening the imagination, or getting to see things from the opponent's side. That indeed is how it should be. But often the results of theoretical war games are accepted subconsciously as a projection of what will happen in 'real life'.

This seems to have happened in the many games played by the United States military planners before and during the Vietnam war, when the nature of their assumptions about political and other human factors was forgotten and the encouraging results contributed to overconfidence in counter-insurgency operations.

War games that yield unpalatable lessons have frequently been ignored or forgotten by national decision-makers in pursuit of alluring goals. Such was the case with the annual war games played by the German General Staff in 1895–1914, which showed the inadequacy of the forces available to execute the Schlieffen Plan, and a naval game whose cautionary outcome was ignored by Japanese commanders on the eve of the Midway disaster.

At the same time even the most comprehensive war-game programmes may fail to prepare the planners for important eventualities, because what turns out to be the critical situation is considered to be too bizarre to merit gaming. In a series of fourteen 'world order scenarios' considered for study by American experts in the early 1960s, the one in which China was allied with the West against the Soviet Union was

dismissed on this score, though now it looks very reasonable. More recently there appears to have been no gaming by the British Ministry of Defence of an Argentine invasion of the Falkland Islands before the events of April 1982. Nor, as far as it is possible to discover, was there any gaming by the Pentagon of an Israeli advance into the Lebanon such as occurred in the same year.

As commonly understood, the term 'war games' includes a wide variety of military exercises, ranging from tactical exercises conducted on the ground by skeletal headquarters staffs, to elaborate representations of a complete nuclear war played entirely by computers. 'Game theory', considered later in this chapter, is a purely mathematical device for the comparison of alternative strategies. Although it uses game models of real-life situations of conflict or co-operation, it has little to do with the other kinds of war game here described.

A distinction can be drawn between purely military tactical games (invented by the British nineteenth-century military reformer, Henry Spenser Wilkinson, and later adopted enthusiastically in Germany) and – a more recent development – politico-military games. As used by the military these deal with the broadest kind of strategic problem ('grand strategy'). They are also used by diplomatic and intelligence agencies (as well as disinterested academic groups) for the study of international relations.

In the most common type of tactical game, the so-called 'closed' type, the 'Blue' and 'Red' commanders are physically separated. Each has a model, generally a map, of the ground over which operations will take place. Symbols for the opposing forces are moved on the model according to the commanders' decisions, and the movements are duplicated on a separate model by the direction staff, or 'Control'. The outcomes of moves are determined by set rules ('rigid assessment') or by the judgment of umpires ('free assessment'). Some rules may be absolute, for example those governing the speed of unopposed movement. Others will be 'probabilistic'; that is, they assign a certain latitude to the outcome of an event and leave it to a random-number device to determine the exact result.

Such 'manual' games, often at the very highest level, continue to be played at SHAPE and other NATO headquarters to assist operational planning, and for operational research purposes by the Pentagon Joint War Games agency and Britain's Defence Operational Analysis Establishment (DOAE). They are relatively faithful in the representation of complex situations. They employ human actors, whose thought processes cannot be simulated mechanically. They include an element of chance, which is an essential ingredient in war. And those who design them are hopefully made aware of parts of a situation about which there may be little or no data.

The limitation of manual war games is the time they take to prepare and conduct, even though several years' 'scenario' may be telescoped into a few days, or even hours. This is particularly felt if it is desirable to replay the same basic situation a large number of times, each time with certain changes in the parameters. Beyond a certain point this becomes possible only with the introduction of computers, which, once the basic scenario has been programmed (an immensely resource-consuming but once-off business), can rerun the game as often as is wanted, the only interruptions being to insert alternative factors, generally sets of figures denoting force levels and so on.

In the case of naval and air-warfare games, in which the mechanical

capabilities of weapons systems and weapons carriers play a predominant part, parts of the 'manual' process can be taken over electronically. A highly developed example is the game model played by the US Navy Electronic War Simulator (NEWS) at the Navy War College at Newport, Rhode Island. In this the movements of up to 48 vessels or aircraft can be electronically represented, together with electronic countermeasures, weapons malfunction, susceptibility of units to radar or sonar detection, and so on, on giant screens.

Computer War Games

But these 'computer-assisted' games are not to be confused with proper computer games like STAGE (Simulation of Total Global Atomic Exchange) developed by the Pentagon in the 1960s to represent a thermonuclear war with the Soviet Union. The STAGE model took three years to prepare and the running of a single game about 30 hours. (Advances in microchip technology have since cut this to a fraction of the time.)

From time to time efforts have been made to develop computer models for more complex situations. Most notable was the attempt at the time of the Vietnam war to construct a computerized counter-insurgency war game based on a manual game called AGILE. But the results have proved unconvincing.

Even the most sophisticated type of computer game involves a high degree of over-simplification. Used to model field operations, the most it can reliably do is to provide information about fire-exchange ratios. This may play an important part in the selection of weapons systems and, particularly in air warfare, the choice of designs for speed, manoeuvrability and so on. But it can never be more than a partial ingredient of strategic planning because of the incalculables concerning human skills and motivation.

The most controversial application of computer gaming has been to model an

East-West strategic nuclear exchange, on the lines of the STAGE game mentioned earlier. Even in the most 'calculable' elements of this there are important theoretical assumptions. One is about systems reliability, highlighted by the recent disclosure that for the greater part of the early 1970s three-quarters of the US Polaris force would have failed operationally because of the jamming of a safety-lock. Another is about the accuracy of long-range ballistic missiles which may be less than is claimed, because of variations in the Earth's gravitational field.

If the nuclear game model is enlarged to include other physical factors that cannot be quantified except within very wide brackets, the variety of possible outcomes becomes enormous.

In the case of a nuclear exchange involving attacks on cities, the many variables requiring to be represented include: accuracy of strikes, burst altitudes, target-population density (dependent on the degree of evacuation), fuel loading (that is, the susceptibility of buildings to fire), weather, time of day, warning time, radiation-protection factors (of buildings), and fallout effects dependent on warhead-type, wind direction and so on. The number of these variables explains the huge latitude in official estimates of the immediate casualties to be expected from a nuclear strike against the United States.

To extend the model yet further to include the long-term effects would make it virtually ungameable, involving, as this would, such unquantifiable factors as civilian morale, survival of public services, maintenance of order and delayed radiation damage to health and agriculture. In short, computer models can do little beyond illuminating nuclear exchange-ratios and some problems of logistics at a fairly basic level. Their outcomes are gravely suspect when quoted to support strategic projections.

Politico-Military Simulations
More indulgence might be extended towards the usefulness of politico-military simulation games, which do not pretend to give cut-and-dried answers and whose main purpose is, in the broadest sense, educational. These remain for the most part manual. A crucial difference from military tactical games is the use of a number of teams to represent the variety of decision centres in an international situation, and often within each team a number of players to represent divisions within the decision centres themselves.

In top-level games, friendly roles may be played by 'real-life' military or foreign service chiefs, or by deputies close enough to represent them faithfully, while agencies go to considerable lengths to obtain realistic players for 'enemy', 'allied' and 'neutral' parts. The Pentagon and the Central Intelligence Agency use outside specialists from universities and other institutions. The Russians do the same and have at least once enlisted a visiting American specialist to play, with State Department approval, in an arms control game. But at the end of the day the worth of any game is determined by the

	BLUE		RED.
Missile Occupancy =	.95		.00
Number of Bombers =	700.00000		435.00000
Warheads per missile =	1.00000	1.00000	
o/o Missile on Missile =	.00000		.20000
o/o Missiles Remaining =	.92443		1.00000
PK Missile on Missile =	.54000	.64000	
Missile Targeting Mode =	2.00000	1.00000	
WH Missile on Missile =	1.00000		1.00000
Effective PK M on M =	.54000	.64000	
o/o Missile on Defense =	.40000	.20000	
o/o Missile on Bombers =	.40000	.40000	
o/o Missile on Cities =	.60000		.20000
PK Missile on Defense =	.46000	.46000	
PK Missile on Bomber =	.45000	.45000	
PK Missile on City =	.43000	.45000	
Number of Defenses =	109.00000	264.00000	
Number of Fields =	64.00000	54.00000	
Number of Cities =	500.00000	400.00000	
Cities Missile Defended =	50.00000		60.00000
Missile Defense Survival =	.25000	.25000	
WH Missile on Defense =	1.00000	1.00000	
WH Missile on Field =	5.18519		2.71875
WH Missile on City =	1.00000		1.00000
WH Missile on Def. City =	1.33333		1.00000
Effective PK M on D =	.46000	.46000	
Effective PK M on B =	.19579	.29542	
Effective PK M on C =	.43000	.45000	
Effective PK M on Def. C =	.10568		.1125
Missiles Remaining =	647.10400		435.0000
Cities Destr. (U) by M =	5.62500	7.81542	
Cities Destr. (D) by M =	16.65000	135.15229	
Number of Bombers =	300.00000	245.00000	
Bomber Occupancy =	3.28125		1.95918
Fighter Kill Prob. =	.56000	.55000	
Fields Remaining =	12.597693		3.32062
Bombers Remaining =	131.33618		145.71022
o/o Bombers Remaining =	.43779		.59474
Defenses Remaining =	21.12195		255.71637
Fighter KP Remaining =	.10852		.53274
Fighter KP Rem. (Int.) =	.35439	.55000	
o/o Bomber on City =	.97097		.84220
o/o Bomber on Defenses =	.02903		.15780
Number Bombs per Bomber =	4.00000	3.00000	
PK Bomber on Defenses =	.97000	.96000	
PK Bomber on City =	.89000		.89000
WH Kill/Bomber Kill =	.80000		.75000

Part of a computer printout of a United States nuclear war-game move. The usefulness of computerized war games — some of which may take years in preparation — is increasingly being questioned, since so many imponderables are involved in the programming.

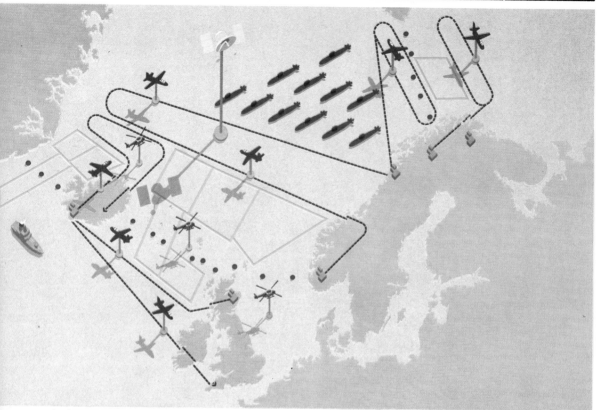

judgment and skill of the Control staff, which by inventing outside events to facilitate or frustrate particular moves, is responsible for guiding the play towards significant decision points.

Simulation games can never teach how events will turn out in real life. They can, however, alert the participants to possibilities for action of which they might otherwise be unaware.

Simulation games may also be useful in preparing their participants for what may become one of the major problems in any future war between the Superpowers. The military command will be called upon to make decisions at extremely high speed in the face of a flood of data, electronically delivered, of a volume unprecedented in warfare. The psychological strain on the decision makers will be extraordinarily intense. No simulation, unfortunately, could possibly duplicate the strain of making 'real-life' decisions, though it might well duplicate technically the pressure of data and the pressure of time that give rise to the strain.

Various attempts have been made to develop computer models for politico-military games, mainly with a view to conflict-avoidance and crisis-management. A system called CASCON for providing information on local conflicts was developed in the United States by Professor Lincoln Bloomfield of the Massachusetts Institute of Technology in the 1970s. Used in a foreign-policy game, it attracted the interest of government and United Nations officials, but was not carried further for want of funds.

Other Planning Techniques
In the context of war-gaming mention must be made of a number of other analytical techniques used to assist military planning. These include systems analysis (the study of particular objectives

Many war-game scenarios are set in the vital Greenland-Iceland-UK gap, through which the Soviet submarines based at the Kola Peninsula have to pass to enter the Atlantic. Each light grey rectangle represents the deployment area of a US attack submarine; the spheres with antennae represent underwater listening systems; the helicopters are capable of dropping sonars into the sea, and also carry depth charges; the CAPTOR minefield can be rapidly sown across choke points; ASW (anti-submarine-warfare) aircraft patrol the area; observation satellites also keep watch. The buildings on land are US ASW-aircraft bases. Few submarines get through unobserved.

in relation to the availability of resources), military case-studies (the analysis of historical, as opposed to simulated, situations), general operational analysis and game theory.

Game theory might be described as war-gaming stripped to the barest essentials. Originally developed for economic analysis by the Princeton mathematicians John Von Neumann and Oskar Margenstern in the 1920s, it postulates a set of players, each with a set

to limit A's gain to a minimum. This maximization of the minimum is known as the max-min. B, on the other hand, must choose the strategy which minimizes the greatest loss that A can inflict. This is known as the min-max.

The way simple game theory works is shown in the figure below. This represents the classic game of Prisoner's Dilemma, which is frequently used to illustrate the paradox of the arms race. Applied to armament/disarmament choices, the game

of strategies (that is, possible courses of action, which may depend on moves made by the others). Each strategy of each player will have a defined outcome, and each player will have a preferred order of outcomes, or 'pay-offs'. Each side's strategies and the outcomes resulting from their intersection can be shown in a rectangular box called a 'game matrix'.

In its simplest form, game theory can be applied to a situation of pure competition involving only two players. In it, each of the two players, A and B, chooses a strategy from a limited number of possibilities, without knowing the strategy the other is choosing. A, to ensure the best result for himself, must assess each strategy by the gain it will give him *regardless of what B may do.* In other words he must pessimistically assume that B knows his plan and will counter it so as

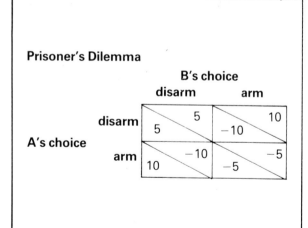

Prisoner's Dilemma

makes it seem rational for each player not to disarm but to arm. For by arming, either player (say A) does better whichever choice the other makes. If B disarms, A

The Strategic Air Command's control room beneath a mountain in Colorado. Here in case of war the game would be played in deadly earnest, but it is also the location for simulated warfare — games played to probe weaknesses in the defence system, and to examine various plausible war scenarios and their possible results.

The classic example of game theory, the Prisoner's Dilemma. There are dangers in applying game theory to real life. Most dual games are 'zero-sum', one side's gain equalling the other's loss. But in practice dual games may be non-zero-sum, as when two nations negotiate a truce benefiting both.

gets 10, the best possible outcome; and if, on the other hand, B arms, he still gets −5 rather than −10. The paradox is that if both sides were to ignore the games-theory prescription of minimizing possible loss and disarm, they would both do better than by both arming, because each prefers mutual disarmament (5/5) to the arms race (−5/−5).

Seeking a more faithful representation of the complexity of strategy choices in real life, game theoreticians have developed models in which one game is joined to another. This may be either in a vertical series, in which successive choices are made in the light of the result of the preceding game (Rapoport), or in a horizontal series known as Hypergame (Bennett and Dando), which represents different ways in which the game may be perceived by A and B respectively. (In a recent analysis Bennett and Dando used the Hypergame to explain the 1940 fall of France by reference to the Allies' and the Germans' different perceptions of the strategic possibilities.)

Although much current literature on game theory comes from peace-research analysts, it can readily be seen that game-theory models are applicable to choices in military planning where data bases are available for what appears to be a more sophisticated weighting of pay-offs. But although arguably helpful in this kind of study, just as in the study of disarmament and arms-control problems, the extreme simplification of game-theory models severely limits their practical usefulness.

So far as is known, no operational decision has ever been taken on the basis of game-theoretical analysis; and, given the opposition of politicians and generals alike to 'theory', none is ever likely to be.

Practical Difficulties of Military Planning

Certainly today in the West (and it may be assumed in the East also) military 'planning' is a much more haphazard process than the playing of war games and other techniques suggest. In practice it is generally a crude compromise between the demands of the military, forever seeking to guard against all contingencies, and the constraints imposed by the available national resources. Into this is thrown the complicating factor of political pressure from the 'supply side' (the arms industry), seeking to enlarge the market for its products.

Nor is 'planning' normally a case of military requirements giving rise to the development of new weapons designs, but rather the other way round. New weapons such as the neutron bomb and the cruise missile tend to emerge from the laboratory long before the military have any clear idea how to use them. Doctrines for their employment come only later, often after considerable funds have been committed to their development, as a result of industrial pressure or from fear that the same weapons are being developed by the opposite side.

Rational planning is further jeopardized

Three examples of war games being carried out in real life. Left: Chinese soldiers under instruction, the educational tool being a model of a United States tank. Such exercises bear little resemblance to strictly theoretical war games, which are over-simplified and have to make often invalid assumptions. Centre: Soviet-bloc naval leaders working out tactical plans during Operation 'Sever' in 1968. Right: children in Feggendorf, West Germany, watching British tanks during Operation 'Crusader 80', a huge NATO exercise, involving about 63,000 men, carried out in 1980.

by the great time now required – up to twenty years – for the development of new strategic systems. By the time these are ready the mission for which they are planned may have changed totally – witness the fiasco of the British Chevaline Polaris warhead, developed at a cost of one billion pounds to evade an anti-missile system that had long been discarded.

Without doubt the coming decade will see innumerable war games devoted to the viability and cost-effectiveness of space-based anti-ballistic-missile systems, new anti-submarine weapons and precision-guided munitions for the European theatre. But any effect they may have on procurement decisions is likely to be secondary. In a famous passage the Elder Moltke once wrote that no plan is likely to survive contact with the enemy. A twentieth-century successor might observe that no plan is likely to be translated into hardware before the situation for which it is intended has passed into history.

Andrew Wilson

References

Bennett, P.G. and Dando, M.R., 'The Arms Race as a Hypergame', **Futures**, Aug. 1982
Bennett, P.G. and Dando, M.R., 'Complex Strategic Analysis: a Hypergame Study of the Fall of France', **Journal of the Operational Research Society**, vol. 30, 1, 1979
Mandel, R., 'Political Gaming and Foreign Policy Making During Crises', **World Politics**, July 1977
Rapoport, A., **Strategy and Conscience**, Harper & Row, New York, 1964
Shubik, M. and Brewer, G., 'R-1060-ARPA/RC' (May 1972) and 'R-732-ARPA' (June 1972), RAND Corporation Reports
Von Neumann, J. and Morgenstern, O., **Theory of Games and Economic Behavior**, 2nd edition, Princeton University Press, Princeton, New Jersey, 1947
Wilson, A., **War Gaming**, Penguin, London, 1970
See also the article on CASCON by Bloomfield, L. and Beattie, R. in **Journal of Conflict Resolution**, vol. XV, 1971, and appendix 'Learning Through Gaming' in Bloomfield, L., **The Foreign Policy Process: a Modern Primer**, Prentice-Hall, New York, 1982

Chapter 14

Governments and Armies

The threat of Future War, or at least of future wars, has a great deal to do with the sometimes symbiotic relationship between armies and governments in the modern world. This relationship varies a lot, of course, in the way it manifests itself. We have already had a good deal to say about military pressures on government in the developed world, in previous chapters, though further points will emerge. Primarily, however, we will look at the nations of the Third World where the government–army relationship is often even more important and direct. We can begin to explain this point with an anecdote.

Military Politics in African States

The woman editor of a little-known newspaper in the sleepy Zimbabwe border town of Murare (formerly Umtali) received a major tip-off. Having lived among the farming community for many years she knew everybody, and when a large contingent of North Korean military advisors' arrived in the exquisite surroundings of the Nyanga mountains it was not long before she heard about it. The *Umtali Post* gained immediate international recognition when it broke the story that the Koreans were training an elite 'praetorian guard', known as the 5th Brigade, answerable directly to Prime Minister Robert Mugabe. Mugabe was furious. The editor was summoned to the capital and hauled over the coals before being sacked by the bosses of the state-controlled press.

Some two years later the latent fears about the existence of such a military instrument of government were brought into sharp focus when the 5th Brigade gained international notoriety because of its suppressionary activities in Matabeleland, home of the 'exiled' opposition leader Joshua Nkomo and the Ndele people. Mugabe, as leader of the majority Shona people, was simply

Crack Zimbabwean troops in training. In recent years it has become widely recognized that the 5th Brigade, trained by North Koreans, has been essentially out of control in Matabeleland.

perhaps the most important factor in the militarization of so many African states (even democracies like Kenya and Zimbabwe), which makes African governments and armies inseparable instruments of power now and in the foreseeable future.

In Angola the social, economic and political vacuum left behind by the Portuguese was filled by warring peoples

following in the traditions of African power politics; historically, the political authority of the African tribal chief has almost invariably derived from military might. It might be said that the chief function of the armed forces in Africa (and many other Third World regions) is not to defend against attack from abroad, but to support the government and keep order at home.

The colonial drawing of arbitrary boundaries, the imposition in some cases of European-style nation statehood and the many bitter wars of independence have not changed African traditions. Instead they have intensified ancient feuds. Hatchets that were temporarily buried by different groups or tribes while there was a common foe were later dug up to be used against each other.

In Nigeria, secessionist forces in Biafra catalysed one of the bloodiest and most bitter civil wars ever in Africa, which led to many more years of direct military rule. Indeed, the existence of tribal conflicts is

split into tribal divisions, which were variously supported by great-power interests. In Zimbabwe the merging of the different guerrilla armies seemed against all the odds. That it was nearly accomplished was due primarily to the expertise and professionalism which was the legacy of the British Army, but later the old strains reappeared, and because Mugabe could not trust the new 'national' army he created his own national guard.

During the past 25 years of turbulence, military depredation and economic deprivation the armed forces have become an entrenched and integral part of independent African government. This is no less true of white-run South Africa where military men hold important positions in government and where the army is, in the final analysis, both mentor and protector of the Afrikaaner tribe and its government. It is also true of many other countries outside Africa – especially those which are not within the Soviet bloc. (In the latter, the military are the

167

A United States Green Beret training Bolivian rangers. There has been considerable international disquiet over the extent of American involvement in South America in recent years. The United States points to the region's instability: Bolivia has had nearly 200 coups to date.

General Jaruzelski, military leader of Poland until the suspension of martial law in the summer of 1983. He enacted his coup almost reluctantly in 1981, impelled by the sight of his country being riven apart by the conflicts between Solidarity's demands and Poland's economic situation.

natural purveyors of authority for an authoritarian system of government.)

The Global Picture

Beyond the Soviet umbrella and the Western democracies (which are touched upon below) the relationship between governments and armies is a complex panoply made up of many disparate elements. It is made up of personalities such as the *caudillos*, the military politicians of Latin America; of economic pressures and the protection of economic resources; of religion and ideologies; of greed and fear; of military coups and palace revolutions; and of the social and economic integration of the military into society, as in China and Indonesia. The threads of this politico-military fabric are loosely woven, and the comparison of government-military relationships within continents and especially between continents can only be made in the broadest possible terms. What may appear to be a common ideological pattern often, under close scrutiny, dissolves into the local weaving of such factors as ambition, religious intolerance and economic crises or natural disaster. But there are two important common denominators: the personalities, including some of the most ruthless and charismatic leaders in the world, and the existence or threat of violence which, according to the Latin American Marxist guerrilla leader Che Guevara, was always justified as the 'midwife of history', and whose instrument, of course, is primarily the military.

A vast number of people have lived under direct military rule since the end of World War Two – one quarter of the world's population at some time or other during this period. The situation is fluid. Some nations, such as Nigeria, have gone back to civilian rule quite recently. Overall, 53 out of the 160 states for which data are available have had direct military rule at some time during the period 1945–82. In 1960 twelve per cent of the world's population was under military rule;

this figure had risen to almost twenty per cent by 1976; by 1981 it had gone down again to fifteen per cent. All these figures would be very much larger if those nations whose governments, though officially civilian, have strong military participation were included. Several examples of this pattern appear later in the chapter.

Military regimes vary a great deal. Some are comparatively benevolent, and

The Emperor Bokassa of the Central African Empire on his famous Eagle Throne. He was overthrown in 1979, as a result of his bringing his country to its economic knees. Both his coming to power and his overthrow were engineered by the French.

General Galtieri, leader of the Argentine military junta, on parade. His nationalistic drive towards the recapture of the Falkland Islands (Malvinas), intended to unite the people by diverting their attention from more pressing matters, led to defeat and his downfall.

MILITARY REGIMES
This includes regimes with substantial military participation

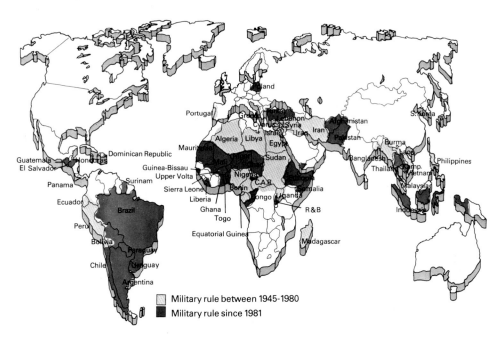

Military rule between 1945-1980
Military rule since 1981

represent a majority ethnic group or a majority class. Others have a well armed minority suppressing an unarmed majority. Some, such as the present military government in Afghanistan, are in essence foreign. In some a military dictator rules only with the tacit agreement of a military junta. In others, a military dictator's authority is largely vested in his own strength of personality or his personal popularity.

The Western Powers

Even in the Western democracies there is room occasionally for uncertainty about the extent to which the military can take political action without political consultation. It is still unclear, for example, who was responsible in the United Kingdom – military or politician – for the decision at the outset of the 1982 Falklands war with Argentina to sink the warship *Belgrano*. This action was a major turning point in escalating the conflict. The United States military seems to have acted independently of its political

masters at times. While the decision to bomb Hanoi during the Vietnam war was taken in the Oval Office, not all US actions in Vietnam had political backing. On the other hand, it was a political decision, determined both by domestic and international pressure, that forced the US military to fight a limited and unwinnable war in Vietnam.

It was the political philosopher Georg Wilhelm Friedrich Hegel who spoke of America as the land of the future '. . . where in the ages that lie before us, the burden of the world's history shall reveal itself . . .'. But whereas in North America the military–industrial establishment must resort to political manoeuvring through Washington's now institutionalized lobby system to persuade government to take a particular course of action, in most of South and Central America military personnel either run the country directly or their armies are an integral part of the government machinery. President Ronald Reagan's success in 1983 in getting Congress to

An indication of the vast numbers of peoples under military rule.

ratify the development of a new generation of MX nuclear missiles was a triumph for the White House, but also for the military lobby. There are other powerful and well-schooled lobbies in the United States, of course, but the military are particularly adept at appealing to national security and exploiting the frailties of politicians who act always with an eye on the next election.

In Europe, the military arm of government is particularly strong in France. Among Europe's nations with a colonial past during which the army was an instrument of aggressive foreign policy, France remains perhaps the most ready today to use such force to protect its international political and economic interests. Its direct participation in first setting up and then overthrowing Emperor Bokassa of the Central African Empire (now Republic) and its intervention in ridding southern Zaire of Katangese rebels who had overrun the mining town of Kolwezi in 1979 were specific examples of the very special relationship the Army has with the Elyse.

It is, however, possible to be over cynical about the degree to which the political servants of the Western democracies are prepared to submit themselves to the influence of the military. To take the most important example, most Americans and indeed the rest of the world derive some comfort from the fact that there are a series of constitutional checks and balances over those in charge of the world's most powerful military machine. In South America, as in most other parts of the world outside the Western alliance, those checks which arise out of the separation of powers between the legislature and the executive very often do not exist.

Latin America

It was Simon Bolivar, 'liberator of South America', who wanted a separation of executive and legislative powers similar to that of the United States, but who came to the disillusioned conclusion that

'America is ungovernable'. Although Latin American countries do not have a monopoly of experience when it comes to changing government by coups and palace revolutions, as a region it has certainly had more experience than most. Bolivia alone has had nearly 200.

At the beginning of the 1980s well over half the governments of Latin America – thirteen of them, including Bolivia, Guatemala, Honduras, Brazil, Chile, Argentina, Paraguay and Uruguay – were under direct or indirect military rule. A military career is traditionally one of the best roads to political power in much of the region. However, the emphasis has been changing. At one time many military governments were in effect the tool of one very powerful dictator. Now military rule is tending to be more institutional, with many members of the high command of the armed forces with a voice in

Fidel Castro of Cuba and Colonel Gaddafi of Libya, the leaders of two highly militarized, leftist nations, symbolically extend the hand of friendship to each other. Castro is the most unusual of Latin American caudillos, in that he has massive popular support and seems to be 'motivated by ethical principles'.

leaders (although in abstract terms he could have spread his net much wider) said that they fell into two categories: the 'doctors' (the politicians enamoured by ideas) and the 'generals'. The latter group was the breeding ground for the *caudillos*, who could come from almost any rank in the officer corps. They could also be civilians with close army or powerful family connections. Of these men he says: 'The general is not interested in principles ... His aim is power, and he feels no qualms as to the ways and means to attain it, or indeed, to retain it. He may be an officer with a certain level of technical military training and education, but not infrequently will be a self-made general, having reached the top of the military ladder by unorthodox ways, and a self-taught man, more self than taught. His knowledge of the roots of the country, the village square, pond, drink shop and police station will be concrete and extensive ... He will be quite astute, ruthless and, if need be, cruel.'

The nature of the *caudillo* and his rise to power in Latin America has changed in the latter half of this century but the style is similar. As Dr Collier points out, the political and social environment in which Colonel Peron climbed to power was '... certainly a great deal more sophisticated and complex than the one in which Juan Manuel Rosas [Argentine dictator 1835–52], for instance, exercised his baleful authority. But there are sufficient similarities between the boundaries of a common tradition.'

Perhaps the most fascinating *caudillo* to have arisen this century is Cuba's president, Fidel Castro. Dr Collier believes that there is little greed in Castro: 'It is most unlikely that he has salted away as much as a single peso in a Swiss bank account.' Most observers believe that Castro is motivated by ethical principles. This does not seem commonly true of Latin American leaders.

Without denying the Marxist or communist nature of the Cuban revolution, one can still emphasize the

government, and with the head of state being subject – to a degree – to their wishes. This is effectively rule by junta.

The Latin American specialist Dr Simon Collier in his book *From Cortes to Castro* (1974) recounts a conversation between a Chilean army officer, Jose Miguel Carrera, and a member of an influential Chilean family. The latter was: '... happily boasting that his various relatives now occupied all the senior positions in the patriot government – one was president of the congress, another president of the junta, a third president of the new supreme court, and so on. This did not amuse Carrera. "But who," he asked bluntly, "is the president of the bayonets?" Within weeks of that conversation, Carrera staged the first of the very few coup d'etats in Chilean history, thus proving *he* was.'

The Spanish author Salvador de Madariaga, speaking of Latin American

The aftermath of the 1979 military coup in Turkey. Upper, military police patrolling the streets of Istanbul enforcing the midnight to 8am curfew imposed shortly before by General Kenan Evren. Right, the seizure and round-up of suspected political terrorists. Evren's rule, while brutal (there were extensive *allegations of torture), may have been the lesser of two evils: before he took over Turkey was in a state of chaos, with widespread indiscriminate murder and a collapsing economy.*

great personal influence of Castro. Dr Collier refers to a distinguished Nicaraguan poet who was told in Cuba in 1970 that the Cubans '... were only superficially Marxist in outlook; what Cubans really were was "*fidelista* and if Fidel were to declare that Marxism is bad in Cuba, all the Cubans would cease to be Marxists".' Not many leaders in history can have had such power. What was once Castro's guerrilla army is now an agent of his foreign policy, which has provided troops to both Ethiopia and Angola in recent years to help prop up Soviet-backed governments.

Other Generals in Power

Military coups can take place in a variety of ways, and sometimes there is very little violence. However, in twentieth-century coups (there have been military coups in more than 40 nations since 1960) the successful insurgents have learned that it is better to risk temporary world opprobrium by killing the luckless incumbent than to have the embarrassing and risky problem of keeping him alive, but incarcerated. Pakistan's General Zia ul Haq will have secretly wished that when he took over Prime Minister Bhutto had been 'killed while resisting arrest'. Instead, in the public glare of the world press, he went through the charade of a political trial. Bhutto was found guilty on a series of trumped-up charges and, in Pontius Pilate style, General Zia washed his hands of the affair saying it was a matter for the courts. Bhutto was eventually hanged.

There are also examples of generals being brought into government reluctantly at first, but then having had a taste of power being reluctant to go. The assassination of South Korea's President Park left this US-supported country with a political hiatus through most of 1979 and 1980. Eventually Lieutenant General Chun Doo Hwan took over and with a mixture of repression, strict fiscal controls and liberal doses of J.M. Keynes's general theory of economics steadied the country's over-heated economic and political temperature. The military is still very much in control of most aspects of South Korean government and will remain so as long as there is a real or perceived threat from within the country or from the old enemy in the north.

Turkey's example of the reluctant generals is perhaps the best. Throughout the whole decade of the 1970s the Army, one of the biggest elements in the NATO alliance, remained committed to Kemalism. (Mustafa Kemal Ataturk was the 'father of the Turks' who dragged Turkey into the twentieth century and into Europe in the wake of the demise of the Ottoman Empire. He believed in civilian-run democratic government.) But the 1970s in Turkey were characterized by growing violence between right- and left-wing factions. Assassinations, indiscriminate bombings, wild gunfire into hotels and restaurants were all part of daily life in Turkey. This and the anachronistic banking system controlled by powerful families and the huge black economy all contributed to the near anarchy that prevailed in 1979 which led the Army to take over once again.

They had taken over on two previous occasions in the same decade to restore order before handing power back to the civilians. Both those attempts failed, and disorder returned. General Evren, his Prime Minister (also a general) Bulent Ulusu and the Supreme Council decided that the experiment had failed. They banned the old political parties and their politicians for ten years. Thousands of politicians and so-called activists were swept up in mass arrests and there were widespread allegations of torture. But by 1983 the streets of Ankara and Istanbul were once again safe at night and the performance of the economy was drawing approving nods from the International Monetary Fund (IMF) in Washington, which had already poured millions of dollars of standby credit into Turkey's coffers.

The IMF itself has been blamed both

fairly and unfairly in the past two decades for being either directly or indirectly the cause of coups and changes of government, especially in such economically crippled countries as Ghana. The IMF's recipe for financial recovery includes a sizeable currency devaluation, and indeed this is regularly a prerequisite for their help. In both developing and developed nations the local currency is part of the country's pride in itself – its national *machismo*. Devaluation is total anathema. (In Ghana, Accra's famous and colourful 'market mamas' wouldn't stand for it.) Today Ghana's leader Flight Lieutenant Rawlings is trying again to run a near-bankrupt economy with the help of inexperienced and ill-educated fellow military officers. (Rawlings had taken power in 1979, then handed the country back to a civilian government; his second coup – largely in response to the economic shambles he saw about him – was on 31 December, 1981.) There have been further approaches by Ghana to the IMF's 'gnomes', but with the political pressure in favour of conservatism that the IMF tacitly receives from the White House and Number 10 Downing Street, Ghana is in for a tough fight (despite the moral support of Libya).

Can Armies Work for the People?
One of the IMF's major adversaries has been the doyen of the Third World movement, Tanzania's president Julius Nyerere. Although not a military man himself, Nyerere is very much in control of his army. But for Nyerere a nation's army does not exist solely for national defence. His army has played a significant role in training the various armed guerrilla movements in southern Africa, and providing them with material support and succour. Here the Tanzanian Army has been a very specific tool for furthering Nyerere's ideologically-based foreign policy in Africa.

Nyerere has always wanted '. . . an army that understands the problems of building a nation, not an army isolated from the people'. This has also largely been the attitude of the older generation of soldiers across the world in the army of Indonesia – the fifth largest nation in the world. They have always worked on the assumption that as an essential part of government the military has a central role to play in uniting the nation and guiding its development. But there is in Indonesia a new generation of soldier, the young professional, more interested in weaponry than in social and political affairs. This division has been highlighted by a growing realization that too many very senior military men held important ministerial posts. In the days of Brigadier General Suharto's 'New Order' (he became President in 1967) the various heads of the armed forces lost their ministerial rank as well as their command function and were put under the direct control of the Defence Minister as chiefs of staff. The thinking behind this move was to cut the direct links between the President and the services and so reduce their role as a political tool. There was also the expedient of divide and rule: combining the jobs of Defence Minister and Commander of the Armed Forces vested far too much power in one man.

The old military establishment in Indonesia, on the other hand, is trying to cope with the vexed problem of integrating the army into society. They introduced the 'Abri Masuk Desa' programme which was meant to create opportunities for young officers to understand social and political affairs. Under the programme the military men help with construction and other social work in the villages. In Indonesia the dual role of the army in society as a military protector and civilian developer is well entrenched. Indeed, in 1981 40,000 military officers (out of a total of 300,000) also held civilian positions. The difficulties lie in different styles of direction between the younger and the older officers. The army is the country's wealthiest and most technologically advanced employer, so that for the time being it will continue to attract the country's best minds.

While Indonesia's army, like some others, is an integrated and integral part of the society it protects, this is not true in many countries. Many governments, notably in Africa, are faced with the problem of maintaining large armies which they know that they cannot dismantle because of the social and economic implications, and above all the danger of creating even worse unemployment. Nigeria, for example, boasts one of the largest armies in Africa (it is quite considerable by world standards), and with a population of one hundred million, huge unemployment and probably the world's worst case of urban drift (people coming from the country to the cities) plus a history of military rule since independence and a disastrous civil war not so long ago there is very little the civilian government can do about it, although official Nigerian policy is to reduce the army's size. Likewise in Zimbabwe: with a population growth of 3.6 per cent a year, the highest in the world, the Harare authorities cannot afford to have such a large and indeed disparate army, but they cannot afford to dismantle it.

These and many other governments have tried to get these rather idle but well-trained men into the civilian sector of the economy. But this in turn causes problems because the cheapness of military labour is often a direct cause of civilian unemployment. There are, however, opportunities for making some projects economically viable by using cheap military labour supplemented by civilian labour. Once again the Indonesian example comes to mind. The military coup in 1966 had terrible consequences – *half a million* supposed communists were massacred and perhaps 200,000 people placed in political detention. In fact the coup, though it certainly had political elements, was largely due to army frustration at the limitations of civilian rule which in the military minds was not keeping pace with the modernization the army wanted. The army regarded itself as

being in the vanguard of change. This caused several tensions, one of them being the necessity to reduce the armed services' aloofness so that they could begin digging ditches and building roads.

Civilian Roles
The image we have of the military in the Third World is largely as an instrument of internal repression. This is quite often an accurate picture, though as we have shown the role of maintaining civil order is sometimes truly necessary, and preferable to chaos or civil war. As we have also suggested in passing, the armed forces can have a constructive role in maintaining the coherence of society and the coherence of the state. It is all too unconsciously easy for those of us who live in relative comfort in the developed Western World to be appalled at the dominating role of military forces in so much of the Third World, but it is often a mistake to stereotype this role as all 'black', or all 'white' if it comes to that. The positive and negative aspects of politico-military power are both suggested by examining the three important 'civilian' roles of the armed forces as proposed by H. Hanning in his book *The Peaceful Uses of Military Forces* (1967).

Hanning argues that the role of the army in civilian life falls into three broad categories, all usually under the direct control of government. First, the army is almost invariably brought in during natural disasters for emergency relief and during domestic civil disturbances such as strikes. In the 1983 British general election much was made by opposition candidates of allegedly secret proposals by the Conservative government to introduce a greater role for the army in terms both of providing emergency relief and of training to take over essential services during strikes. During a 1982 water workers' strike in the United Kingdom there were widespread calls from the ranks of the ruling Conservative party for a ban on strikes in the essential services and for the use of the army in such cases. But this brought considerable disquiet in certain quarters: a cursory glance at the world's more authoritarian states – such as those of the Soviet bloc, and South Africa – shows that the rulers of those countries also ban such civilian activity as strikes and have the army well prepared to take over should it be necessary.

Hanning's second point involves using the military for education and training which should be integrated into any national manpower policy and resettlement programme.

Hanning's third point involves the use of the army in economic and social programmes. David K. Whynes in his study *The Economics of Third World Military Expenditure* (1979) says that the need for such military integration is both familiar and important. The reasons include the issue of allocation of scarce resources (the 'guns versus butter' dichotomy). They also include the sad fact '. . . that cuts in military expenditure and manpower seem to be impossible to

make, owing to the vested interests of military personnel'. Whynes believes that the use of the military by governments in such civilian activity would humanize the army by improving its image and by developing a spirit of co-operation rather than maintaining an image of oppression and aggression. He admits that there are problems of what he calls 'deprofessionalization'. This is of particular concern among the younger army officers in Indonesia who as discussed above believe that their 'socialization' detracts from the true purpose of their job.

In those regimes ruled directly by the military it can be expected that many of the top domestic and foreign appointments will be of a military nature. There are, indeed, examples (such as the Philippines) where although the primacy of civilian government and control is continually stressed, the military has been so integrated into society that many of the top government and diplomatic positions are also held by military personnel.

The President of the Philippines, Ferdinand Marcos (in power since 1965), has cleverly used carrot and stick to keep the military Leviathan in check. Nevertheless the army has been given a taste of power that it will find hard to give up. Certainly the upper echelons of the military hierarchy have received what by now may be an insatiable taste for the fringe economic benefits that go with their expanded role in society. After 1972 and martial law, the army's more favoured

Upper left and right: the two faces of Saudi Arabia, the old and the new. On one side a Sa'udi soldier, probably American-trained, wears the latest in military gear; on the other, a Sa'udi prince makes ready for falconry. Lower left: President Ferdinand Marcos of the Philippines, flanked by military associates, reviews a military parade. The powerful Philippine military, *which contains several Marcos relatives, was much publicized in September 1983 when they failed to prevent the assassination of an opposition leader supposedly under their protection; one Japanese reporter said he saw soldiers do the shooting, but this is unlikely.*

sons began to acquire lucrative fishing and logging interests. They became board members of various banks and companies, and although they have never quite cracked the snobbish old-boy network that would give them access to high society and the clubs of Manila, they still remain an important if not the most important element of President Marcos's elite entourage. Marcos has worked hard to keep the army on his side as a part of his government machinery. He continually stresses how much army salaries have gone up and what he does for army widows.

Marcos is cast in similar mould to that of the Latin American military heads of state, the *caudillos*. He is the Philippines' most decorated World War Two soldier and he continually plays up his own achievements as a guerrilla leader and brave soldier. He is typical of the innumerable personalities who have provided that umbilical link between governments and armies in the history of modern nation-states.

The Middle East

Personalities have also been at the centre of the intricate politico-social-military relationships of the Middle East, both at home and abroad. Perhaps the most durable of these complex systems is that of the House of Sa'ud which has governed the now immensely rich desert kingdom of Sa'udi (Saudi) Arabia for most of this century. It was the extraordinarily charismatic Abdul Aziz Ibn Sa'ud who with a small band set out in 1901 across the desert from Kuwait to capture Riyadh, today the capital of Sa'udi Arabia. The history of Arabia shows clearly that he who dominated and controlled the most powerful military force ruled the longest.

Today the Kingdom can afford to buy the latest in military technology but it suffers from a shortage of manpower. They have 'bought' the services of Asian brigades to protect the country, and the Europeans and Americans are present in large numbers introducing Sa'udis to the complexities of their weapons. But despite the length of its rule and its seemingly impregnable position the House of Sa'ud has been and still considers itself to be under threat. For this reason it has its own praetorian guard known as the National Guard. While in the mid-1970s lavish sums of money were spent on US weaponry, partly in response to the Iraqi threat and partly because of the Sa'udi concern at the grandoise military build-up undertaken by the Shah of Iran, this did not all go into the national army. The National Guard has played an important part in the Kingdom's political in-fighting. Run by the very senior and powerful Prince Abdullah, son of one of the survivors of the Rashid clan whom Abdul Aziz married after capturing the Rashid-held city of Hail with the National Guard, this personal army was involved closely with the final abdication of King Sa'ud and in putting down coup attempts in the 1950s and 1960s.

In 1975 a 330-million-dollar deal was signed by the Sa'udis and the United States to boost the National Guard into a highly efficient fighting force. Nearly one thousand US servicemen, many of whom were Vietnam veterans, took part in the training programme. David Holden and Richard Johns in their definitive work *The House of Saud* (1981) recall speculation at the time that the arrangement had greatly furthered the CIA's penetration of the Kingdom.

The region's 35 years of Arab–Israeli conflict has led to the military playing a vital role in the decision-making process of government throughout the region, but worries about Israel are only one factor leading to the political strength of the military. Just as important a factor for the security-minded Arab leaders, some of whom hold office by the skin of their teeth, has been the Islamic revival in the 1960s and 1970s culminating in the siege of Makkah (Mecca), the crushing of the Muslim Brotherhood and the destruction of Hamra City by the Syrian Army, the rise to power in Iran of a devout and

the men at the top, and are likely to be upset from time to time by splits within themselves – by palace revolutions and army coups. It is probable that those who come to power in this way will continue to rule within the same broad framework of "national development" as those whom they replaced.'

This statement could effectively apply, with few exceptions (the democratically elected nations and the Soviet bloc) to most regions and many countries throughout the world.

The presence of armed forces so close to the seats of government and the hearts of power around the world is one of the major factors that could lead to Future War. The reduction of regional conflict should be a global priority, and where regional conflicts (often involving military governments) do occur, the great powers must take every possible precaution against being sucked in.

Gavin Shreeve

fundamentalist monk, the Ayatollah Khomeini, and the assassination of Egyptian President Anwar Sadat by the Muslim Brothers.

Albert Hourani of St Antony's College, Oxford, believes that though there is more than one possible view of what Islam really is and what it imposes on believers, the consensus of opinion about the area is that '. . . the state will always win'. Hourani takes a wholly realistic view of the region: 'In modern circumstances, whoever controls the machinery of government has such a vast power of coercion in his hands that he can always suppress opposition. This does not mean that he who has power will have it forever; although on the whole there has been stability, at least in the Arab countries, during the 1970s, most regimes have no deep root in popular sentiment and loyalties; they rest in the end on armed force and the solidarity of

References

Collier, Simon, **From Cortes to Castro**, Martin Secker & Warburg, London, 1974
de Madariaga, Salvador, quoted in Collier, Simon, **From Cortes to Castro**
Hanning, H., **The Peaceful Uses of Military Forces**, Praeger, New York, 1967
Holden, David and Johns, Richard, **The House of Saud**, Sidgwick and Jackson, London, 1981
Hourani, Albert, in Royal Institute of International Affairs, **Islam in the Political Process**, Cambridge University Press, Cambridge, 1983
Whynes, David K., **The Economics of Third World Military Expenditure**, Macmillan, London, 1979

The Ayatollah Khomeini holds one of his weekly sessions at which invited guests come to hear him speak. Before the dais stands a rank of 'Pasdarans', the Guardians of the Revolution. The regime of Khomeini is the most overt manifestation of the Islamic revival of the 1960s and 1970s.

Chapter 15

Problems and Prospects

Preventing Future War is not quite the same thing as preventing future wars. The disaster we all fear, of course, is a Future World War Three: a global holocaust that would probably set back the cultural evolution of mankind by many hundreds of years and put an end to civilization as we now know it.

The black absurdity of the situation is that such a war could take place even though nobody – except a tiny handful of psychopaths – wants it. Many of the economic, political and technological mechanisms that make such a war more likely have already been described in these pages, notably the advances in ballistic-missile sophistication that make the concept of nuclear weapons as a deterrent less and less likely to be workable. Thus the uneasy rationale for the building up of the Superpowers' nuclear arsenals is rapidly losing its logic, but the weapons remain.

Many political leaders, of course, point to the fact that there has been no global conflict since the end of the World War Two. The proof of the pudding is in the eating, they say; the nuclear deterrent has worked. Be that as it may (and there can be no proof that the unstable and rickety world peace of the past three decades or so is the direct result of the nuclear arsenals rather than other factors), the system is unlikely to retain its teetering balance for very much longer, and now ways of ensuring world peace are urgently needed. Public perception of this instability has been growing rapidly, as is demonstrated by the present renewed vitality of the anti-nuclear movements after years of comparative quiet. This is especially evident in Europe, which, it has become clear, is the likeliest first victim in World War Three.

A demonstration by members of CND (Campaign for Nuclear Disarmament) and of END (European Nuclear Disarmament) against the deployment in Europe of American cruise missiles.

The problem then becomes that of communicating public disquiet to the politicians and the military establishment who collaborate in maintaining the nuclear *status quo*. A major obstacle in achieving this is that many of the potential leading actors in such a conflict are partially insulated from the unglamorous realities of the mundane world.

An illuminating digression: a tourist driving westwards out of Death Valley in California rises up from the valley floor through a barren but beautiful desert landscape as he slowly climbs across a plateau to the Nevada state line. A little further on he encounters, against a fantastically contorted backdrop of buttes and rocky spurs – perhaps glowing bright red in the dying sunlight – signs warning him that he has reached the perimeter of the Nuclear Testing Grounds. It is alarming to consider that it is in this primeval, utterly inorganic seeming setting with practically no visible evidence of human occupation – like something from the face of the Moon – that the weapons of tomorrow are put to trial. The point is that it must be all too easy amid this apocalyptic, tormented scenery, to imagine nuclear weapons as being almost 'natural'. The craters left by the underground tests are not unlike the volcanic indentations that already mark nearby desert areas.

We might feel more comfortable about the prospects of world peace if the nuclear elite were less isolated. Deep in shelters under the Rockies, or in submarines beneath the sea, or thousands of feet aloft in airborne command planes, the people who may have to press the buttons must find it all too easy to see themselves as playing a role in some sort of fiction. An analysis of the psychological factors that might lead to Future War is outside the brief of this book – and too speculative, perhaps, to be really meaningful. But it can be said with some confidence that if military and political leaders were less cut off from the ups and downs of everyday life, they would be less likely to translate their cold, hypothetical war-gaming theories into action.

Local Wars

Future wars – the smaller variety – may be less dreadful than the possible finality of the ultimate Future War. But we cannot afford to be smug about them. It would be a mistake to suppose that it is only high-technology war on a global scale that poses the final threat. Just as in geology, the slow action of wind and tide has done as much to reshape the face of Earth as the more spectacular eruptions of molten magma and the clashes of tectonic plates, so, in modern civilization, it may be that irreparable damage to our moral stature as human beings might be created by the continuous abrasion around the globe of localized conflicts. At any one time these smaller wars are leading to an intolerable life for people in, say, twelve different areas of the world. It is appalling to realize just how many people have died in warfare and acts of genocide during the long 'peace' since the end of World War Two: millions upon millions. Hot spots, especially in the Middle East, in Africa, in Central America and in South East Asia, flicker continuously, sporadically blazing up and never quite dying away.

As we have pointed out, there is an ever-present danger that any one of these conflicts could erupt (because of the interests of the Superpowers) into general war. But even if they do not, the conditions they create for far too many of the World's people must remain a dreadful stain on the conscience of the World as a whole – and particularly (it could be argued) on the consciences of the major arms-producing nations: in the West the big seven of the United States, the Soviets, France, Italy, the United Kingdom, West Germany and (surprisingly to some) neutral Sweden; in the Third World the big seven (comparative midgets) of China, Brazil, Argentina, Israel, India, Taiwan and South Africa. No citizen of these fourteen nations in particular can affect an air of moral superiority to the barbarities taking place in small, impoverished nations like Chad or Guatemala, or even rather stronger ones like Iraq and Iran. Firefighters are not supposed to make money on the side by selling the fuel that maintains the blaze.

Military technology is not only developing superweapons for use in nuclear war. The comparatively light armaments used around the world in many brushfire wars are also increasing in sophistication and deadliness: light missiles, radar and laser rangefinders, fragmentation bombs and so on. More people have been and are being killed by rifles and grenades than by atomic weapons. Indeed, attempts to import high technology into low-technology conflicts have often been unsuccessful. In August 1983 it was reported that American ground-to-air missiles given to the government of Chad to use against the Libyan-backed rebels in the north of that wartorn country failed completely. According to some reports the weapons themselves were defective, but the more likely report is that the Chad military did not have the expertise to maintain and use the weapons correctly.

Science Fiction Warfare
The popular media during the 1970s and early 1980s gave great publicity to the science-fictional aspects of future warfare. These were, after all, the years in which *Star Wars* became the most successful film ever made. Fortunately perhaps, the prospects of science-fictional superweapons do not look particularly bright in practice. Much has been made (*see* Chapter Eight) of the possibility of mounting laser and particle-beam weapons on platforms in space, but the practical difficulties are immense, and the idea (used in several James Bond movies) of a villainous power holding the world to ransom from a fortress in the sky is likely to remain fictional for a long time, despite the apparent *imprimatur* that Ronald Reagan gave to the idea in his 'Star Wars'

speech of March 1983. For one thing, space satellites are not highly manoeuvrable, and would be extremely vulnerable to attack from Earth-launched missiles.

The technology of warfare is indeed becoming science-fictional in many respects, but the reality is far from the futuristic super-weapons envisaged by comic-book artists and movie directors. The sophisticated microelectronics that are at the heart of most new weapons systems lie cradled in boring black boxes, and tanks, aircraft, submarines and even missiles look much the same as they ever did. The much-feared cruise missiles, whose introduction into the European theatre by the Americans led to widely spread demonstrations in the early 1980s do indeed have remarkable capabilities. But in essence they consist of a cylinder with a jet engine, almost identical to the German V-1 flying bomb of World War Two. The new developments – the amazingly sophisticated guidance system and the nuclear warhead – are covered up and not reflected in any outward futurism of design. These instruments of death look considerably less sleek, say, than a modern automobile or power boat, and their flight appears lumbering and cumbersome.

Another science-fictional aspect of modern warfare is the use of 'drones' – robot aircraft. They do not, however, look like anything from *Star Wars*; rather, they resemble rickety monoplanes from the early years of powered flight.

In a perverse sort of way it would be exciting to catalogue the military marvels of tomorrow with the kind of awestruck breathlessness that sometimes appears in articles on the subject in the popular press, but aside from the dubious morality of such armchair applause for instruments of death, it is not especially easy to do. It is difficult to imagine any really plausible, really new kind of weapon that will be developed in the next decade or two. There has been much talk in science fiction about the use of robots, cyborgs and even androids (artificially created beings of flesh and blood) in future conflict, but the military utility of such devices is doubtful. We *already* have war-robots – 'smart' machines, as the Americans call them. The cruise missile and the Assault Breaker anti-tank missile are two examples. They may not have arms and legs, but then arms and legs are not very useful in high-technology warfare.

The cliches of science fiction, then, may bear no obvious relationship to fact, either now or in the immediately foreseeable future. Yet the science fiction writers did get it right when they foretold the progressive automation of war. It used to be that the greatest need for military manpower was in the front lines, but in any likely scenario for high-technology future war, the primary need for manpower will be behind the lines, especially for the maintenance of extremely delicate automated equipment. The actual battlefield of the future may be quite sparsely populated so far as human beings go, though thickly sown with sensors and mines, and heavily bombarded by quasi-intelligent missiles. This, at least, is the scenario as it can be deduced from the contents of the Superpowers' arsenals. In practice, this rather hygienic form of war seems as far away as ever.

The continuing conflict between Iraq and Iran, for example, has been marked by mass assaults by twelve-year-old Iranian boys against well-entrenched Iraqi fortifications, despite the fact that both nations at the beginning of the war had access to many sophisticated weapons. The bloody and horrible slaughter that ensued may in terms of chronology be one of the nearest approaches to a future war that we can observe today, but in terms of its nature it is remarkably reminiscent of such events as the Charge of the Light Brigade in the Crimea (not so very far away from Iraq) more than a century ago.

Other futuristic methods of waging war have been suggested, many of them based on triggering or directing 'natural' disasters against an enemy – perhaps by altering the path of a hurricane, or creating tidal waves or even setting off earthquakes. There is a recent treaty against the use of such weapons (*see below*), but this means little, since nobody in practice knows how to do the triggering. There were many American attempts at rainmaking in Vietnam and Cambodia, but these were feeble in comparison and may not have worked at all.

We are so used to thinking of nuclear explosions as the biggest kind of explosion there is that we forget how much raw energy can be supplied by Nature herself. A major earthquake will release many hundreds of times more energy than the explosive power of the largest nuclear bombs. Even the energy contained in a hurricane dwarfs that of nuclear weapons. Our most potent weapons may well be inadequate as triggers for natural calamities, and even supposing that such a calamity were triggered, its results would be unpredictable and possibly harmless. Surprisingly few people were injured, for example, by the explosion of Krakatoa.

Glitches

We already possess 'futuristic' weapons. The question is, will they work in battle? Fortunately, there have been few really high-technology conflicts so far, and so the opportunities for testing modern weaponry in battlefield conditions have been relatively few. That is one reason why nations such as the United States followed the Falklands conflict with such close attention, and indeed much was learned, for example, about the difficulties of defending warships against air-launched missiles during that short war. The battle exercises in which weapons are tested may not approximate the actual conditions of war.

As we showed in Chapter Eleven, the more sophisticated modern weaponry becomes, the longer the maintenance periods that are required and the shorter the periods of trouble-free operation. Many main battle tanks and modern fighter aircraft operate only for very short periods before breaking down. Back-up circuits are often designed into such weapons in case the primary circuits fail, but this added complexity not only adds to the expense, it may create yet more opportunities for things to go wrong.

Anti-militarists may well find this problem more amusing than dismaying when it applies to tanks and aircraft, but it may not be at all funny when it comes to the radar and computer networks that warn of an enemy nuclear attack. There are many instances already on record of electronic equipment giving false warning of such an attack, and it is a horrifying thought that a badly programmed computer or a short circuit might, through the false information it imparts, be the direct cause of war. There are, of course, a great many precautions against such accidents leading to 'retaliation', and so far nothing too terrible has happened, but the possibility remains.

The difficulty is in checking whether or not the electronic systems are working correctly. Some computer systems are so massively complex that they cannot be directly checked by humans; special computer programs are used to check the computers, and this can be a lengthy business. The communications networks on which Future War must rely –especially for Early Warning of attack –have become so automated that their workings are becoming less and less susceptible to human intervention.

To put the quandary bluntly: the intensity with which the technological arms race is being conducted is leading to the production of unreliable and erratic equipment. Futuristic weaponry sometimes appears designed by Heath Robinson rather than George Lucas.

Will There Be a World War Three?

The answer, of course, is that nobody knows, but the factors for and against can be summarized. The following factors (all of them discussed elsewhere in this book) increase the threat of nuclear war:

* The arsenals of the Superpowers contain weaponry capable of destroying the entire population of the world many times over
* These arsenals are growing
* Although the Superpowers have demonstrated a measure of self-restraint over the past decades, nuclear weapons may soon be available to more overtly fanatic nations
* The Superpowers defend the interests of their client states, with the result that local conflicts have the potential for flaring up into much larger wars
* The defence industries generate great profits and employ many people: thus they constitute a potent political lobby
* The Third World nations, especially those of the Middle East, are buying more arms than ever before, and the major arms-supplier nations are happy with this
* Unrest (often caused by deprivation) is increasing in the Third World
* Improvements in the accuracy of nuclear-weapon delivery systems have made the temptation to win a war by striking first stronger than before
* A fiery patriotism is strongly encouraged by the governments and media of all major world powers; the result is a climate of opinion that encourages aggression if national interests, no matter how remotely, seem to be threatened
* Existing strategies for arms control have consistently proved ineffective.

And these are some of the factors that make such a Future War less likely:

* Nobody wants a war in which both sides are decimated and few can readily contemplate a war in which only one side is destroyed; such a result would anyway be difficult to guarantee

* Nuclear war threatens the stability of the entire population of the world
* Military spending is severely affecting the economies of the great powers, and the old argument that defence industries create employment is looking shaky
* Technological developments are beginning to shift the balance of power from offensive to defensive weapons, especially in conventional weaponry
* Modern weapons are both expensive and unreliable
* Tanks, aircraft and warships are becoming more vulnerable to attack from missiles
* Some weapons systems, notably fighter aircraft, have become so complex that it is becoming very difficult indeed to find people fast and clever enough to operate them; the limits of human capacity are being reached
* The Superpowers have not yet gone to war against one another, and there is no evidence that they wish to
* Civilian protests against militarization are becoming more powerful, and the time may be coming when governments can no longer dismiss such protests.
* The economic boom during which the major arsenals were built up is over; it has become clear that the world economy, currently in great difficulties, will have to find new priorities, especially in terms of fighting economic and ecological deprivation in the Third World; the result may be to force a reduction in defence spending.

These factors can not be quantified. One might guess that at present the likelihood of nuclear war is much less than 50 per cent, but a guess is all it is. On the other hand, local wars are likely to increase in scale and ferocity. The situation is critical but not hopeless. The war industries around the world have a terrible

momentum, but it is still possible that the mighty energies that have produced that momentum can be redeployed. What has the community of nations actually managed to achieve in this respect?

Disarmament
'Disarmament' refers to getting rid of arms – making the present arsenals smaller – and 'arms control' refers to not buying or building new ones. During the 1950s the concept of disarmament was still very much alive. During the 1960s the emphasis shifted to arms control.

Arms-control advocates claim that in a world of security-conscious sovereign states, disarmament can only come about – if at all – as the end product of a lengthy process. Although the language used in the hundreds of international meetings on the topic is more formal, the gist is that it makes sense to start small and work up to bigger things, as mutual confidence between the powers grows.

The actual measures that have been negotiated are not very spectacular. There are eight major multilateral arms-control treaties, and in addition some important bilateral treaties negotiated directly between the USA and the USSR.

The eight treaties are:

1 The Antarctic Treaty (1961); it prohibits the militarization of the Antarctic;
2 The Outer Space Treaty (1967), which does the same for space; it forbids the placing of weapons of mass destruction in Earth orbit;
3 The Treaty of Tlatelolco (1967), which makes Latin America a nuclear-free zone; or it would do, except that neither Argentina nor Brazil have fully acceded to the treaty, which gravely weakens it;
4 The Partial Test Ban Treaty (1963) which (the most important of the eight) bans nuclear-weapon tests in the atmosphere and outer space, and under water; this has reduced contamination, but has not slowed

testing; it has merely changed the venues; underground tests continue at about the same rate as had previously been the case for other kinds of test – around 1300 tests from 1945 to 1982, of which 833 were since the treaty; France and China have not signed;

5 The Non-Proliferation Treaty (1970); this is discussed in Chapter Four; it is a fragile instrument because of the number of non-signatories;

6 The Sea-Bed Treaty (1972) prohibits the emplacement of nuclear weapons on the sea bed but says nothing about submarines;

7 The Biological Weapon Convention (1975) prohibits the development, production and stockpiling of biological and toxin weapons; the USA has announced the destruction of its stockpiles; the USSR has not, never having admitted having them in the first place;

8 The Environmental Modification Convention (1978) prohibits such techniques as creating tidal waves, hurricanes and earthquakes – techniques which anyway do not exist.

The Hot Line and Bilateral Agreements

The first bilateral arms-control treaty between the USA and USSR set up the 'hot line', a direct communications link between Washington and Moscow, in 1963. A second hotline agreement came into force in 1971 to improve the reliability of the system by the use of communications satellites. This may have been influenced by the surreal event of the late 1960s when a Danish farmer severed the hot line while ploughing his field! Since no back-up system was in force at the time, an international crisis might well have had some very worried telephonists trying to fight their way through the conventional telephone system to reach the unlisted numbers at the other end.

A rapid communications link between the Superpowers is obviously valuable in clarifying intentions at times of crisis, and

avoiding misunderstandings. The hot line has been officially used on several occasions, including the Middle East crises of 1967, 1970 and 1973.

Other bilateral agreements include measures for reducing the likelihood of any accidental outbreak of nuclear war (1971) and a Treaty on the Limitation of Underground Nuclear Tests (1974). The latter has not yet been ratified by the US Senate, although its mild provisions (no testing of weapons with a yield greater than 150 kt – about twelve times the size of the Hiroshima bomb) appear to be adhered to.

SALT I and II

By far the most familiar and important bilateral agreements are those that have come from the Strategic Arms Limitation Talks (SALT) that began in 1969. The first SALT agreement (SALT I) came into force in 1972, by which time the nuclear arms race had already shifted from a race for quantity to a race for quality. SALT I can be said to have legitimized this shift, since there are no restrictions on the increasing sophistication of weapons, such as the building of multiple warheads.

The main restrictions of SALT I were on the building of anti-ballistic missile systems (ABM systems) and on the total number of ICBM and SLBM launchers. Under a 1974 protocol each power is limited to the deployment of one hundred ABMs at only one site. In fact, the USA has not yet deployed any ABMs. The Soviets have deployed fewer than one hundred ABMs around Moscow.

The SALT II Treaty, which supersedes SALT I in some of its provisions, was signed by Carter and Brezhnev in 1979, and is to remain in force until 1986. It has not yet been ratified by the US Senate, but both powers appear to be obeying its provisions, although President Reagan has said that SALT II is 'fatally flawed'.

The SALT II Treaty limits each side to 2,500 strategic nuclear delivery systems. These include ICBMs, SLBMs and nuclear-armed long-distance aircraft. A sub-limit totalling 1,320 is placed on MIRVed ICBMs and SLBMs and on the number of aircraft equipped with long-range (over 600 km) cruise missiles. Of these 1,320, no more than 1,200 may be MIRVed ICBMs and SLBMs, and of these 1,200 no more than 820 can be MIRVed ICBMs. Current bombers are limited to 20 air-launched cruise missiles each.

How effective?
The multilateral treaties are not wholly ineffective, but they are gravely weakened by the absence of some nations' signatures. It is notable that they ban nuclear weapons from environments in which there is anyway little or no interest. Similarly, biological weapons (which are tricky and could rebound on the user) are banned, but the equally dreadful chemical weapons are not.

The Partial Test Ban Treaty is useful, but the only really efficient way of putting an ultimate end to the arms race in this manner would be by way of a *comprehensive* test ban treaty. In the long run such a ban would be essentially equivalent to nuclear disarmament because of the military need to test, from time to time, a nuclear warhead taken at random from the stockpile. If governments were unable to do this, they would eventually lose confidence that the weapons would work satisfactorily in war and would thus become unwilling to use them. Trilateral talks between the USA, the UK and USSR on a comprehensive test ban were indefinitely adjourned in 1980.

The SALT process (which left the Superpowers with ample nuclear arms for mutual destruction) has for all practical purposes been abandoned. In June, 1982, the two Superpowers began the Strategic Arms Reduction Talks (START) in Geneva. Current American proposals would eliminate about 2,250 missiles and (taking MIRVs into account) about 4,700 warheads. The Soviets under this system would be forced to alter their 'mix' of weapons more substantially than the Americans, since the Soviet nuclear arsenal is largely land-based, whereas the Americans make greater use of submarine- and air-launched missiles. The American proposals leave air-launched cruise missiles to one side in the first phase. There are few present signs of a possible agreement.

To summarize: arms-control measures over the past two decades have failed to produce *any* nuclear disarmament or even to halt the nuclear arms race between the USA and USSR. In spite of this, many ordinary people are under the impression that steady progress is being made – largely because each new measure is greeted by political leaders with pomp, ceremony and euphoria.

It may be that only well-informed pressure on governments from ordinary people will finally force the adoption of more stringent measures. In the meantime, it can only be said that unless arms control leading to disarmament is achieved, the Future War that is the subject of this book must be regarded as the greatest and most immediate threat that the world has ever faced.

Frank Barnaby and Peter Nicholls

In 1979 President Jimmy Carter and Premier Leonid Brezhnev signed the SALT II Treaty, shook hands and then embraced. However, the treaty has yet to be ratified by the US Senate. Until recently, nevertheless, the two Superpowers seemed tacitly to have agreed to abide by its terms.

Most of the trouble is with acronyms — words made up entirely of initials — like the 'CIA' (Central Intelligence Agency). The list below is not exhaustive by any means, but it includes all the jargon acronyms that have crept into this book. We thought of banning acronyms altogether, but this would have meant repeating long and cumbersome phrases over and over again, and would in any case have been unrealistic, since these are the actual terms most often used by the military themselves, and indeed in newspapers and books.

ABM	Anti-Ballistic Missile
AIRS	Advanced Inertial Reference Sphere
AIS	Avionics Intermediate Shop
ALCM	Air-launched Cruise Missile
ASW	Anti-Submarine Warfare
AWACS	Airborne Warning and Control System
CD	Committee on Disarmament
CEP	Circular Error Probability
C31	Command, Control, Communications and Intelligence (the first three are sometimes called C^3, pronounced see-cubed)
DOAE	Defence Operational Analysis Establishment
ECM	Electronic Countermeasures
Elint	Electronic Intelligence
EMP	Electromagnetic Pulse
GCD	General and Complete Disarmament
GNP	Gross National Product
IAEA	International Atomic Energy Agency
ICBM	Intercontinental Ballistic Missile
IFF	Identification — Friend or Foe
IMF	International Monetary Fund
MIRV	Multiple Independently-targetable Re-entry Vehicle
NATO	North Atlantic Treaty Organization
NEWS	Navy Electronic War Simulator
NMC	Not Mission Capable
NPT	Nuclear Non-Proliferation Treaty
R and D	Research and Development
RPV	Remotely Piloted Vehicle
SALT	Strategic Arms Limitation Talks
SIPRI	Stockholm International Peace Research Institute
SLBM	Submarine-launched Ballistic Missile
START	Strategic Arms Reduction Talks
TERCOM	Terrain Contour Matching System (used in programming missiles to recognize the landscape)
TNT	Trinitrotoluene (an explosive)
TOW	Tube-launched, Optically-tracked, Wire-guided missile

There are a number of references to specific topics given after most of the individual chapters. Some of these – those with a more general application – are repeated below.

The Annuals
These are books with a new edition every year. The most recent edition only is cited, but in many cases back issues contain still relevant material.

International Institute for Strategic Studies, **The Military Balance – 1982-1983**, IISS, London, 1982

Sivard, Ruth Leger, **World Military and Social Expenditures – 1982**, World Priorities, Leesburg, Virginia, 1982

Soviet Military Power, US Government Printing Office, March 1983

Stockholm International Peace Research Institute, **World Armaments and Disarmament, SIPRI Yearbook 1983**, Taylor and Francis, London, 1983

United Nations, **United Nations Disarmament Yearbook**, UN, New York, 1983

Whence the Threat to Peace, Military Publishing House, Moscow, 1982

Other References
Barnaby, C.F. and Thomas, G.P. (eds), **The Nuclear Arms Race: Control or Catastrophe**, Francis Pinter, London, 1982

Boston Study Group, **The Price of Defense**, Times Books, New York, 1979

British Medical Association, **The Medical Effects of Nuclear War**, Wiley, Chichester, UK, 1983

Dickson, Paul, **The Electronic Battlefield**, Indiana University Press, Bloomington, Indiana, 1976

Gunston, W., **Encyclopedia of Rockets and Missiles**, Salamander, London, 1979

Hanning, H., **The Peaceful Uses of Military Forces**, Praeger, New York, 1967

Kaldor, Mary, **The Baroque Arsenal**, Andre Deutsch, London, 1982

Kidron, Michael and Smith, Dan, **The War Atlas: Armed Conflict – Armed Peace**, Pan, London, 1983

Melman, Seymour, **The Permanent War Economy: American Capitalism in Decline**, Touchstone, New York, 1974

Myrdal, Alva, **The Game of Disarmament**, Pantheon, New York, 1976

Newhouse, John, **Cold Dawn: the Story of SALT**, Holt Rinehart and Winston, New York, 1973

Pierre, Andrew J., **The Global Politics of Arms Sales**, Princeton University Press, New Jersey, 1982

Pringle, Peter and Spigelman, James, **The Nuclear Barons: the Inside Story of How they Created our Nuclear Nightmare**, Michael Joseph, London, 1981

Sampson, Anthony, **The Arms Bazaar**, Hodder & Stoughton, London, 1977

Sanger, Clyde, **Safe and Sound – Disarmament and Development in the 80's**, Zed Press, London, 1982

Stockholm International Peace Research Institute (SIPRI), **The Arms Race and Arms Control**, Taylor and Francis, London, 1982

Stockholm International Peace Research Institute (SIPRI), **Nuclear Energy and Nuclear Weapon Proliferation**, Taylor and Francis, London, 1979

Whynes, David K., **The Economics of Third World Military Expenditure**, Macmillan, London, 1979

York, Herbert, **Race to Oblivion: a Participant's View of the Arms Race**, Simon & Schuster, New York, 1971

Index

35-7, 69; Trident, 36-7; Typhoon, 35-6, 85
Suharto, Brig. Gen., 173
Sweden, 70, 96, 114, 127, 154, 179

Taiwan, 8, 24, 51-2, 70, 179
tanks, 76, 129, 131, 137
Teller, Edward, 103
terrorism, 23, 26, 44
Third World: and arms trade, 149, 151, 155, 156-7, 158,
        182; defence industries in, 70-1, 154, 155, 158;
        dependence on Superpowers, 8; development in, 7,
        158; military politics, 166-8; military spending, 7,
        125, 146; navies 94-5; nuclear energy in, 46-7, 50-1,
        55; nuclear weapons in, 53; wars in, 9, 72
Tlatelolco Treaty, 51, 183
Turkey, 115, 172

United Kingdom, 174; arms trade, 149, 157, 158, 179;
        military research spending, 57, 144; and nuclear
        weapons, 29, 31, 41, 54, 59
United States: and Afghanistan, 23-4, 110; arms trade, 149,
        151, 158, 179; bilateral arms control with Soviet
        Union, 183-5; and China, 24; military bases
        overseas, 152; military communications, 67-70;
        military research spending, 56, 141-3; military
        spending, effect of on, 138-40, 143-4, 146; military
        technology compared to Soviet Union, 43, 67;
        nuclear policy, 41-2; and South Africa, 54; strategic
        nuclear weapons, 28-31, 33, 36, 42, (openness about
        own) 29, (planned) 30-1, 36-7; and Taiwan, 24; and
        Vietnam, 23-4, 109, 169; see also missiles, US; naval
        forces, US

Vietnam, 22, 23, 72, 106, 109, 116-7, 152, 169

Wallop, Sen. Malcolm, 101-2
wars: causes, 7-13, 14, 22, 24, 26, 116; damage done,
        (non-nuclear) 9, 114-7, (nuclear) 117-24; fatalities,
        114-7; location of, 14-28, (future) 20
war games, 159-65
Warsaw Pact, 14, 24, 80, 82, 85-6, 185
weapons, 80; cost, 125-47; future, 9-11, 82; technological
        improvements, 56-71; unreliability, 130-2; see also
        arms trade; and individual headings
West Germany, 24, 40-1, 50, 51, 179; military research
        spending, 57, 143
Westmoreland, Gen. W.C., 72
World War One, 14, 18, 23, 106, 115
World War Two, 14-16 passim, 22, 23, 106, 115-6
Wyatt, Dr Vivian, 111

Zia ul Haq, Gen., 172
Zimbabwe, 23, 166, 167, 174